Sharon,
Love
Zella Rogers Patton

Some
RUSSELL COUNTY, VIRGINIA
Records

Births & Deaths 1853-1866

Compiled by:
Thomas Colley

Southern Historical Press, Inc.
Greenville, South Carolina
1996

Please Direct all Correspondence & Orders to:

Southern Historical Press, Inc.
P.O. Box 1267
375 West Broad Street
Greenville, S.C. 29602-1267

ISBN # 0-89308-087-X

Printed in the United States of America

An abstract from Virginia State Library & Archives m/film:

Russell County, Virginia Register of Births, 1853-1866
Russell County, Virginia Register of Deaths, 1853-1866
(Filmed 10 Sep 1953, Lebanon, Russell County, VA)

The Birth register lists no entries for 1863-1864
The Death register lists no entries for 1863-1864 and only six entries
for 1865.

The entries are arranged alphabetically by the creative and phonetic
spelling as found in this handwritten register. No attempt was made
to convert this spelling to the modern conventional. All "sounds
like" entries should be checked as some entries indicate a different
surname spelling for child and parents.

Ex: p11, Ln 55 states:
*Sarah V. Renolds; d/o Philip Renalds & Elizabeth Reynolds; reported by
father, Philip Reynolds*

Mistakes and off-line entries are abundant in this register copy. An
example from the birth register, page 20, Line 8; the mother of
Margaret Matilda (Breeding) appears to have been missed, making the
register off line for mother's information for lines 9 thru 47.
Mistakes on this page, and others, indicates that confirmation from
additional sources is needed to verify the information as stated.
Possible register errors, when identified, were noted by the compiler
within *() and in italics*.

i

Some Russell County Records
Births & Deaths   1853–1866

Table of Contents:

Some Russell County Records

Format for Births:

Child's Name: Date of Birth: Place of Birth: Parents
(Reference Code)

Many parents have multiple entries under creative and phonetic
spelling. Be sure to check all "sounds like" entries.
See Footnotes for additional information from Death Register and
1850 - 1860 Russell County census.

Abbreviations:

Ages: y = years **m** = months **d** = days
b. = born
d. = died
d/o = daughter of
f/o = father of
m/o = mother of
s/o = son of
tw = twin
Un/M = Unnamed Male
Un/F = Unnamed Female
Un/Child = Unnamed Child
♀ = Female
♂ = Male

SOME RUSSELL COUNTY RECORDS

Reference Codes for Place of Birth:

ACo = Alleghany County, NC
Ca = "Car's Creek"
Cc = Copper Creek
CC = Cedar Creek
Cl = Clinch River
CM = Cook's Mill
CMt= "C. Mountain"
CR = Copper Ridge
Cr = Castle's Run
CS = Corner Settlement
Cw = "Castlewoods"
DC = Dumps Creek
EG = Elk Garden
FS = Field's Settlement
Gc = Grassy Creek
GH = Glade Hollow
Gl = Gravelly Lick Creek
Ha = Hayter's Valley
HCo= Hawkins Co., TN
HG = Hayters Gap
HV = Horton's Valley
IC = Indian Creek
JCo = Johnson Co., KY
KR = Kents Ridge
LC = Lewis Creek

LCo= Lee Co., VA
Le = Lebanon
Li = Lick Creek
Lo = Loop
LR = Little River
Mo = "Moccasin"
NF = Nashes Ford
NG = New Garden
RC = Russell County
Re = Reeds Valley
RF = Russell Fork
RG = Rye Grass Mountain
RV = River Valley
Sa = Sandy
SCo= Scott Co., VA
Sm = Swords Creek
SM = Sword's Mill Creek
SR = Sandy Ridge
TCo= Tazewell Co., VA
TN = Tennessee
TNc = Claiborne Co., TN
WC = Weavers Creek
WCo = Washington Co., VA
WNc = Wilkes County, NC
WY = Wythe Co., VA

SOME RUSSELL COUNTY RECORDS
BIRTHS 1853-1866

Child	Date of Birth	Birth Place	Parents
ADAMS			
Andrew	03 Apr 1856	RC	Joel & Elizabeth Adams
Louisa J.	08 Mar 1858	RC	Joel R. & Elisterely Adams
Lucy (tw)	27 Mar 1854	RC	Thomas & Sarah Adams
Matilda (tw)	27 Mar 1854	RC	Thomas & Sarah Adams
Rebecca Ellen	09 Jun 1853	RC	"Unknown" & Julia Ann Adams
ADDAMS			
James	07 Nov 1860	RC	Joel & Elistaritta Addams
ADDERSON			
(Un/M)[1]	03 Dec 1857	RC	Hiram & Lucinda Adderson
ADDISON			
(Un/M)	15 Jul 1865	NG	Rodden & Arminda Addison
(Un/M tws)	12 Jul 1866	EG	Rodin & Armilda Addison
Hiram	10 Sep 1861	EG	William F & Mary J Addison
James W	01 May 1860	EG	Osker G & Mary Addison
Margaret S.	11 Sep 1853	EG	Hiram & Susannah(?) Addison
Martha W	10 Jun 1861	EG	Roddin & Mary J Addison
Michael	07 Jun 1860	EG	William F & Mary J Addison
Nancy J.	10 Aug 1865	NG	Granville Addison & Manerva Ferguson
Rush F.	01 Apr 1860	EG	James G. & Cosby Addison
Susanah V.	25 Oct 1857	RC	Oscar & Polly Addison
William T.	17 Mar 1860	EG	Hiram & Ellen F. Addison
ADESON			
George C.	10 Sep 1855	HV	Hiram J. & Lucinda Adeson
ADINGTON			
Malvina	06 Nov 1854	RC	John & Lucinda Adington
ADKINS			
(Un/F)	19 Mar 1865	NG	William & Hannah Adkins
AKERS			
Elvina J.	24 Mar 1856	RC	William & Margaret Akers
John H.	24 Jun 1860	RC	William & Margaret Akers
Margaret Isabel	08 Dec 1862	RC	William & Margaret Akers
Nathan W.	02 Apr 1854	RC	Thomas & Mary Akers

---

1 1860 Russell County Census Rose Dale Hh# 700: Hiram & Lucinda Addison lists a Margaret, 6; George <u>Chrisman</u> Addison, 5; <u>Elbert S.</u>, 3; et al.

1

SOME RUSSELL COUNTY RECORDS
BIRTHS 1853-1866

Child	Date of Birth	Birth Place	Parents
Ransom H.	27 Nov 1856	RC	Thomas & Mary Akers
Sarah E.	15 Feb 1858	RC	William & Margaret Akers
William R.	05 May 1859	RC	Thomas & Mary Akers
William P.	25 Oct 1854	RC	William & Margaret Akers
ALDERSON			
(Un/M)[1]	02 Jun 1854	RC	T.C.M. & Nancy Alderson
(Stillborn/M)	01 Sep 1857	RC	John D. & Martha Alderson
Isabell J.	17 Mar 1854	RC	John D. & Martha Alderson
Nannie Isabella	__ Aug 1861	RC	T.C.M. & Nancy J. Alderson
Nannie J.	08 Jul 1860	RC	Thomas C.M. & Nancy J. Alderson
ALEXANDER			
(Un/M)	16 Jul 1861	EG	David & Nancy E. Alexander
Anna Lisa	18 Oct 1854	RC	David & Elizabeth Jane Alexander
George	01 Sep 1856	RC	David & Elizabeth Alexander
Mary J.	10 May 1856	RC	_____ & Elizabeth Garrett
AMBURGY			
Martha	24 Feb 1857	RC	William & Cyntha Amburgy
Martha A.	__ Dec 1862	RC	William & Sarah Amburgy
AMOS			
Eliza	02 Jun 1856	RC	Merideth & Mary A. Amos
ANDERSON			
Andrew	01 May 1854	RC	Samuel & Elizabeth Anderson
Elias	08 Jun 1853	RC	Nickademus & Nancy Anderson
George W.	25 Nov 1857	RC	James G. & Cosby Anderson
Hazy	15 Jul 1854	RC	Charles & Matilda Anderson
Henry	16 Oct 1856	RC	Charles & Matilda Anderson
Isaac	__ Jul 1862	RC	Nichodemus & Nancy Anderson
Robert J.	27 Feb 1862	RC	Isaac & Mahala Anderson
Whitley	11 Jan 1853	RC	Joseph & Elender Anderson
ARTRIP			
Andrew	15 Jun 1854	RC	Joseph & Mary Artrip
Eliza S.	__ May 1860	RC	Harvey & Rachel Artrip
Francis M.	07 May 1853	NG	Harvey & Rachel Artrip
Fredrick	06 Mar 1853	WC	James & Elizabeth Artrip
Fullen	03 Dec 1855	Cl	Joseph & Rachel Artrip
George W.	18 Jun 1855	Cl	James Jr. & Mary Artrip

---

1 1860 Russell County Census lists a William H., age 5.

SOME RUSSELL COUNTY RECORDS
BIRTHS 1853-1866

Child	Date of Birth	Birth Place	Parents
James	03 Feb 1857	RC	William & Mary Artrip
Joseph	23 Nov 1856	RC	Joseph & Mary Artrip
Martha A.	__ Sep 1860	RC	James Jr. & Sarah Artrip
Marty E.	17 Dec 1856	RC	Jasper & Mary Artrip
Mary	__ Dec 1860	RC	Jasper & Mary Artrip
ASCUE			
(Un/M)	05 Jul 1856	RC	Ancil & Prida Ascue
Elenor	10 Apr 1854	RC	Ancel & Pruda Ascue
Mary S.	16 May 1853	HV	Arvil & Prudence A. Ascue
ASHBY			
Henry T.	25 Jul 1853	RC	Charles M. & Eliza Ann Ashby
Mary Jane Elizabeth	14 Apr 1862	RC	Charles & Liza Ann Ashby
Oliver	27 Feb 1860	RC	Charles M. & Eliza Ashby
ASTON			
Eddy Larcena	22 Jun 1860	NG	Henry D. & Rachel Aston
Henry	09 Oct 1862	NG	Henry D. & Rachel Aston
ATHEY			
Malinda	02 Jan 1861	EG	_____ & Susan Athey
Mary E.	02 Sep 1858	RC	_____ & Malinda Athey
AUSTIN			
Abbaty S.	08 Sep 1855	EG	James A. & Mary E. Austin
Flemming	02 Dec 1859	RC	Thomas & Jane Austin
Mary E.	18 Apr 1858	RC	John & Eliza Austin
Robert	18 Jul 1862	RC	John & Elizabeth Austin
AYERS			
(Un/F)	05 Oct 1865	NG	George & Elizabeth Ayers
BAILEY			
Florence R.	03 May 1860	RC	George W. & Katherine Bailey
William	10 Apr 1859	RC	John & Elizabeth Bailey
William G.	10 Feb 1861	RC	James & Elizabeth Baily
BAKER			
(Un/F)[1]	15 Nov 1861	RC	George A. & Julian Baker

---

1 See Death Register: indicated to be an unnamed male; died at age 14 days, __ Nov 1861; "s/o" George A. & Julian Barker

SOME RUSSELL COUNTY RECORDS
BIRTHS 1853-1866

Child	Date of Birth	Birth Place	Parents
Caroline E.[1]	17 Jun 1860	RC	John H. & Malissa Baker
Caroline J.	05 Sep 1853	RC	John & Elizabeth Baker
Charles	29 Nov 1853	RC	Samuel & Malinda Baker
Frances H.[2]	15 Jun 1861	RC	William C. & Edieth Baker
John G.	27 Mar 1861	RC	"Base"[3] & Mary E. Baker
John G.	11 Oct 1856	RC	John H. & Malissa Baker
John L.	20 May 1860	RC	George A & Julia Baker
Jonas J.B.	07 Mar 1866	Mo	George A & Julia Ann Baker
Joseph A.M.	02 Dec 1866	Mo	William C. & Edidth Baker
Mary E.C.	15 Oct 1856	RC	William C. & Edith baker
Thomas J.	08 Aug 1858	RC	John C. & Melissa Baker
William C.	13 Jan 1862	RC	George A & Julia Ann Baker

BALDEN

William	24 Nov 1857	RC	Jacob & Orpha Balden

BALDWIN

Elisha	16 Aug 1853	SR	Stephen & Phoebe Baldwin
Rebecca J.	24 Jun 1856	RC	Stephen & Phoebe Baldon

BALL

Andy	11 Feb 1856	RC	Andy & Sarah Ball
Drusillar	04 Jun 1860	NG	John T. & Margarett Ball
Elihue	20 Sep 1853	NG	John T. & Sarah Ball
Eveline	14 Feb 1853	NG	Andrew & Margaret Ball
Fullen J.	06 Mar 1856	RC	John T. & Mary Ball
George W.	27 Oct 1855	Cl	Cornelious & Nancy Ball
Isaac	14 Sep 1853	EG	William M. & Susannah Ball
Isaiah M.	10 Apr 1860	NG	William L. & Sydna Ball
James F.	06 Jul 1857	RC	William L. & Synna J. Ball
James M.	19 May 1860	NG	John Jr. & Milley Ball
James W.	27 Nov 1857	RC	William H. & Rebecca Ball
John T.[4]	21 Jan 1853	NG	Moses & Mary Ball
Joshua	30 Dec 1859	RC	William M. & Susannah Ball
Leah	30 Jun 1859	RC	John & Rebecca Ball
Lucinda	24 Feb 1861	NG	James & Rebecca Ball
Margaret	11 Jan 1857	RC	Cornelious & Nancy Ball

---

1 See Death Register

2 Frances <u>Helen</u>; See Death Register

3 "Base": speculatively, out of wedlock

4 See Death Register

SOME RUSSELL COUNTY RECORDS
BIRTHS 1853-1866

Child	Date of Birth	Birth Place	Parents
Margaret A.	27 Sep 1854	RC	William & Susan Ball
Martha	06 Nov 1859	RC	Robert S. & Cynthia Ball
Martha	12 Oct 1862	NG	John W. & Rebecca Ball
Mary Ann	29 Mar 1861	NG	Moses & Mary Ball
Mary	29 Mar 1858	RC	Robert S. & Louiza Ball
Robert S.	10 May 1859	RC	James H. & Mary J. Ball
Larrah	11 Nov 1855	Cl	James H. & Mary Jane Ball
Sousannah	26 Nov 1855	Cl	William M. & Sousan Ball
Unice	11 Sep 1865	RC	Isaac D. & Rebecca Ball
Vastine (♀)	10 Oct 1862	WC	Cornelius & Nancy Ball
Victory	27 Dec 1860	WC	Cornelious & Nancy Ball
Virginia	17 Mar 1859	RC	Moses & Mary Ball
William J.	21 Dec 1857	RC	William & Susanah Ball

BANNER

Child	Date of Birth	Birth Place	Parents
Camel	16 May 1854	RC	Berry R & Martha J Banner
Edward	03 Oct 1857	RC	Berry R & Martha C Banner
George W.	26 Dec 1858	RC	George & Priscilla M. Banner
James N.	11 Apr 1856	RC	George & Priscilla Banner
Jefferson J.	12 Jan 1861	RC	George & Priscilla M. Banner
John T.[1]	13 Jul 1854	RC	George & Priscilla M. Banner
Sarah	15 Oct 1853	RC	Stephen & Sarah Banner
Steven W.	15 Dec 1866	Cw	George & Pricilla Banner

BARGER

Child	Date of Birth	Birth Place	Parents
Sarah J.	07 Jun 1860	EG	Jerome & Mary Barger

BARKER

Child	Date of Birth	Birth Place	Parents
(Un/F)[2]	08 Jan 1856	RC	Robert & Sarah Barker
Henry	__ Oct 1858	RC	Robert C. & Sarah Barker
Isaac B.	19 Sep 1858	RC	William C. & Edith Barker
Lucinda	07 Jun 1858	RC	David W. & Nancy E. Barker
Sarah P.	07 Aug 1855	RC	David & Nancy E. Barker
William R.	07 Sep 1853	RC	David W. & Nancy C. Barker

BARRETT

Child	Date of Birth	Birth Place	Parents
Bildona W.F.	12 May 1865	RC	Robert Barrett & Margaret Bar
Mary Allis	16 Mar 1860	NG	James & Rebecca F. Barrett

---

1 See Death Register

2 1860 Russell County census Dicksonville Hh# 1185:
Robert & Sarah Barker, lists a Nancy Barker, age 5;
Henry Barker, age 1.

SOME RUSSELL COUNTY RECORDS
BIRTHS 1853-1866

Child	Date of Birth	Birth Place	Parents
BARTEE			
(Stillborn/M)	05 Aug 1862	RC	James & Mary C. Bartee
Christener E.	28 Dec 1860	RC	James M. & Nancy E. Bartee
BARTLEY			
Newbern	14 Aug 1856	RC	John & Winney Bartley
Roling	20 Sep 1853	RC	Pleasant & Nancy Bartley
Andrew F.	12 Jun 1854	RC	Revel & Nancy Bartly
Drewry	07 Nov 1854	RC	Jessee & Jemimy Bartly
Vive (♂)	14 Mar 1854	RC	John & Winy Bartly
BARTON			
(Male)	10 May 1865	NG	William & Margaret Barton
(Un/M)[1]	01 Jun 1859	RC	Washington & Elizabeth Barton
Abram	27 Jan 1861	NG	George & Matilda Barton
Angeline	11 Dec 1857	RC	William & Margaret Barton
Charles	07 Oct 1860	NG	Jacob & Lucinda Barton
John W.	18 Nov 1862	NG	Jacob & Louisa Barton
Martha	14 Jul 1860	EG	William & Margaret Barton
William	14 Apr 1865	RC	George W. & Matilda Barton
BAUGH			
Martha E.	01 Oct 1862	RC	John J. & Louisa Baugh
Nancy	08 Jan 1859	RC	John J. & Louisa Baugh
Nancy W.	08 Jan 1860	RC	John J. & Louisa Baugh
BAULDWIN			
Elihu K.	25 Oct 1855	Cl	Stephen & Nancy Bauldwin
BAUSELL			
John C.	__ Jul 1860	RC	William T & Hannah F Bausell
BAYS			
(Un/M)	10 Jul 1854	RC	John H. & Malinda Bays
(Un/M)	07 Apr 1854	RC	William & Adaline Bays
Beverly T. (♂)	26 Sep 1854	RC	James H. & Julia Bays
James W.	02 Oct 1860	EG	James H. & July Ann Bays
John E.	25 Jan 1860	Le	Isaac Mc. & Elizabeth Bays
Nancy V.	02 Jun 1856	RC	James J. & Mary Bays
BAZZLE			
Charles W.	__ Jun 1860	RC	Joseph C. & Eliza Bazzle

---

1 See Death Register

SOME RUSSELL COUNTY RECORDS
BIRTHS 1853-1866

Child	Date of Birth	Birth Place	Parents
BEGLEY			
Emily F.	20 Mar 1866	LCo	Elijah & Mary Begley
BELCHER			
Braniel	04 Jun 1865	RC	John T. & Frances Belcher
Cyntha A.	12 Sep 1855	EG	John T. & Elvina Belcher
George H.	08 Nov 1854	RC	William & Caroline Belcher
Joseph	14 Sep 1859	RC	Charles W. & Eliza Belcher
Joseph H.	03 Jan 1860	NG	Charles W. & Eliza Belcher
Lucy Elizabeth	05 Jun 1854	RC	Joseph & Nancy Belcher
Sarah M.	___ Jan 1860	RC	Samuel H. & Nancy Belcher
Stephen A.D.	10 Oct 1860	NG	John T & Frances A Belcher
William P.	18 Oct 1859	RC	Hopkins & Frances Belcher
William P.	04 Oct 1858	RC	John F & Frances S Belcher
BENNETT			
Ransy (♀)	10 Dec 1854	RC	Wirah(?) & Mary Bennett
BEVERLEY			
John R.	13 May 1853	RC	Robert & Mahaley Blevens
Malinda	05 Mar 1854	RC	Elijah & Nancy Beverly
BICKLEY			
Charles M.	20 May 1862	RC	Marion T & Mary J Bickley
Eliza A.	01 Nov 1855	RC	William C & Harriet B Bickley
Georgia E.	09 Dec 1857	RC	John F. & Eliza A. Bickley
Henry D.[1]	23 Jan 1853	RC	Marion T & Martha B Bickley
James O.	20 Apr 1860	RC	M.T. & Mary J. Bickley
John B.F.	01 Feb 1858	RC	James M. & Eveline Bickley
John F.	07 Jul 1858	RC	Marion T & Mary J Bickley
John Walter	05 Jul 1866	Cw	John F. & Eliza Bickley
Martha M.	17 Oct 1854	RC	Marion T & Mary J Bickley
Mary A.	___ Jun 1860	RC	James M. & Evaline Bickley
Thomas Jefferson	11 May 1862	RC	William C & Harriet B Bickley
William	05 Nov 1859	RC	William & Harriet B Bickley

---

1 Death register states:[p4;Ln32] Henry D. Bickley,
died <u>01</u> Aug 1853; age <u>6m</u>; Flux; Russell County; s/o
Marion T. & Martha Bickley; reported by grandfather,
Charles Bickley.
A double entry in death register for Henry D. Bickley,
reported by his father states: died <u>21</u> Aug 1853, age <u>9</u>
months of Flux . [p4:Ln38]

SOME RUSSELL COUNTY RECORDS
BIRTHS 1853-1866

Child	Date of Birth	Birth Place	Parents
BIRD			
Polly	?? Nov 1856	RC	John & Elizabeth Bird
Sarah J.	28 Aug 1853	NG	William & Margaret Bird
BLACK			
Mary S.	04 Feb 1862	RC	Lawrence & Rhoda Black
BLAIR/(? BLAIN)			
James H.	06 Oct 1856	RC	Jacob & Louisa Blair/Blain
Jasper (twin)	06 May 1854	RC	William & Frances Blair
Newton (twin)	06 May 1854	RC	William & Frances Blair
BLEAR			
Saban	28 Jun 1855	RC	David & Mary A. Blear
BLESSING			
(Un/M)[1]	20 Apr 1853	RC	Crockett & Mary Blessing
BLEVINS			
John	22 Oct 1862	RC	David & Alcy Blevins
Mary	06 Apr 1860	RC	David A. & Aley Blevins
Matilda	29 Oct 1853	RC	Linkhorn & Sarah Blevins
BLIZZARD			
Elihu	16 Jun 1857	RC	Sidner & Ruth Blizzard
Elizabeth J.	15 Apr 1860	RC	Sidner & Rutha Blizzard
Hannah E.	14 Dec 1861	RC	William & Margaret Blizzard
Louisa J.	__ Apr 1860	RC	William & Margaret Blizzard
Lydia	28 Nov 1861	RC	Sydner & Rutha Blizzard
Mary E.[2]	14 Jul 1856	RC	Sidney & Lucy Blizzard
Nancy	__ Oct 1858	RC	Sidner & Ruth Blizzard
Robert	24 Nov 1854	RC	Sidner & Rutha Blizzard
Stephen H.	06 Nov 1853	RC	Eliza Jane Blizzard
BOBB			
Robin (twin)	01 Apr 1855	Cl	Benjamine & Marinda Bobb
William (twin)	01 Apr 1855	Cl	Benjamine & Marinda Bobb

---

1   Birth was reported by grandfather, Jeremiah Fields. [p4;Ln4]
   Death register states:[p2;Ln28] Unnamed male Blessing, died age 1 day from unknown cause; s/o Crockett & Mary Blessing; reported by grandfather, Jeremiah Fields.

2   See Death Register

8

SOME RUSSELL COUNTY RECORDS
BIRTHS 1853-1866

Child	Date of Birth	Birth Place	Parents
BOGGS			
Abel	25 Nov 1853	RC	William & Rebecca Boggs
BOND			
(Un/M)[1]	23 Aug 1855	RC	Charles F. & Mary J. Bond
Peter L.	21 Jan 1853	RC	(Parents not named)
BOOHER			
Robert R.	27 May 1857	RC	Thomas & Mariah Booher
William L.B.	13 Feb 1853	RC	Thomas P & Matilda M Booher
BOOTH			
Celina R.	30 Sep 1859	RC	John & Susannah Booth
Rebecca J.	08 Jul 1858	RC	Stephen & Jane Booth
BOOTHE			
Alfred	10 Oct 1853	RC	Alfred & Loucretia Boothe
BOSWELL			
George F.	06 Dec 1853	RC	John C. & Nancy Boswell
Mary Catherine	13 Feb 1853	RC	Wm. T. & Hannah F. Boswell
BOWLING			
Reuben J.	23 Mar 1853	TCo	James B & Elizabeth J Bowling
BOWMAN			
Charles F.	07 Jan 1866	Cc	_____ & Mary E. Bowman
James E.[2]	05 Feb 1860	RC	Peter & Mary Bowman
William J.	01 Jun 1853	RC	Peter & Mary J. Bowman
BOYD			
(Un/M)[3]	10 Feb 1854	RC	John H. & Malinda Boyd
(Un/M)	05 Jul 1853	NG	Jonathan & Mary Boyd
Isaac M.[4]	26 Dec 1858	RC	Charles D. & Martha Boyd

---

1 Death Register states: (unnamed male) Bond, died at age 4 <u>days</u>(sic; *months*) on 03 Dec 1855; s/o Charles F. & Mary J. Bond

2 See Death Register

3 1860 Russell County census New Garden Hh# 953 of John H. & Melinda Boyd lists a <u>Sparrell</u> Boyd, age 5

4 See Death Register

SOME RUSSELL COUNTY RECORDS
BIRTHS   1853-1866

Child	Date of Birth	Birth Place	Parents
John H.	05 Mar 1853	NG	John & Malinda Boyd
Levina G.	02 Jun 1861	NG	Joseph & Presly Boyd
Margaret A.	10 Jul 1861	RC	Charles D. & Martha Boyd
Mary E.	01 Sep 1853	CR	Robert C & Rebecca E Boyd
BRADLEY			
Martha A.	06 Oct 1853	RC	Lewis & Rachel Bradley
William N.	2_ May 1862	RC	Jno. A & Winney C Bradley
BRADSHAW			
(Un/M)	10 Sep 1854	RC	John & Nancy Bradshaw
William	10 May 1858	RC	John & Isabella Bradshaw
BRANHAM			
James S.	28 Feb 1854	RC	Martin & Matilda Brandham
Martha	01 Nov 1853	RC	Tandy & Elizabeth Branham
BRATTIN			
George H.	10 Jul 1856	RC	Alexander L & Susanah Bratton
BREEDING			
Albert	24 Apr 1856	RC	James H. & Margaret Breeding
Elizabeth	02 Apr 1854	RC	Bryant & Elizabeth Breeding
James	10 Feb 1861	DC	Briant & Elizabeth Breeding
John	15 May 1853	RC	George & Rebecca Breeding
John H.	___ Nov 1860	RC	Spencer & Hannah Breeding
Margaret Matilda	16 May 1856	RC	Elijah Breeding & _____
Nancy J.	06 May 1856	RC	Briant & Elizabeth Breeding
Noah	06 Jul 1856	RC	George & Rebecca Breeding
Phoebe	06 May 1859	RC	George & Rebecca Breeding
BREEDLOVE			
Jefferson	01 Jan 1858	RC	Charles & Elizabeth Breedlove
BROMETT			
Margaret	10 Oct 1857	RC	Henry & Eliza Bromett
BROWN			
Thomas J.	27 Dec 1857	RC	Henry N. & Nancy Brown
BROWNING			
(Un/M)[1]	15 Aug 1857	RC	John C. & Elizabeth Browning

---

1 1860 Russell County census Gibsonville Hh# 1333 of
John C. & Elizabeth M. Browning lists: George W., age 3;
James, age 6; et al.

SOME RUSSELL COUNTY RECORDS
BIRTHS 1853-1866

Child	Date of Birth	Birth Place	Parents
(Un/M)	18 Jul 1853	RC	Wm. McR & Susan C. Browning
Charles L.	27 Feb 1859	RC	Francis A. & Mary E. Browning
Charles W.	05 Sep 1860	RC	John C & Elizabeth M Browning
Howard H.C.	24 Sep 1866	Mo	Francis A. & Mary E. Browning
James	15 Aug 1865	NG	Jacob & Margaret Browning
James F.	25 Jun 1854	RC	John C & Elizabeth M Browning
James H.	18 Oct 1862	EG	Jacob & Margaret Browning
James S.	06 Dec 1855	EG	Jesse & Rebecca Browning
Jasper N.	16 Sep 1853	RC	William & Rebecca Browning
Jessee	10 Sep 1860	EG	John P. & Armiter Browning
John P.	22 Nov 1862	EG	John P. & Arminta Browning
Joseph	01 Dec 1855	RC	Wm. M.R. & Susan Browning
Malissa[1]	27 May 1853	RC	"Unknown" & Martha J Browning
Mary A.	16 Nov 1862	EG	John B. & Rachel Browning
Mary Ann	06 Jun 1853	RC	Jesse & Biddy Browning
Mary E.	24 Nov 1860	EG	James H. & Martha E. Browning
Sally P.	09 Nov 1862	EG	James H. & Martha E. Browning
Sarah E.	18 May 1858	RC	John P. & Minte Browning
Taylor S.	18 Dec 1855	EG	John P. & Minta Browning
William J.	29 Sep 1854	RC	Francis A. & Mary E. Browning
Wilson E.	18 Oct 1857	RC	Jessee & Rebecca Browning

BRUCE

Child	Date of Birth	Birth Place	Parents
Lizzie L.	26 May 1866	Le	Garland S & Sarah E Bruce

BRUMMIT

Child	Date of Birth	Birth Place	Parents
Nancy A.	22 Jan 1862	RC	John & Malinda Brummit

BUCKHANAN

Child	Date of Birth	Birth Place	Parents
Elbert W.	09 Oct 1855	RC	James L. & Mary Buchanan

BUCKLES

Child	Date of Birth	Birth Place	Parents
Ellen A.	___ Jul 1860	RC	Edward L & Mary J Buckles
James A.	02 Jun 1857	RC	Abraham & Rebecca Buckles
Mary J.	01 Jul 1855	TN	Edward & Mary Buckles
Mary Derinda	23 Aug 1862	RC	Eli & Elizabeth E. Buckles

BUMGARDNER

Child	Date of Birth	Birth Place	Parents
Valandingham[2]	05 Jul 1862	WNc	Wm. S. & Elizabeth Bumgardner

---

1 Birth of Malissa Browning was reported by grandfather, Jessee Browning. [p7;Ln17]

2 See Death Register

SOME RUSSELL COUNTY RECORDS
BIRTHS 1853-1866

Child	Date of Birth	Birth Place	Parents
BUNDY			
(Un/M)[1]	30 Sep 1856	RC	Daniel & Rebecca Bundy
Samuel P.	___ Aug 1862	RC	Sampson & Sarah Bundy
William F.	18 Jul 1855	RC	Samuel & Sarah Bundy
BUNTY			
Julaeth[2]	09 Aug 1854	RC	Daniel & Rebecca Bundy
BURCHETT			
Francis M.	14 Mar 1853	RC	Meredith & Mary Burchett
BURDINE			
(Stillborn/F)	23 Apr 1862	RC	John W & Stella C Burdine
Elen	07 Jul 1862	TNc	Patton & Elizabeth Burdine
Henry D.	14 Jul 1857	RC	John & Nancy Burdine
James P.	22 Feb 1854	RC	John W. & Stilly Burdine
Nathan E.	05 Nov 1859	RC	John W & Stillia C Burdine
BURGESS			
Margaret Ann	03 Jul 1855	Lo	Robert & Sarah Jane Burgess
Susan[3]	10 Jun 1858	RC	Thomas & Ann Burgess
BURK			
(Un/M)	02 Jun 1854	RC	Isaiah & Mary Burk
(Un/M)	23 Dec 1862	RC	Samuel & Nancy Burk
Etella	07 Apr 1858	RC	Isaiah & Martha A. Burk
Henry S.	02 May 1854	RC	Archer & Sarah P. Burk
Henry L.F.	08 Apr 1860	RC	Isaiah & Martha Burk
Isaiah	02 Jul 1854	RC	John & Nancy Burk
James	04 Sep 1853	RC	Samuel & Nancy Burk
Jefferson Davis	02 Aug 1861	EG	Archer & Sally P. Burk
Joseph F.	03 Mar 1856	RC	Samuel & Nancy Burk
Mary C.	08 Jul 1856	RC	Isaiah & Martha A. Burk
Mary Amelia	12 Oct 1862	RC	John & Nancy Burk
Rebecca J.	11 May 1860	EG	Isaiah J. & Mary E. Burk
Sarah E.	28 Mar 1862	EG	William & Lourinda Burk

---

1 See Death Register entry for Lilburn H. Bundy, s/o Daniel & Rebecca

2 1860 Russell County census Dickensonville Hh# 1268 of Daniel & Rebecca Bundy lists a Julia, age 5; et al.

3 Birth of Susan Burgess was reported by "brother", Alex. Caldwell. [p28;Ln29]

SOME RUSSELL COUNTY RECORDS
BIRTHS 1853–1866

Child	Date of Birth	Birth Place	Parents
Thaddius	07 Jun 1859	RC	Archer & Sarah Burk
William[1]	13 Oct 1865	NG	Winton W. & Dorcas Burk
Louisa	30 Jul 1866	Mo	John & Nancy Burke
Nancy J.	07 Nov 1866	Cc	Samuel & Nancy Burke

BURNETT

(Stillborn/F)	03 Jan 1853	NG	Samuel & Mary Burnett
John	06 Nov 1856	RC	Samuel B & Mary J Burnett
Mary E.	05 Oct 1854	RC	Obediah M. & Anna Burnett

BURTON

Johnson C.	09 Jun 1855	RC	John & Louisa Burton

CALDWELL

Alexander	10 Aug 1859	RC	William & Margaret Caldwell

CAMPBELL

(Un/child)[2]	29 Oct 1858	RC	James H. & Mary Campbell
(Un/M)[3]	23 Sep 1857	RC	James & Elizabeth Campbell
(Un/F)	17 Feb 1853	RC	Geo. W. & S.C. Campbell
Andrew W.	26 Nov 1857	RC	James C & Eliza A Campbell
Charles B.	08 Feb 1859	RC	John W C & Mary E Campbell
Charles P.	20 Sep 1860	EG	Joelle & Mary E Campbell
Clinda (tw)	10 Apr 1856	RC	George W & Sidney Campbell
Cyntha	01 Jun 1858	RC	William Jr & Susan Campbell
David W.	08 Mar 1856	RC	James C & Eliza A Campbell
Edward T.	23 Sep 1853	SM	James H & Mahala J Campbell
Eliza	18 Jul 1860	EG	William J & Susan Campbell
George C.	28 Feb 1861	RC	George W & Sidney E Campbell
George A.	04 Jun 1854	RC	Fountain & Malinda Campbell
Henry F.C.	24 Apr 1858	RC	George W & Sidney Campbell
James (tw)	10 Apr 1856	RC	George W & Sidney Campbell
Jasper N.	21 Dec 1853	GH	William & Susan Campbell
Joel R.	12 Feb 1854	RC	James H. & Mary Campbell
John	13 Sep 1861	RC	Fountain & Malinda J Campbell

---

1   See Death Register

2   1860 Russell County census Lebanon Hh# 234 of James H. & Mary W. Campbell lists; Margaret A., 8; Joel R., 6; William, 3; Rachel P., 1

3   1860 Russell County census Lebanon Hh# 206 of James & Eliza A. Campbell lists; David W., 4; Andrew W., 2; Nancy E., 9/12

SOME RUSSELL COUNTY RECORDS
BIRTHS 1853-1866

Child	Date of Birth	Birth Place	Parents
John F.	08 Jan 1856	RC	James H. Jr & Mahala Campbell
John C.	12 Aug 1857	RC	Andrew J. & Floranze Campbell
Laura W.	28 Sep 1866	Ca	G.W. & Sydney E. Campbell
Mary E.	14 Sep 1859	RC	James C & Eliza A Campbell
Mary J.	04 Oct 1858	RC	Jas. H. & Eliz Campbell
Rachael	04 Jan 1859	RC	James H. & Mary Campbell
Rachel A.	09 Sep 1860	RC	James H. & Elizabeth Campbell
Rachel E.	28 Aug 1860	EG	Wilson E & Leah C Campbell
Sarah Elen	16 Mar 1862	RC	George W & Elizabeth Campbell
W.S.	20 Mar 1857	RC	Fountain & Malinda Campbell
William P.	04 Dec 1859	RC	Fountain J. & Jane Campbell
William W.	07 Jul 1857	RC	Henry & Syntha Campbell
Wilson E.	29 Jul 1856	RC	James H. Sr. & Mary Campbell

CANDLER

Child	Date of Birth	Birth Place	Parents
Sarah A.	23 Oct 1859	RC	Singleton & Adline H. Candler
Thomas A.	05 Sep 1854	RC	Singleton & Adaline H Candler

CANTRELL

Child	Date of Birth	Birth Place	Parents
Levi	01 May 1853	RC	Hiram & Nancy Cantrell
Polly	21 Apr 1866	Gl	Joseph & Nancy Cantrell

CARICO

Child	Date of Birth	Birth Place	Parents
Florence	10 Jul 1854	RC	Joseph & Elener Carico

CARRELL

Child	Date of Birth	Birth Place	Parents
(Un/F)[1]	01 Aug 1854	RC	Lorenzy D. & Harriet Carrell
George[1]	15 Jan 1853	RC	Lorenzo D. & Harriet Carrell
Mary	10 Mar 1859	RC	Charles Sr. & Mary V. Carrell
Nancy F.	02 Jul 1858	RC	Thomas & Jane Carrell

CARRICO

Child	Date of Birth	Birth Place	Parents
(Un/M)	20 Dec 1855	RC	Alexander & Martha J. Carrico
Elbert S.	04 Jul 1859	RC	Joseph & Eleanor Carrico

CARROLL

Child	Date of Birth	Birth Place	Parents
Whitfield	08 Jul 1856	RC	Thomas & Jane Carrell

CARSON

Child	Date of Birth	Birth Place	Parents
Joseph H.	25 Dec 1858	RC	Robert P. & Marah C. Carson

---

1 1860 Russell County census Bickleys Mill Hh# 1439 of
L.D. & Hariet Carrell lists: Nancy, 9; George, 7; <u>Leah</u>,
6; Stephen, 5; Priscilla, 1; et al.

SOME RUSSELL COUNTY RECORDS
BIRTHS 1853-1866

Child	Date of Birth	Birth Place	Parents
CARTER			
Archer	18 Nov 1855	RC	Dale & Elizabeth Carter
James M.	16 Dec 1853	RC	Granville C. & Martha Carter
James H.	17 Jan 1860	RC	_____ & Elizabeth M. Carter
John W.H.	06 Sep 1860	RC	James O. & Elizabeth Carter
Margaret S.	14 Dec 1861	RC	James O. & Elizabeth Carter
Tasville H.(♂)	25 Oct 1854	RC	Granville C. & Martha Carter
CARTEY			
Easther	09 Jul 1859	RC	John B. & Liley Cartey
CARTY			
Elbert F.[1]	13 Jul 1854	RC	Thomas J. & Caroline Carty
Elizabeth	04 Sep 1862	RC	John B. & Delila Carty
James L.	__ Mar 1862	RC	Samuel G.W. & Mary Carty
Jenial H.	16 May 1853	RC	James P. & Jane Carty
John W.	06 Nov 1853	RC	Robert D. & Nancy Carty
Joseph	07 Sep 1861	RC	John B. & Delila Carty
Margaret Sarency	__ Jun 1862	RC	Robert D. & Nancy Carty
Mary E.	29 Aug 1854	RC	John & Delily Carty
Mary	__ __ 1858	RC	Robert D. & Nancy Carty
Nancy E.	03 Apr 1857	RC	Thomas & Caroline Carty
Nancy	19 Feb 1857	RC	John B. & Delila Carty
Patcy	15 Jul 1854	RC	James L. & Lydda Carty
Sarah E.	31 Jan 1855	RC	Robert D. & Nancy Carty
William	06 Mar 1860	RC	Samuel G.W. & Mary Carty
CASE			
Newton	01 Mar 1853	RC	James & Jane Case
CASEY			
Nancy E.	09 May 1860	EG	Henry D. & Sally Casey
CASSELL			
Ralph J.	06 Jun 1854	RC	Calvin M. & Lydda Cassell
CASTLE			
(Un/F)[2]	__ May 1860	RC	Ralph S. & Sarah L. Hicks

---

1 See Death Register

2 1860 Russell County census Dickensonville Hh# 1314 of Ralph & Sarah Castle lists; Sarah E., age 1; et al.

SOME RUSSELL COUNTY RECORDS
BIRTHS 1853-1866

Child	Date of Birth	Birth Place	Parents
(Un/M)[1]	07 Mar 1853	RC	Ralph S. & Sarah Castle
(Un/M)[2]	02 Apr 1854	RC	John & Lucinda Castle
(Un/M)	17 May 1856	RC	Ralph S. & Sarah Castle
Charlotte	03 Apr 1858	RC	Zachariah & Lucy Castle
Darthula[3]	22 Sep 1859	RC	"Unknown" & Lucy Castle
James M.	30 Dec 1853	RC	Silas & Elizabeth Castle
James B.	01 Feb 1866	Cc	Calvin M. & Malinda J. Castle
John A.	01 May 1859	RC	Calvin M. & Lydia J. Castle
Joseph W.B.	20 Dec 1861	RC	Ralph & Sarah Castle
Lucinda	26 Dec 1860	NG	John & Lucinda Castle
Lydia Jane	14 Apr 1862	RC	Calvin M. & Lydia Castle
Malinda	__ May 1861	RC	Zachariah & Lucy Castle
Manford B.	11 Mar 1861	JCo	James C. & Katherine Castle
Nathaniel David	15 Jun 1862	RC	Silas & Elizabeth Castle
Polly Ann	26 Feb 1862	RC	Alexander & Mary Castle
Ralph L.	25 Dec 1859	RC	Silas & Elizabeth Castle
Robert	01 Apr 1860	RC	Alexander & Mary Castle
Samuel B.	__ Aug 1860	RC	Calvin M. & Lydia Castle
William R.	04 Dec 1857	RC	Silas & Elizabeth Castle
William A.	08 May 1856	RC	Alexander & Mary Castle

CATRON

Child	Date of Birth	Birth Place	Parents
(Un/M)[4]	01 Nov 1855	Le	Felix G. & _____ Catron
James Henry	22 Apr 1860	EG	Felix G. & Elizabeth Catron

---

1 Death register states:[p2;Ln36] Unnamed male Castle, died at age 1 day of unknown cause in Russell County; s/o Ralph & Sarah Castle; reported by father.

2 1860 Russell County census New Garden Hh# 871 of John & Lucinda Castle lists; Major A., 6; et al.

3 Birth of Darthula Castle reported by grandfather, Zachariah Castle. [p36;Ln17]

4 1860 Russell County census Lebanon Hh# 94 of Felix G. & Elizabeth Catron lists: John W., 6; et al.

SOME RUSSELL COUNTY RECORDS
BIRTHS 1853-1866

Child	Date of Birth	Birth Place	Parents
CHAFFIN			
(Un/M)[1]	__ Sep 1858	RC	Oliver & Rebecca Chaffin
Floyd	__ Apr 1858	RC	James & Margaret Chaffin
CHAFIN			
(Un/M)[2]	20 Sep 1857	RC	James & Susanah Chafin
(Un/M)	09 Dec 1862	RC	James & Peggy Chafin
Charles (tw)	25 Jun 1853	RC	Oliver & Rebecca Chafin
Elizabeth	10 May 1857	RC	Oliver & Rebecca Chafin
Frances Jane(tw)	25 Jun 1853	RC	Oliver & Rebecca Chafin
Henry Fletcher	08 May 1862	RC	Oliver B. & Rebecca Chafin
Rolson B.	15 Jun 1855	RC	Oliver & Rebecca Chafin
Sarah	10 Feb 1855	RC	James & Margaret Chafin
CHANY			
James H.	27 Mar 1854	RC	Jacob C. & Anny Chany
Joseph	15 Aug 1857	RC	Jacob & Anna Chany
CHAPMAN			
(Un/F)[3]	__ Oct 1858	RC	Jason & Margaret Chapman
(Un/F)[4]	01 Oct 1857	RC	William H. & Lucinda Chapman
(Un/F)[5]	23 Jul 1853	HG	Benjamine & Mary Chapman
(Un/M)	30 Sep 1862	EG	Benjamine F. & Martha Chapman
Bartholomew	18 May 1862	RC	William & Minerva Chapman
James H.	17 Mar 1857	RC	Benjamine & Jane Chapman
John B.	15 Jul 1855	Lo	John & Rebecca Chapman
Joseph	14 Dec 1858	RC	Benjamine Jr. & Jane Chapman
Joseph	26 Jan 1853	EG	William & Manerva Chapman
Margarett	01 Oct 1860	NG	B.F. & Martha Chapman

---

1   1860 Russell County census Dickensonville Hh# 1235 of Oliver & Polly Chafin lists: Charles, 8; Frances J., 8; Roslon B., 5; Thomas K., 1; et al.

2   1860 Russell County census Lebanon Hh# 449 of Sousannah Chafin lists: Charles, 4; Andrew J., 2; et al.

3   1860 Russell County census Hansonville Hh# 1123 of Jasen & Margaret Chapman lists; Mary Jane, age 2

4   1860 Russell County census Bickleys Mill Hh# 1498 of William H. & Lucinda Chapman lists: Margaret E.J., age 3

5   1860 Russell County census Hendricks Mill Hh# 535 of Benjamin & Mary Chapman lists; Catherine, age 6; et al.

17

SOME RUSSELL COUNTY RECORDS
BIRTHS 1853-1866

Child	Date of Birth	Birth Place	Parents
Virginia C.[1]	24 Sep 1855	Lo	Benjamine Jr & Martha J. Chapman
William O.	20 May 1858	RC	John & Rebecca Chapman
CHASE			
(Un/child)	24 Jun 1855	RC	Jeramiah T. & Sarah Chase
CHILDERS			
Archer L.	19 Sep 1857	RC	John H. & Rebecca Childers
Martha V.	___ Sep 1862	RC	John H. & Rebecca B. Childers
Mary S.	30 Dec 1855	RC	John H. & Rebecca B. Childers
Rebecca	___ Apr 1860	RC	John H. & Rebecca Childers
CHILDS			
George R.	10 Oct 1866	Cc	A.L. & Thursy J. Childs
CHISENHALL			
Marion[2]	10 Jun 1854	RC	James & Nancy Chisenhall
CLARK			
(Un/M)	03 Feb 1860	NG	Patrick & Eliza Clark
(Un/M)[3]	11 May 1860	EG	Daniel O. & Leah Clark
Evaline	06 Jan 1862	NG	Daniel O. & Lear Clark
Martha	10 Aug 1861	NG	John P. & Elizabeth Clark
Montriville	03 Apr 1858	RC	Daniel O. & Leer Clark
Salina	12 Dec 1856	RC	Patrick C. & Louisa Clark
Samuel J.H.	11 Aug 1858	RC	Andrew D. & Margaret Clark
Sarah A.	27 Nov 1857	RC	John P. & Elizabeth Clark
William	20 Aug 1854	RC	William & Polly Clark

---

1   1860 Russell County census Hendricks Mill Hh# 536 of Benjamin F. & Martha J. Chapman lists; (Virginia) Catherine, age 4; et al.

2 Birth of Marion Chisenhall (male), reported by Unkle, Galen Roberts. [p12;Ln13] (Note: 1850 Russell County census household #1415: Lewis Roberts, 50; Penelope, 48; Gailen, 22; Nancy, 24; William, 16; Catherine, 14; Anna, 11; Ira, 7; James, 4; Louisa Roberts, 42.   Living near in household #1406 of Arthur Wheatley was James Chisenhall, 22, listed as a laborer and born Grayson Co., Va.).

3   See Death Register

SOME RUSSELL COUNTY RECORDS
BIRTHS 1853–1866

Child	Date of Birth	Birth Place	Parents
CLIFTON			
Charles W.	26 Sep 1866	Mo	Elias & Barbarry Clifton
Isaac[1]	15 Jun 1853	Le	Martin & Adeline Clifton
James E.	13 Jun 1854	RC	Elias & Baberry Clifton
Mary Ann	13 May 1853	RC	Elias & Barbara Ann Clifton
Nancy J.	03 May 1854	LCo	Martin & Martha Clifton
Sarah C.	14 Aug 1859	RC	Martin J. & Matilda Clifton
CLOUD			
(Stillborn/M)	20 Apr 1865	RC	John & Sussa Cloud
COATS			
(Un/M)	17 Mar 1862	EG	Thompson & Gelana Coats
COCHRAN			
Jackson	05 Apr 1860	NG	Edward & Malinda Cochran
William L.	09 Nov 1856	RC	Marvel & Lucinda Cochran
COCHRUN			
Sureena	03 Feb 1865	NG	Peter & Nancy Cockrun
COCKRENE			
Cornelius	08 Mar 1862	NG	Marvel & Ruth Cockrene
COLE			
Florence	26 Jan 1866	WCo	Jonas & Hannah Cole
COLEMAN			
Malinda Ann	15 Sep 1854	RC	_____ & Abaegil Coleman
Sarah	30 Mar 1856	RC	Richard & Nancy Coleman
COLLEY			
David	05 Jun 1853	RC	Joshua & Didamey Colley
Joseph	18 Apr 1857	RC	Joshua & Naeleanna Colley
Malisa	12 Dec 1855	RC	James & Ema Colly
COLLINGS			
Nancy A.E.	20 May 1859	RC	John A. & Sarah Collings
COLLINS			
(Un/M twins)	20 Dec 1866	Mo	William H. & Mary Collins
James	01 Aug 1855	RC	Edward & Elizabeth Collins
Margurett M.	18 Feb 1857	RC	John A. & Sarah Collins

---

1 Birth of Isaac Clifton was reported by neighbor, Tabitha Cowan. [p2;Ln38]

SOME RUSSELL COUNTY RECORDS
BIRTHS 1853-1866

Child	Date of Birth	Birth Place	Parents
Rebecca E.	15 Apr 1853	RC	Riley & Emaline Collins
Rebecca	15 Apr 1853	RC	Releya & Emeline Collins
William Edward	23 Jul 1862	RC	William H. & Mary Collins

COMBO

Child	Date of Birth	Birth Place	Parents
(Un/M twins)	26 Oct 1861	RC	William & Eliza A. Combo

COMBOW

Child	Date of Birth	Birth Place	Parents
(Un/F)	27 May 1854	RC	William F. & Sary E. Combow

COMBS

Child	Date of Birth	Birth Place	Parents
Ann Eliza	13 Feb 1860	NG	Cullen D. & Ann Combs
Asa A.	___ ___ 1858	RC	William & Mary A. Combs
Elbert	08 Dec 1862	NG	Samuel & Sarah G. Combs
Elen	18 Jan 1855	Ha	William & Salina Combs
Emily Alice	16 May 1862	RC	John & Margarett E. Combs
Evaline	10 Sep 1861	NG	Timothy & Rebecca Combs
Jacob	08 Nov 1854	RC	Fielden & Sarah Combs
James L.	16 Mar 1857	RC	Joseph & Nicy Combs
James M.	10 Jan 1861	NG	W J. & Ella Combs
John F.	07 Aug 1853	RC	William & Mary Ann Combs
John W.	12 Nov 1860	RC	John & Margaret E. Combs
Margaret Elen	15 Feb 1862	RC	Joseph & Nicy Ann Combs
Martha M.D.V.	07 May 1859	RC	Joseph & Nicy A. Combs
Mary E.	24 Feb 1860	NG	Cullen Sr. & Sally Combs
Melissa C.	26 Dec 1858	RC	Wm. J. & Eliza "Combo"
Pary (♂)	28 Dec 1860	NG	Benson & Rebecca Combs
Rachel[1]	14 Apr 1857	RC	Fielding & Sally Combs
Robert	08 May 1861	RC	William & Mary Ann Combs
Susan	28 Sep 1860	NG	Thompson Jr. & Anna Combs
Tonia	28 Sep 1859	RC	Timothy & Sarah Combs
Victoria	20 Apr 1856	RC	Thompson & Ann Combs
William E.	?? May 1866	RC	Samuel A. & Elizabeth Combs

COMPTON

Child	Date of Birth	Birth Place	Parents
(Un/M)	01 Mar 1859	RC	Stephen & Ailcy Compton
Aaron	17 Aug 1853	NG	Jeremiah & Martha Compton
Catherine	01 Oct 1856	RC	Bartley & Catherine Compton
Eliza Ann	14 Apr 1854	RC	Sterlin & Manerva Compton
Elizabeth	01 Apr 1855	NG	James H. & Phebe Compton
Ira	11 Aug 1857	RC	David & Jane Compton
James	09 Oct 1862	NG	James & Amy Compton
Jeremiah	06 Mar 1854	RC	Bartin & Catherine Compton

---

1 See Death Register

SOME RUSSELL COUNTY RECORDS
BIRTHS 1853-1866

Child	Date of Birth	Birth Place	Parents
Martha	04 Apr 1860	EG	Paton & Mary Compton
Marthy	04 Apr 1860	NG	Paton & Mary Compton
CONNER			
Nancy A.	05 Sep 1860	WCo	James M. & Julia Conner
COOK			
(Un/F)[1]	07 Aug 1859	RC	James & Catherine Cook
(Un/F)[2]	___ Jul 1854	RC	James & Polly Cook
(Un/M)	10 Dec 1861	NG	James & Anna Cook
Angeline	17 Nov 1862	NG	William & Frances Cook
Eliza	21 May 1853	NG	James & Mary Cook
Elizabeth	10 Apr 1861	NG	William C. & _____ Cook
Evan K.	03 Jul 1859	RC	Jasper & Sarah Cook
Hannah	09 May 1855	NG	John & Hannah Cook
Isabel	03 Mar 1862	NG	James & Christen Cook
Jacob A.	31 Mar 1859	RC	John & Hannah Cook
James C.	14 Mar 1861	NG	Jasper & Elizabeth Cook
Lucinda	12 Mar 1861	NG	Newton & Lear Cook
Simeon E.	08 Jun 1859	RC	James & Anna Cook
COOPER			
(Un/F)	01 Mar 1866	Cw	William P. & Tabitha Cooper
Edmond	15 Jul 1854	RC	David & Sarah Cooper
Susan P.[3]	09 Aug 1858	RC	William & Rhoda Cooper
COUCH			
Caroline	17 Feb 1861	RC	Jeremiah Jr. & Lutitia Couch
Charles W.	___ Apr 1860	RC	Archibald & Mary Couch
Henry	___ Sep 1862	RC	Jeremiah & Luticia Couch
Martha E.	06 Apr 1866	Cl	Jeremiah Jr. & Lucretia Couch
Thomas H.	08 Jul 1858	RC	Jeremiah & Margaret Couch
Winney A.	12 Oct 1861	RC	Archibald & Mary Couch

---

1 Possible error;   1860 Russell County census Bickleys Mill Hh# 1436 of James & Catherine Cook lists; Rachel, 3; Buchanan, 2; John, 10/12; et al.

2   1860 Russell County census Lebanon Hh# 478 of James & Polly Cook lists: Anna, 8; Eliza, 6; Rachael, 3; Leah, 1; et al.

3 See Death Register

Child	Date of Birth	Birth Place	Parents
COUNCE			
Eliza J.	28 Jan 1853	RC	William G. & Martha B. Counce
Joshua	23 Mar 1853	RC	Elijah & Catherine Counce
COUNTISS			
(Un/M)	13 Sep 1853	RC	Ezra Countiss & Margaret Counts
COUNTS			
(Un/M)	21 Oct 1858	RC	John & Eliz Counts
(Un/F)[1]	12 May 1857	RC	William F. & Patsey Counts
(Un/F)	02 Aug 1859	RC	David & Nancy Counts
Aley	21 Jun 1858	RC	Joshua & Margaret Counts
Benjamine F.	20 Oct 1853	RC	Ezekiel R. & Harriet Counts
Charles B.	30 Jan 1856	RC	William S. & Patsey Counts
Eliza C.	11 Jan 1866	Cw	Jas. M. & Eliza Counts
Etha A. (♂)	04 Jun 1854	RC	John & Elizabeth Counts
Floyd	23 Aug 1860	RC	Canaan & Ann Counts
Floyd	01 Oct 1859	RC	John B. & Elizabeth Counts
George L.	28 Apr 1862	NG	David & Nancy Counts
Joshua	___ Sep 1860	RC	Ezekiel & Abigail Counts
Margaret E.	25 May 1854	RC	John C. & Elizabeth Counts
Margaret	20 Feb 1856	RC	Noah & Aley Counts
Nancy J.	21 Feb 1856	RC	David & Nancy Counts
Nancy	29 Jan 1855	RC	William & Pasy Counts
Nelson	11 Jan 1857	RC	John N. & Elizabeth Counts
Priscilla	04 Oct 1859	RC	John Jr. & Eliza A. Counts
Sebastian C.	___ Dec 1862	RC	Ezekiel K. & Harriet Counts
William T.	17 Apr 1856	RC	John & Elizabeth Counts
COX			
(Un/M)	14 Oct 1859	RC	Wilson & Eliza Cox
Edward H.	30 Jan 1853	RC	David & Ann Cox
Helbert	25 Oct 1860	NG	John & Elizabeth Cox
John	07 Jul 1855	EG	Alfred & Mary Cox
Martha J.	07 May 1853	RC	Isham & Louisa Cox
Martha	15 Jun 1855	EG	Wilson & Eliza Cox
Mary	22 Feb 1860	EG	Alfred & Polly Cox
Nealy E. (♀)	01 Mar 1855	RC	Isham & Louisa Cox
Sarah J.	20 Sep 1853	EG	Alfred & Mary Cox
Thomas	22 Jul 1858	RC	Joseph & Menerva Cox
William F.	06 Apr 1855	NG	Joseph & Manerva Cox

---

1 See Death Register

SOME RUSSELL COUNTY RECORDS
BIRTHS 1853-1866

Child	Date of Birth	Birth Place	Parents
CRABTREE			
Charlotts	10 Sep 1861	NG	William & De_?_ Crabtree
George M.	13 Aug 1855	NG	Jacob & Elen Crabtree
Jeremiah	20 Mar 1861	NG	Soloman & Mary Crabtree
Mary E.	19 Jul 1853	RC	John & Jane Crabtree
Rebecca	11 Dec 1856	RC	Soloman & Nancy Thomas Crabtree
CRISMON			
John J.[1]	24 Oct 1853	RC	Thomas & Artamitia Banion
CROSS			
John R.	30 May 1858	RC	Mordica & Jane Cross
Margaret	07 Jul 1862	RC	John B. & Martha Jane Cross
Mary E.	21 Oct 1854	RC	Modecai & Jane Cross
CROSSWHITE			
Andrew J.	11 Oct 1856	RC	Jacob & Elizabeth Crosswhite
W.G.[2]	31 May 1860	EG	Jacob & Elizabeth Crosswhite
(Stillborn/F)	27 Feb 1859	RC	Jacob & Elizabeth Crosswhite
CUBBERTSON			
Nathaniel J.	02 Dec 1855	RC	Henry & Mary M. Cubbertson
Harriet C.	02 Dec 1853	RC	Henry & Nancy E. Culbertson
Martha W.	10 Oct 1860	RC	Thomas & Martha E. Culbertson
Telia V.	09 Sep 1860	Le	E.J. & Martha E. Culbertson
CUMBO			
Andy F.	15 Apr 1853	RC	William & Eliza Ann Cumbo
Charles C.	20 Oct 1853	RC	Nancy Jane Cumbo
Charles Wilson	01 Mar 1862	RC	George W. & Edith Cumbo
Cleaminda(?)	01 Jun 1853	RC	Francis & Sarah E. Cumbo
Eliza	04 Jul 1859	RC	William Sr. & Eliza A. Cumbo
CUMBOW			
(Un/M)	17 Dec 1857	RC	Francis & Sarah E. Cumbow
CUNNINGHAM			
Benjamine P.	15 Dec 1856	RC	Thomas & Louisa Cunningham
Rachel C.	02 Feb 1853	RC	Thos. & Louisa Cuningham

---

1 See Death Register

2 1860 Russell County census Lebanon Hh# 304 of Jacob & Elizabeth Crosswhite lists; William G., 1/12; et al.

SOME RUSSELL COUNTY RECORDS
BIRTHS 1853-1866

Child	Date of Birth	Birth Place	Parents
DALE			
(Un/M)	01 Oct 1861	RC	"Base" (born) & Margaret Dale
David F.[1]	14 Mar 1858	RC	_____ & Margaret E. Dale
Doctor P.[2]	23 May 1853	RC	Hiram & Elizabeth D. Dale
Merican E. (♀)	___ Feb 1861	RC	"Base" (born) & Eliza Dale
Noah R.	15 Nov 1854	RC	Hardin & Anny Dale
William P.[3]	05 Mar 1853	RC	Samuel P. & Sena M. Dale
DANNER			
John W.	05 Apr 1855	RC	Daniel & Mary A. Danner
Nancy E.	02 Aug 1853	RC	David & Mary Ann Danner
DARNELL			
Cowan W.	29 Dec 1858	RC	_____ & Rebecca Darnell
DAUGHERTY			
May	01 Oct 1860	CS	Andy & Mary Daughtery
Susannah	23 Apr 1859	RC	Andrew & Mary Daugherty
DAVENPORT			
Charles W.	24 May 1859	RC	Isham & Frances Davenport
DAVIS			
Caleb	15 Oct 1853	GH	Thomas J. & Sarah Davis
Charles	22 Dec 1853	EG	Daily C. & Louisa Davis
Florence E.B.	26 Apr 1860	RC	John C. & Mary C. Davis
Hannah	01 Feb 1859	RC	Thomas J. & Sarah Davis
Jesse	22 May 1854	RC	Robert & Hester Davis
John H.	12 Jan 1858	RC	Isaac W.M. & Eliz. S. Davis
John W.	19 Jul 1855	RC	Eli & Henny Davis
John H.	12 Jan 1859	RC	Isaac W M & Elizabeth L Davis
Margaret R.	06 Aug 1857	RC	Calhound & Eliza Davis
Nancy C. (tw)	12 Nov 1861	RC	Calhoun & Eliza Davis
Nancy E.	21 Feb 1853	RC	Robert T. & Hester Ann Davis
P. (♂)	24 Dec 1857	RC	Eli & S.(? L.) Davis
Rachel E. (tw)	12 Nov 1861	RC	Calhoun & Eliza Davis
Robert P.	07 Apr 1853	RC	Jesse & Mary H. Davis

---

1 Birth of David F. Dale reported by friend, Rebecca Darnell. [p31;Ln25]

2 See Death Register

3 Birth of William P. Dale was reported by Uncle, Hardin Dale. [p6;Ln16]

SOME RUSSELL COUNTY RECORDS
BIRTHS 1853-1866

Child	Date of Birth	Birth Place	Parents
Thomas	04 Oct 1858	RC	Henry C. & Levisa Davis
William D.	30 May 1856	RC	Dale C. & Louisa Davis
William	08 Sep 1853	Le	Thomas & Jane Davis
William Rees	20 Jan 1861	NG	Thomas W. & Isabel Davis
William A.	06 Nov 1866	Ca	Isaac W. & Elizabeth Davis
DEAL			
Amanda	07 Mar 1853	Sa	Fredrick & Louisa Deal
David A.	26 Mar 1853	Sa	George & Martha Deal
Franklin	18 Oct 1856	RC	Jacob & Louisa Deal
Henry H.	20 Dec 1853	Sa	Harvey & Louisa Deal
John	06 Dec 1857	RC	Wiloby & Frances Deal
Joshua	13 Jan 1853	Sa	Willis & Frances Deal
Malvina	10 Feb 1856	RC	Harvey & Vicy Deal
DEAN			
Mary E.	07 Jul 1855	RC	Ellis & Manervy A. Dean
Wesley F.	30 Dec 1854	RC	William H. & Isibell Dean
DEEL			
Charles A.	15 Dec 1857	RC	David & Mary Deel
Priscilla	02 Jun 1853	RC	David & Nancy Deel
DENISON			
Christopher	10 Apr 1858	RC	Phillip & Martha V. Denison
George W.	08 Nov 1855	EG	Philip & Martha V. Denison
DENISTON			
Lear J.	10 Mar 1865	NG	George & Eliza Deniston
DENNISTON			
Ann L.	15 Sep 1859	RC	James & Jane Denniston
DICKENSON			
(Un/M)	07 Jun 1857	RC	J.H. & Nancy Dickenson
(Un/F)[1]	27 Nov 1856	RC	Samuel C. & Rebecca J. Dickenson
(Un/M)[2]	___ Jul 1861	RC	Charles & Nancy C. Dickenson
(Un/F)	23 Oct 1854	RC	James H. & Nancy G. Dickenson

---

1 1860 Russell County census Hansonville Hh# 1056 of
Samuel C. & Rebecca J. Dickenson lists: Martha C., 3;
Henry N., 1/12.

2 See Death Register

25

SOME RUSSELL COUNTY RECORDS
BIRTHS 1853-1866

Child	Date of Birth	Birth Place	Parents
(Un/F)[1]	06 Nov 1856	RC	John N. & Sarah Dickenson
(Un/M)	14 Jan 1853	RC	Charles C. & Catherine Dickenson
(Stillborn/M)	25 May 1861	RC	John N. & Sarah J. Dickenson
Alice Virginia	31 May 1862	RC	__? N. & Sarah S. Dickenson
Asa C.	20 Jun 1858	RC	S.R. & Ferreba Dickenson
Carmelia C.F.	06 Dec 1853	RC	Charles H. & Nancy C. Dickenson
Catherine P.	__ Nov 1862	RC	Charles C. & Catherine Dickenson
Charles	29 Aug 1860	RC	Nathan E. & Catherine Dickenson
David O.	23 Apr 1854	RC	Newberry & Ferrbe Dickenson
Eliza	18 Oct 1857	RC	Samuel & Elizabeth Dickenson
Henry M.	21 Apr 1853	RC	George W. & Frances Dickerson
Henry B.	26 May 1854	RC	Nathaniel E. & Catherine Dickenson
Henry S.[2]	06 Feb 1858	RC	Charles & M.J. Dickenson
Henry C.	16 Mar 1860	RC	Henry P. & Mary J. Dickenson
Henry P.	10 Aug 1860	RC	Thomas F. & Josephine Dickenson
Henry	__ May 1860	RC	Charles & Mary J. Dickenson
James A.	06 Dec 1854	RC	Henry J. & Elen J. Dickenson
Josephine	11 Nov 1856	RC	L.R. & Ferraba Dickenson
Mary E.	08 May 1858	RC	Henry J. & Ellen Dickenson
Mary M.	12 Jun 1862	RC	Thomas P. & Elizabeth Dickenson
Mary E.	11 Dec 1856	RC	Nathan E. & Catherine Dickenson
Nancy V.	02 Aug 1861	RC	Henry P. & Mary J. Dickenson
Nancy R.	01 Nov 1854	RC	Samuel & Elizabeth Dickenson
Nathaniel H.	19 Apr 1860	RC	Samuel C. & Rebecca J. Dickenson
Noah C.	__ May 1860	RC	Charles C. & Katherine Dickenson
Susan M.J.	10 Sep 1853	RC	Rosannah Dickenson

---

1   1860 Russell County census Dickensonville Hh# 1236 of John M. & Sarah J. Dickenson lists: Sally T., 5; Emit A., 1; et al

2   1860 Russell County census Bickley Mill Hh# 1382 of Charles & Margaret J. Dickenson lists: Henry S., 2; John F., 1/12.

SOME RUSSELL COUNTY RECORDS
BIRTHS 1853-1866

Child	Date of Birth	Birth Place	Parents
Temperance V.	10 Dec 1854	RC	Thomas P. & Elizabeth Dickenson
Thomas	14 Aug 1854	RC	Charles C. & Sarah Dickenson
Thomas F.	22 Aug 1857	RC	C.C. & Catherine Dickenson
Thomas N.	31 Jan 1859	RC	Charles & Margaret J. Dickenson
William A.	30 Oct 1866	Cw	Samuel C. & Rebecca Dickenson
William F.	16 Apr 1853	RC	James H. & Nancy G. Dickenson

DILLS

Child	Date of Birth	Birth Place	Parents
Emmett	06 Dec 1860	CR	James & Rosanah Dills
Henry	28 Oct 1854	RC	James & Rosanah Dills
Juda	10 Mar 1853	CR	James & Rosanah Dills
Mary Allis	15 Aug 1861	EG	John W. & Martha Dills
Mary E.	10 Jun 1861	CR	James & Nancy J. Dills

DORTON

Child	Date of Birth	Birth Place	Parents
(Un/M)	08 Aug 1857	RC	Jacob & Elizabeth Dorton
(Un/M)	29 Dec 1853	RC	George W. & Nancy Dorton
(Un/M)	16 Aug 1854	RC	Jacob & Elizabeth Dorton
(Un/M)[1]	01 Dec 1854	RC	Joseph C. & Cosby A. Dorton
Charles W.	14 Apr 1861	RC	Joseph C. & Cosby Ann Dorton
Edith Alice	04 Sep 1862	RC	Samuel B & Sina Elvira Dorton
Emily F.	03 Sep 1866	Cc	Joseph C. & Cosby A. Dorton
Jemimy	01 Nov 1854	RC	George W. & Nancy Dorton
Martha E.	23 Apr 1866	Cc	Oliver V. & Nancy Dorton
Mary	Feb 1859	RC	Joseph C. & Cosby Dorton
Nathan W.	25 May 1862	RC	William B & Margaret K Dorton
Robert C.	25 Apr 1859	RC	William B. & Margaret Dorton
William A.	08 Aug 1855	RC	Jacob B. & Elizabeth Dorton

DOTSON

Child	Date of Birth	Birth Place	Parents
Mary	12 Dec 1858	RC	Stephen & Dicy Dotson
Nathan	13 Dec 1854	RC	William & Cela Dotson
William H.	25 Jul 1853	RC	Henderson H. & Susan Dotson

DRAPER

Child	Date of Birth	Birth Place	Parents
Elizabeth[2]	21 Sep 1866	Cc	Charles & Nancy C. Draper

---

1 1860 Russell County census Dickensonville Hh# 1276 of Joseph C. & Causby Dorton lists: Martha A.E., 7; <u>Elbert G.H.</u>, 5; Samuel J., 3; Mary E.R., 1; et al.

2 Birth of Elizabeth Draper was reported by grandfather, Robert Boyd. [p57;Ln7]

SOME RUSSELL COUNTY RECORDS
BIRTHS 1853-1866

Child	Date of Birth	Birth Place	Parents
DUFF			
Diannah T.	12 Aug 1855	NG	John G. & Rosanna Duff
Mary	16 Feb 1858	RC	John G. & Rosanah Duff
DUNCAN			
Jackson L.	05 Sep 1855	NG	William P. & Lucinda Duncan
Mary	10 Sep 1862	NG	Alexander & Newly Duncan
Thomas H.	21 Oct 1854	RC	John W. & Lear Duncan
William	03 Dec 1853	RC	William & Lucinda Duncan
DUNKIN			
William	03 Dec 1853	RC	William P. & Lucinda Dunkin
DUTY			
(Un/M)[1]	18 Mar 1857	RC	John L. & Sarah Duty
Noah L.	17 Jun 1857	RC	Lemuel & Mary Duty
DYE			
(Un/M)	15 Jul 1860	SM	Absalom & Susan Dye
Aaron	04 Nov 1861	NG	Prior & Sarah Dye
Abram	___ Jun 1861	RC	Thomas J. & Margaret Dye
Catherine	01 Nov 1858	RC	Henry & Rachel Dye
Charles C.	14 Dec 1858	RC	Richeson & Eliza Dye
Ellen	10 Sep 1860	EG	Thomas & Martha Dye
Enelz(? Emelz)	18 Aug 1857	RC	Absalon & Rachel Dye
Francis A.	05 Sep 1862	NG	Jefferson & Sally Dye
Harvey C.	14 May 1860	EG	Jefferson & Sally Dye
Henry P.	12 Nov 1856	RC	Thomas & Nancy Dye
John M.	04 Dec 1858	RC	William & Rosan Dye
Lihue	19 Dec 1856	RC	Thomas & Martha Dye
Lilbern L.	19 Oct 1854	RC	William & Nancy S. Dye
Lilburn	17 Sep 1860	NG	William & Rosanah Dye
Lucy	18 Oct 1859	RC	Harvey & Cynthia Dye
Malissa	15 Aug 1861	NG	Absalem & Rachel Dye
Margaret H.	25 Apr 1860	RC	James & Martha Dye
Mariah F.	11 Nov 1856	RC	William & Nancy Dye
Martha E.	___ Dec 1858	RC	Jas. L. & Martha Dye
Mary E.	14 Nov 1859	RC	Prior Jr. & Sarah Dye
Mary	15 Jul 1856	RC	Henry & Cyntha Dye
Nancy	10 Sep 1854	RC	Bransen & Polly Dye
Nancy	15 Dec 1854	RC	Absolom & Rachel Dye
Polly	15 Sep 1861	NG	James & Nancy Dye
Rachel	11 Mar 1859	RC	Thomas C. & Nancy Dye
Sarah Ann	15 Apr 1854	RC	Thomas G. & Margaret Dye

---

1 See Death Register

SOME RUSSELL COUNTY RECORDS
BIRTHS 1853-1866

Child	Date of Birth	Birth Place	Parents
Thomas K.	27 Oct 1856	RC	Jefferson & Sarah Dye
Thomas	15 Nov 1862	NG	James & Sarah Dye
Thomas	02 Jun 1853	NG	James L. & Martha Dye
William	30 Dec 1858	RC	William & Nancy Dye

DYER

Child	Date of Birth	Birth Place	Parents
Mary F.	30 Jun 1856	RC	Sumpson & Ritter Dyer
Unicey	15 Sep 1853	RC	Symson & Riter Dyer

EAKIN

Child	Date of Birth	Birth Place	Parents
John W.	15 Jan 1859	RC	James G. & Sarah A. Eakin
Virginiabelle	17 Sep 1858	RC	William G. & Camantha Eakin

EASTEP

Child	Date of Birth	Birth Place	Parents
Joseph	01 Sep 1854	RC	Joseph & Elizabeth Eastep

EASTERLY

Child	Date of Birth	Birth Place	Parents
Francis E.B.	27 Sep 1861	RC	Christian & Sarah A.C. Easterly
Nancy	12 Sep 1860	RC	John Eli & Margaret A. Easterly

EDWARDS

Child	Date of Birth	Birth Place	Parents
Brice	02 Oct 1857	RC	A.T. & Christenah Edwards

ELAM

Child	Date of Birth	Birth Place	Parents
Enoch B.	05 Jun 1858	RC	Absalem & Susan Elam
James	27 Jan 1856	RC	Absalom & Susanah Elam

ELKINS

Child	Date of Birth	Birth Place	Parents
Nancy A.	03 Mar 1860	LR	William O. & Rachel Dye

ELLIOT

Child	Date of Birth	Birth Place	Parents
John F.	__ Sep 1860	RC	_____ & Susan Elliot

ELLIOTT

Child	Date of Birth	Birth Place	Parents
John	10 Mar 1862	NG	James A. & Permelia Elliott
Wilson E.	11 Nov 1855	CS	James H. & Permalia Elliott

ESTILL

Child	Date of Birth	Birth Place	Parents
Sarah Ann	30 Apr 1862	RC	Peter & Levina Estill

Faliegh

Child	Date of Birth	Birth Place	Parents
Baughzel (♂)	07 Jul 1854	RC	James O. & Margaret Fraley

29

SOME RUSSELL COUNTY RECORDS
BIRTHS 1853-1866

Child	Date of Birth	Birth Place	Parents
FARMER			
(Un/M twins)[1]	25 Jul 1853	RC	John & Sarah Farmer
Marthart	30 Sep 1853	FS	Burdine & Sarah Farmer
FARRIS			
Mary Elizabeth[2]	05 Jul 1853	RC	John & Nancy C. Farris
FERGUSON			
(Un/M)[3]	30 Jun 1855	EG	Anthony M. & Catherine Ferguson
(Un/M)	10 Jun 1861	EG	D. & Ellen M. Ferguson
(Un/F)	17 Apr 1862	EG	Anthony M. & Catherine Ferguson
(Un/F)	11 Apr 1853	CC	Anthony & Catherine Ferguson
Albert A.C.	10 Sep 1862	NG	David H. & Helen Ferguson
Catherine	15 Jul 1861	EG	Granville A. & Maneva Ferguson
Charles	___ Jun 1861	RC	Hugh D. & Fanny A. Ferguson
Charles W.	29 Nov 1859	RC	Anthony M. & Polly Ferguson
Elihu	09 Mar 1853	Lo	Andrew & Rebecca Ferguson
George A.	26 Jul 1857	RC	Andrew C. & Susan Ferguson
George B.	10 Oct 1858	RC	Hugh D. & Frances Ferguson
James H.	24 Nov 1859	RC	Benjamine H & Mary F Ferguson
John C.	05 Mar 1856	RC	Benjamine & Mary Ferguson
John J.	02 Feb 1856	RC	Granville & Manervy Ferguson
Mary A.	18 Mar 1857	RC	Benjamine & Mary Ferguson
Mary A.	17 Feb 1859	RC	Granville H. & Minerva Ferguson
Mary E.	22 Jan 1854	RC	David C. & Elen M. Ferguson
Sarah A.	06 Jun 1858	RC	David C. & Melisa Ferguson
Susannah C.	26 Mar 1859	RC	Andrew Jr. & Susan Ferguson

---

1 Death register states:[p3;Ln40] Unnamed male Farmer; died 01 Aug 1853, age 4 days; Russell County; Cause Unknown; s/o John & Sarah Farmer; b. Russell County; reported by father, John Farmer.

2 Death register states: Mary Elizabeth Farris, died 26 Aug 1853; age 1m 21d; of Flux; d/o John & Nancy C. Farris; reported by mother. [p2;Ln19].

3 1860 Russell County census Lebanon Hh# 223 of Anthony M. & Catherine Ferguson lists: Barbary E., 8; Charles W., 6; Henry B., 4; Joseph M., 5/12; et al.

SOME RUSSELL COUNTY RECORDS
BIRTHS 1853-1866

Child	Date of Birth	Birth Place	Parents
FERRELL			
(Un/M)[1]	28 Mar 1860	EG	William & Juline O. Ferrell
FERRILL			
Oscar M.	02 Oct 1855	EG	William & Julia Ann Ferrill
FICKEL			
Elizabeth D.	11 Mar 1860	Le	Isaac B. & Elizabeth Fickel
Elbert L.	02 Apr 1858	RC	Isaac B. & _____ Fickle
FIELDS			
(Un/Child)[2]	20 Jan 1858	RC	Calvin Fields & Lucinda Ferguson
(Un/M)	01 Aug 1861	EG	Joseph & Mary Fields
(Un/child)	24 Dec 1859	RC	Richard & Mary Fields
(Un/M)	08 May 1855	CMt	Mitchel & Martha Fields
Andy F.	04 May 1860	EG	Randolph & Rosanah Fields
Cynetha J.	__ Oct 1860	RC	John & Rosanah Fields
Doctor	15 Jan 1859	RC	Mitchell & Martha Fields
Edmondson W.	22 Jan 1859	RC	Calvin T. & Lucinda Fields
Frances M.	10 Jul 1859	RC	Andrew F. & Milly Fields
Jane	08 May 1858	RC	James J. & Jane Fields
John Henry	25 Apr 1854	RC	James J. & Biddy Fields
Joseph	15 Nov 1859	RC	Joseph & Margaret Fields
Leah	22 Oct 1860	EG	Joseph T. & Mary Fields
Lilburn T.[3]	__ Sep 1860	RC	Russell & Rachel Fileds
Mary	10 May 1865	NG	Joseph & Mary Fields
Mary E.	14 Dec 1855	CMt	Russell & Rachel Fields
Mary	08 Oct 1853	SM	John & Rosanah Fields
Nancy	09 Apr 1854	RC	Ader & Rebecca Fields
Reece B.	15 Oct 1854	RC	Joseph & Celia Fields
Richard	29 May 1855	RC	John & Rosanah Fields
Robert	07 Feb 1855	EG	Randolph & Rosannah Fields
Russell	__ Feb 1862	RC	John & Rosanah Fields
Sarah C.	02 Dec 1861	EG	A.F. & Milly Fields

---

1   1860 Russell County census Rose Dale Hh# 721 of William & Jelina O. Ferrell lists: Oscar M., 4; William S.H., 3; Not named _female_, 3/12.

2   1860 Russell County census Lebanon Hh# 173 of Calvin T. & Lucinda Fields lists: Margaret A., 8; Andrew, 4; David C., 2; Edwinson W., 1; et al.

3   See Death Register

SOME RUSSELL COUNTY RECORDS
BIRTHS 1853-1866

Child	Date of Birth	Birth Place	Parents
Sarah C.	03 Jun 1857	RC	Russell & Rachel Fields
Thomas	__ Sep 1858	RC	John & Rosanna Fields
William Russell	22 Aug 1862	RC	Russell & Rachel F. Fields
Wilson C.	08 Nov 1855	CMt	James J. & Biddy Jane Fields

FINNEY

Eliza	09 May 1853	NG	James & Dorcas Finney
Nancy	10 Aug 1866	NG	Lilburn & Malissa Finney

FLETCHER

(Un/M)	25 Oct 1861	NG	William C. & Arena Fletcher
Beverly Parott	05 Jun 1855	NG	James H. & Elenor S. Fletcher
Charles W.	30 Sep 1856	RC	William & Mary Fletcher
Isaac F. (tw)	01 Sep 1855	NG	William & Martha Fletcher
James M.	02 Feb 1853	NG	William & Martha Fletcher
John	08 Jun 1859	RC	Milton & Virginia Fletcher
John Bedford	03 May 1855	NG	William T. & Mary Fletcher
L.D.	30 Nov 1866	CR	Abraham & Elizabeth C. Fletcher
Mary R.	19 Apr 1853	NG	Bazil & Sarah Fletcher
Matilda	21 May 1860	NG	Vanburon & Dicy Fletcher
Nordillas (♀)	16 Sep 1861	NG	L.D. & Mary A. Fletcher
Robert Lee	04 Nov 1861	NG	Thomas L & Pessenape Fletcher
Serrilda Jane	01 Dec 1854	RC	John W. & Celia Fletcher
Thomas J. (tw)	01 Sep 1855	NG	William & Martha Fletcher
Thomas	05 Oct 1858	RC	William & Mary Fletcher
Virginia C.	10 Jul 1859	RC	Thomas L & Elizabeth Fletcher

FOGLEMAN

(Un/child)[1]	13 Dec 1859	RC	David A. & Lucy J. Fogleman
(Un/F)	16 Apr 1861	EG	Henry & Mary A. Fogleman
(Un/M)	22 Dec 1861	RC	David A. & Lucy Fogleman
Charles	24 Aug 1860	EG	Samuel P. & Sarah Fogleman
John W.	09 Mar 1861	EG	Samuel P. & Sarah Fogleman
Palina A.	30 May 1865	RC	Samuel & Sarah Fogleman
Samuel P.	01 Nov 1862	EG	Samuel P. & Sarah Fogleman
William H.	26 Dec 1858	RC	Patten & Sarah Fogleman

---

1 1860 Russell County census Lebanon Hh# 114 of David
N. & Lucy Jane Fogleman lists: "not named", 6/12 _male_

SOME RUSSELL COUNTY RECORDS
BIRTHS 1853-1866

Child	Date of Birth	Birth Place	Parents
FRALEY			
(Un/F)[1]	20 Jun 1854	RC	"Not named" & Nancy Fraley
(Un/M)	22 Jan 1853	RC	Martin & Mary Fraley
(Un/M)	12 Aug 1856	RC	Boon & Mary Fraley
Elizabeth E.	24 Jan 1855	RC	Boon & Mary Fraley
George M. P.	15 Feb 1853	RC	James A. & Abigail Fraley
Nicy O.	08 Apr 1855	RC	James & Abigale H. Fraley
Rebecca S.	08 Sep 1866	Li	James O. & Margaret Fraley
Susana	27 May 1858	RC	James O. & Margaret Fraley
FRANKLIN			
(Stillborn/M)	08 Dec 1859	RC	John & Sarah Franklin
Charles	03 Nov 1855	RC	John & Sarah Franklin
Martha J.	06 Mar 1862	RC	John & Sarah Franklin
Mary	21 Jan 1866	Li	John & Sarah Franklin
Nancy	07 Jun 1854	RC	William & Nancy Franklin
Nicy	02 Apr 1856	RC	William L. & Nancy Franklin
FREEMAN			
William	12 Aug 1855	RC	Joseph T. & Sarah Freeman
FUGATE			
(Stillborn/M)	21 Apr 1861	RC	Joseph C. & Elizabeth Fugate
Easter S.	20 Jul 1857	RC	Jo. C. & Elizabeth Fugate
Edith	13 Sep 1866	Mo	Joseph C. & Elizabeth Fugate
Elbert C.	24 Jul 1853	RC	Joseph C & Elizabeth E Fugate
J.F. (♂)	20 Dec 1866	Mo	Jas. C. & Elizabeth Fugate
James B.	30 Jan 1854	RC	Isaac B. & Sarah Fugate
Mary E.	26 Sep 1866	Mo	Elbert S. & Mary P. Fugate
Rufus C.	01 Nov 1855	RC	James C. & Elizabeth Fugate
Virginia Summers	05 May 1862	RC	F.S.C. & Permelia S. Fugate
William P.	20 Nov 1857	RC	James C. & Elizabeth Fugate
FULLEN			
(Stillborn/F)	25 Jul 1853	Lo	James & Sarah Fullen
Aminta	06 Jun 1856	RC	James & Sarah Fullen
Andrew	15 Dec 1854	RC	James & Sarah Fullen
Arminda	15 Jan 1854	RC	Fowler & Anna L. Fullen
Hiram	25 Feb 1865	NG	Fowler & Fanna(?) Fullen
Martha Jane	15 Feb 1855	Lo	Andrew & Rachel Fullen
Thomas K.	26 Aug 1856	RC	Fowler & Lizy Fullen

---

1 Birth of (Unnamed female) reported by Un<u>k</u>le, Andrew
J. Farley. [p10;Ln47]

SOME RUSSELL COUNTY RECORDS
BIRTHS   1853-1866

Child	Date of Birth	Birth Place	Parents
FULLER			
(Un/M)[1]	01 Sep 1853	RC	Jonas & Rhoda Fuller
Cosby J. (♀)	07 Dec 1854	RC	Noah R. & Cyntha Fuller
Fielden C.	15 May 1854	RC	Abraham S. & Martha Fuller
Fleming G.	11 Jun 1853	RC	Fleming G. & Martha J. Fuller
Franklin	02 Nov 1855	RC	George & Sarah Fuller
George B.	22 Jan 1859	RC	Beverly J. & Mary Fuller
James	21 Jun 1856	RC	Jacob & Margaret Fuller
Mariah S.	10 Aug 1856	RC	Beverley J. & Mary Fuller
Martha A.	08 Mar 1857	RC	Abraham & Nancy Fuller
Rebecca E.	09 Sep 1854	RC	Abraham & Nancy Fuller
GARDNER			
Elijah A.	23 Jun 1854	RC	Pentecost & Stacy Gardner
Long Law	18 Sep 1862	NG	Zadock N. & Jane Gardner
GARRETT			
(Un/M)	12 Jul 1865	NG	John A. & Matelan Garrett
Eunice E.	13 Apr 1857	RC	William G. & Sarah A. Garrett
Henry (tw)	03 Jun 1853	EG	William & Mary F. Garrett
Leah E.	06 Apr 1856	RC	William & Mary Garrett
Loucinda	19 Apr 1862	EG	John A. & Loucinda Garrett
Mary E.	06 Feb 1859	RC	William L. & Sarah Garrett
Nancy M.	12 Nov 1861	EG	Napoleon & Louisa Garrett
Patton	07 May 1860	EG	John F. & Paulina Garrett
Sarah A.	18 Sep 1862	EG	William L. & Sarah E. Garrett
Sarah	16 Oct 1865	NG	William & Sarah A. Garrett
William H.	27 Mar 1861	EG	John W. & Rebecca Garrett
William (tw)	03 Jun 1853	EG	William & Mary F. Garrett
GELESPIE			
Lydia J.	14 Feb 1862	NG	William L. & Lydia Gelespie
GENT			
Rush F.	01 Jul 1862	NG	Fielding & Jane Gent
Whitley	25 Nov 1857	RC	Fuling & Jane Gent
GIBSON			
(Un/F)	___ Nov 1861	RC	Spencer & Sarah Gibson
(Un/F)	0̄3̄ Nov 1854	RC	George R. & Sarah Gibson
Charles A.	20 Feb 1860	RC	John C. & Sarah A.W. Gibson

---

1 Death register states:[p3;Ln46] Unnamed male Fuller,
died 03 Sep 1853, age 3 "months"; s/o Jonas & Rhoda
Fuller. It would appear this child died at age 3 <u>days</u>.

34

SOME RUSSELL COUNTY RECORDS
BIRTHS 1853–1866

Child	Date of Birth	Birth Place	Parents
Florence A.	03 Apr 1862	RC	Henry S. & Mary J. Gibson
George T.	07 Jun 1853	RC	James C. & Jerusha Gibson
Harriet V.	18 Feb 1861	RC	William P. & Elizabeth B. Gibson
Margaret A.	__ Jul 1860	RC	Henry L. & Mary J. Gibson
Martha J.	27 Apr 1853	RC	William Jr. & Sabra Gibson
Melvil A.	01 Sep 1858	RC	Henry & Mary J. Gibson
Nancy D.	04 Jan 1866	Cc	John C. & Sarah Ann Gibson
Samuel P.	25 Aug 1856	RC	John C. & Sarah Gibson
Sarah N.	08 Sep 1854	RC	Thomas & Rachel Gibson
William T.	17 Feb 1853	RC	James H. & Mary J. Gibson
William	18 Dec 1866	Le	Henry S. & Mary J. Gilmer
GILBERT			
(Un/F)[1]	18 Apr 1860	NG	William & Polly Gilbert
(Un/F)	12 Nov 1862	NG	Samuel & Louisa Gilbert
James	09 May 1853	CS	James & Jane Gilbert
John D.	24 Apr 1854	RC	Samuel & Lucinda Gilbert
John P.	10 Apr 1862	NG	Joseph Jr. & Vina Gilbert
Margaret J.	17 Nov 1859	RC	Samuel & Lucinda Gilbert
Samuel	01 Apr 1865	RC	William G. & Mary Gilbert
Sidna J.	09 May 1853	NG	William & Mary Gilbert
Vesta	10 May 1861	WC	Joseph & Vena Gilbert
GILISPIE			
(Un/M)[2]	01 Mar 1854	RC	John C. & Mary Gilispie
GILLISPIE			
Marion	12 Oct 1856	RC	John C. & Mary Gillispie
GILLUM			
David	26 Apr 1853	RC	Ira & Nancy Gillum
GILMER			
Anna A.	26 Nov 1861	CC	Isaac & Mary P. Gilmer
Ballard P.	30 Aug 1860	RC	William Jr & Margaret A. Gilmer

---

1 1860 Russell County census Lebanon Hh# 514 of William & Mary Gilbert lists: Sydney, 7; Mary, 6; Lavinia, 4; Irena, 2/12; et al.

2 1860 Russell County census New Garden Hh# 929 of John C. & Mary E. Gillispie lists: Rees B., 9; Ellan O., 7; Thomas H., 5; Maria A., 3; et al.

SOME RUSSELL COUNTY RECORDS
BIRTHS 1853-1866

Child	Date of Birth	Birth Place	Parents
Cynthia A.	24 Jul 1866	Mo	Daughtery & Mary E. Gilmer
Emely F.	24 May 1860	EG	Isaac & Mary Gilmer
Harriet C.	10 Oct 1866	CC	Isaac & Mary Gilmer
Isaac A.	29 Jul 1858	RC	Isaac & Mary P. Gilmer
James L.	28 Nov 1862	RC	John W. & Mary M. Gilmer
James Oliver Beauregard	11 Mar 1862	RC	William W & Sarah Jane Gilmer
Joseph H.	21 Nov 1855	RC	Wesley & Martha E. Gilmer
Mary Jane	29 Jan 1853	RC	Daugherty & Nancy C. Gilmer
Mary Ann	13 Mar 1860	RC	Morgan & Mary Ann Gilmer
Nathaniel D.	07 Apr 1857	RC	Daughtry & Nancy C. Gilmer
Neuton H.	01 Nov 1857	RC	Joseph & Caroline Gilmer
Rebecca J.	10 Jan 1856	RC	Isaac & Mary P. Gilmer
Rebecca J.	10 Jan 1857	RC	Isaac & Mary T. Gilmer
Robert L.	10 Sep 1866	Mo	Joseph B. & Caroline Gilmer
William C.	12 Sep 1855	RC	Joseph & Caroline Gilmer

GILUME

Child	Date of Birth	Birth Place	Parents
Shaderick W.	21 Dec 1854	RC	Ira & Nancy Gilum

GLENN

Child	Date of Birth	Birth Place	Parents
Elisha	09 Sep 1860	RC	David & Eliza Glenn
John W.	05 Nov 1861	RC	William & Esther Glenn
Levina	07 Dec 1860	RC	Alexander E. & Levina Glenn
Thurey Ann Rebecca	31 Mar 1860	RC	William L. & Easter S. Glenn

GOSE

Child	Date of Birth	Birth Place	Parents
George P.	27 ??? 1854	RC	George C. & Marial Gose
Henry	05 Nov 1856	RC	Aaron & Nancy P. Gose
John T.	27 Jul 1854	RC	Aaron & Nancy T. Gose
Nancy A.	18 Oct 1858	RC	Aaron & Nancy Gose
William C.	__ Oct 1861	RC	George C. & Maria F. Gose
William H.	03 Jul 1860	RC	Nathaniel D & Rebecca G Gose

GRACE

Child	Date of Birth	Birth Place	Parents
Caldonia	11 Dec 1859	RC	James M. & Rosannah Grace

GRAGG

Child	Date of Birth	Birth Place	Parents
Armilda M.	30 Mar 1854	RC	William H. & Cynda A. Gragg
Francis R.	27 Apr 1858	RC	William H. & Cyntha A. Gragg

SOME RUSSELL COUNTY RECORDS
BIRTHS   1853-1866

Child	Date of Birth	Birth Place	Parents

GRAY

Child	Date of Birth	Birth Place	Parents
(Un/child)	12 Dec 1859	RC	Archer J. & Mary E. Gray
John E.R.C.R.A.[1]	22 Sep 1858	RC	John E.R. & Rachel Gray
Martha E.J.	12 Sep 1856	RC	Napoleon B. & Rebecca Gray
Martha A.	18 May 1857	RC	John & Rachel Gray
Mary Belle	22 Dec 1866	Le	A.J. & Mary E. Gray
Mary E.	04 May 1866	Cw	John T. & Sarah L. Gray
Polly A. (tw)	22 Sep 1858	RC	John E.R. & Rachel Gray
Rachel E.	18 May 1857	RC	John & Rachel Gray

GREEN

Child	Date of Birth	Birth Place	Parents
James W.	02 Jan 1853	SCo	Hiram & Gorilada Green
James M.	27 Nov 1855	RC	Elias & Sarah Green
Nancy J.	15 Sep 1854	RC	Hiram & Zarida Green
William	15 Oct 1853	RC	Elias & Sarah Green

GRIFFETH

Child	Date of Birth	Birth Place	Parents
Eliza	16 May 1860	NG	Isaac & Sarah Griffeth
Mahala E.	02 Jun 1860	EG	Calvin W. & Mary E. Griffeth
Mahala	04 Jun 1860	NG	Joshua & Ruth Griffeth
Richard	13 Aug 1860	EG	Harden P. & Nancy Griffeth
Sarah R.	09 Nov 1854	RC	Calvin W. & Mary E. Griffeth
Sparrell	05 Feb 1856	RC	Harden & Nancy Griffith

GRIFFITH

Child	Date of Birth	Birth Place	Parents
(Un/M)	22 Aug 1856	RC	_____ & Elizabeth Griffith
Anna	10 Feb 1854	RC	Isaac & Sarah Griffith
Evans	15 Nov 1862	EG	Calvin W. & Emaline Griffith
Femming	07 May 1865	NG	Isaac & Sarah Griffith
Henry F.	09 Mar 1857	RC	Calvin & Mary E. Griffith
John F.	15 Jan 1858	RC	Tazewell & Leviner Griffith
Laveniah	19 Aug 1858	RC	Calvin W. & Mary E. Griffith
Louisa	10 Nov 1862	NG	Isaac & Sarah Griffith
Mary	11 Sep 1858	RC	Isaac & Sarah Griffith
Susan	10 Sep 1862	EG	Harden P. & Nancy Griffith
William C.	15 Aug 1861	EG	Calvin W. & Mary Griffith

GRIZZLE

Child	Date of Birth	Birth Place	Parents
(Un/M)	12 Apr 1862	RC	John H. & Martha Grizzle
George W.	17 Jun 1866	DC	Elam & Nancy Grizzle
James M.	23 Apr 1862	RC	Elam & Nancy Grizzle

---

1 Twin of Polly A. Gray

SOME RUSSELL COUNTY RECORDS
BIRTHS 1853-1866

Child	Date of Birth	Birth Place	Parents
John N.[1]	09 Mar 1856	RC	George & Elizabeth Grizzle
Lorenzo D.	11 Jan 1861	WC	George & Elizabeth Grizzle
Lydia E.	21 Feb 1858	RC	Jesse & Nancy Grizzle
Margaret	04 Mar 1857	RC	Elam & Mary Grizzle
Martha	16 Jul 1856	RC	Jesse & Nancy Grizzle
Mary A.	01 Sep 1854	RC	"Not known" & Nancy Grizzle
Mary	08 Jul 1854	RC	Jessee & Nancy Grizzle
Nancy J.	___ Jun 1860	RC	Elam & Nancy Grizzle
Rebecca	06 Apr 1854	RC	George & Polly Grizzle

HACKNEY

Child	Date of Birth	Birth Place	Parents
Floyd	___ Jul 1862	RC	Jno. G. & Susan Hackney
George W.	___ May 1860	RC	Anderson & Mary Hackney
Hawkins	09 Feb 1859	RC	John G. & Susannah Hackney
Ibby	12 Oct 1854	RC	Anderson & Mary Hackney
James	08 Mar 1857	RC	Anderson & Margaret Hackney
Jas. P.	20 Aug 1856	RC	Rural P. & Westing Hackney
John A.	27 Feb 1861	SCo	Archibald & Elizabeth J. Hackney
Joseph E.	08 Mar 1861	RC	John W. & Sarah L. Hackney
Lucinda	10 Sep 1853	RC	John G. & Susanna Hackney
Mary	17 Dec 1866	Mo	John W. & Sarah Hackney
Samuel E.	07 Apr 1858	RC	George W. & Catherine Hackney

HALE

Child	Date of Birth	Birth Place	Parents
(Stillborn/F)[2]	06 Apr 1853	RC	"Unknown" & Nancy D. Hale
Clark	18 Feb 1857	RC	J.F. & Fanener(?) Hale
Eleander	01 Jun 1866	Li	Wilbourn & Eleader Hale
Elizabeth	___ Jun 1862	RC	James & Fanissi(?) Hale
Emeline	11 Jun 1860	NG	Sparrel H. & Martha Hale
James	16 Dec 1855	NG	Sparrell & Martha Hale
Malisa	12 May 1856	RC	Henry D. & Ruthy Hale
Noah	22 Oct 1862	RC	James & Eleanor Hale
Sarah J.	05 Apr 1853	RC	William G. & Anna Hale
Sarah	14 Apr 1854	RC	Henry & Ruthe Hale
Tennessee	___ ___ 1858	RC	Jas. F. & Fannie Hale
William	16 Nov 1860	RC	Henry & Mariah Hale

---

1 a possible error: Death Register states John N. Grizzle died at age 2y 3m on 09 Mar 1856; s/o George & Elizabeth Grizzle

2 Birth of (Stillborn female) reported by grandfather, James Hay. [p7;Ln13]

SOME RUSSELL COUNTY RECORDS
BIRTHS 1853-1866

Child	Date of Birth	Birth Place	Parents
HALL			
Absalom	03 Nov 1856	RC	William & Sarah Hall
Elbert (tw)	20 Jul 1857	RC	William & Elizabeth Hall
George W.C.[1]	06 Oct 1853	RC	John & Anna Hall
Mary (tw)	20 Jul 1857	RC	William & Elizabeth Hall
HAMILTON			
James Hopkins	09 Oct 1853	RC	Nathan & Zeph Roan Hamilton
Matilda M.	08 Nov 1858	TN	George M. & Virginia S. Hamilton
Richard R.	15 Apr 1862	RC	George M. & Virginia S. Hamilton
Robert P.	07 Dec 1855	RC	Nathan & Suffrana Hamilton
HANEY			
Martha J.	12 Nov 1860	Le	John W. & Sarah E. Haney
HANSON			
Ellen	05 Sep 1853	RC	James M. & Margaret S. Hanson
Frank M. (twin)	07 Mar 1858	RC	Jas. M. & Margaret L. Hanson
John (twin)	07 Mar 1858	RC	Jas. M. & Margaret L. Hanson
HARGIS			
Martha W.	26 Jun 1860	CS	Leonard S. & Rebecca Hargis
Mary Ann	08 Sep 1862	EG	Leonard S & Rebecca R Hargis
Thomas J. Davis	27 Aug 1861	CS	Leonard & Rebecca Hargis
HARMON			
Charles	02 Feb 1859	RC	Henry & Rebecca Harmon
Robert	___ Jun 1859	RC	Wilson & Elizabeth Harmon
HARRIS			
Eliza	06 Sep 1853	EG	Thomas H. & Rebecca J. Harris
Eunice	23 Oct 1857	RC	John & Elizabeth Harris
Hill	06 Sep 1855	Sa	James & Jane Harris
James B.	27 Dec 1855	Lo	Thomas H. & Rebecca Harris
Jessee F.	02 Aug 1854	RC	John & Elizabeth Harris
Jinney E.	28 Mar 1860	EG	Thomas H. & Rebecca J. Harris
Laura C.	25 Jul 1866	Mo	John & Elizabeth Harris
Sarah	08 Mar 1860	EG	Francis M. & Mary Harris
Sarah M.	16 Mar 1860	RC	John & Elizabeth Harris
Thomas Jefferson	09 Nov 1862	RC	John & Elizabeth Harris
Thomas J.	03 May 1862	EG	Thomas H. & Rebecca J. Harris
Virginia	15 Sep 1865	NG	Thomas H. & Rebecca J. Harris

---

1   See Death Register

SOME RUSSELL COUNTY RECORDS
BIRTHS 1853-1866

Child	Date of Birth	Birth Place	Parents
William F.	12 Feb 1853	RC	Johnston & Martha Harris
HARRISON			
Anna	26 Jul 1856	RC	Samuel & Mary Harrison
Carline V.	08 May 1861	RC	Samuel & Manerva Harrison
Charles C.	08 Apr 1853	RC	Leander L. & Mary M. Harrison
Joel C.	16 Jun 1861	EG	Henry & Rebecca Harrison
John	07 Jun 1853	RC	James & Mary Ann Harrison
Matilda M.	14 May 1855	RC	Saml. & Mary Harrison
HARRISS			
George W.	26 Oct 1862	EG	_____ & Nancy Harriss
Priccilla	22 Oct 1862	EG	_____ & Rachel Harriss
HART			
July (♀)	01 Jun 1856	RC	William & Salina Hart
HAWKINS			
(Un/M)[1]	06 Jun 1853	RC	Thomas T. & Jane Hawkins
(Un/M)	09 May 1857	RC	Thomas T. & Jane Hawkins
Abraham L.	04 Mar 1866	CMt	William R. & Rebecca Hawkins
Cornelia E.	11 Feb 1866	Ca	A.G. & Cornelia Hawkins
Elizabeth	09 Mar 1854	RC	Thomas & Sibba Hawkins
Ellen[2]	07 Mar 1857	RC	Thomas L. & Sibba Hawkins
Jasper N.	___ Sep 1862	RC	Thomas T. & Jane Hawkins
John A.C.	04 Sep 1862	RC	Alex C. & Milla Milissa Hawkins
Mary A.	___ Aug 1858	RC	Alexander & Milla Hawkins
Mary J.	03 Jul 1866	CMt	T.T. & Jane Hawkins
Sarah C.[3]	28 Feb 1859	RC	Thomas L. & Sibby Hawkins
Sarah	09 May 1853	RC	Bluford & Lydia Hawkins
HAY			
(Stillborn/M)	15 Feb 1853	RC	James & Elizabeth J. Hay
Harriet	15 Oct 1853	RC	Ambrose & Phoebe Hay

---

1   1860 Russell County census Lebanon Hh# 383 of Thomas T. & Jane Hawkins lists: George W., 7; Lafayette L., 5; Thomas J., 3; not named, 3/12 male; et al.

2   See Death Register

3   1860 Russell County census Dickensonville Hh# 1248 of Thomas L. & Sibba Hawkins lists; Nancy, 8; Betty, 6; (Sarah) Catherine, 1; et al.

SOME RUSSELL COUNTY RECORDS
BIRTHS 1853-1866

Child	Date of Birth	Birth Place	Parents
John	08 Oct 1855	RC	Ambrose & Phebe Hay
Martha	29 Jun 1856	RC	John W. & Rachel Hay
Sarah J.	17 Oct 1855	RC	William & Mary Hay
HAYNES			
(Un/M)	17 May 1854	RC	Robert & Susan Haynes
HEABERLIN			
Griffith	05 Oct 1857	RC	Samuel B. & Martha J. Heaberlin
HELBERT			
A.C. (♂)	21 Jul 1862	RC	Jacob & Mary M. Helbert
Martha E.	08 Nov 1860	RC	William & Frances Helbert
Thomas J.	15 Dec 1860	RC	Jacob & Malla Helbert
HELTON			
(Un/M)	20 Dec 1855	Lo	Whitley F. & Sarah Helton
Benjamine (tw)	07 May 1865	NG	Whitley F. & Malissa Helton
John H.	23 Sep 1856	RC	_____ & Juda Helton
Joseph (tw)	07 May 1865	NG	Whitley F. & Malissa Helton
Louisa E.	10 Dec 1862	EG	Whitley F. & Milissa Helton
Nathaniel Richeson[1]	23 Jan 1856	RC	Whitley F. & Melissa Helton
HENDERSON			
Bitura (♀)	24 May 1855	RC	Elbert & Sarah Henderson
HENDRICKS			
(Un/F)[2]	04 Apr 1858	RC	Andy F. & Melisa Hendricks
(Un/F)	01 May 1857	RC	George W. & Frances S. Hendricks
(Un/F)	07 Aug 1855	EG	A.F. & Jane Hendricks
Ira F.	06 Nov 1860	EG	Aaron L. & Martha M. Hendricks
John R.	10 Feb 1853	EG	Jas. W. & Eunis Hendricks

---

1   1860 Russell County census Hendricks Mill Hh# 559 of Whitley F. & Melissa Helton lists: Nathaniel R., 4; Julia Ann, 2

2   1860 Russell County census Lebanon Hh# 189 of Andy F. & Melissa O. Hendricks lists: Melissa L., 10; Florence N., 4; Sarah E., 2; not named, 7/12 female; et al.

SOME RUSSELL COUNTY RECORDS
BIRTHS 1853-1866

Child	Date of Birth	Birth Place	Parents
Martha J.[1]	28 Nov 1858	RC	Thomas P. & Margaret H. Hendricks
Whitley F.	20 Aug 1857	RC	Aaron S. & Martha Hendricks
HENLEY			
James M.	12 Jul 1853	RC	William H. & Nancy Henley
Samuel E.	27 May 1859	RC	Stephen & Grace Henly
HENNRITZIE			
Minney	12 Feb 1860	Le	Peter B. & Hannah E. Hennritzie
HENNY			
Ida	05 Oct 1856	RC	John & Mary Elizabeth Henny
HENRITZE			
Peter B.	15 Nov 1857	RC	Peter B. & Hanner Henritze
HENSLY			
Mary A.	__ Aug 1860	RC	Eli & Nancy Hensly
HERNDON			
Mary Jane	15 Dec 1855	EG	John G. & Mary A. Herndon
Nancy B.	20 Apr 1857	RC	John & Ann Herndon
William L.	18 Mar 1858	RC	John G. & Mary A. Herndon
HERRELL			
Allice	08 Oct 1859	RC	John & Sarah Herrell
Thomas J.	15 Nov 1861	EG	John & Sarah Herrell
HESS			
(Un/M)[2]	15 Oct 1853	NG	Isaac & Susannah Hess
(Un/M)	20 Jul 1859	RC	Matthias & Susan Hess
(Un/F)[3]	10 May 1854	RC	John & Sally Hess
(Un/M)	12 Nov 1860	SM	Jacob & Celia Hess
(Un/M)	05 Sep 1854	RC	James & Nancy Hess
(Un/M)	15 Nov 1862	NG	Patten & Sally Hess
Caroline	11 Jun 1865	RC	Patton & Sarah Hess

---

1 See Death Register

2 See Death Register

3 1860 Russell County census Rose Dale Hh# 738 of John & Sally Hess lists: Harvey, 9; Elizabeth, 7; Martha, 5; Sylvester A., 3; et al.

Child	Date of Birth	Birth Place	Parents
Catherine	18 Sep 1858	RC	Patten & Sarah Hess
Charles	07 Apr 1865	NG	Isaac & Susana(?) Hess
Cyntha	16 Apr 1856	RC	James & Milley Hess
Darthula	11 Oct 1860	CS	James & Elizabeth Hess
Elijah (tw)	10 Jul 1854	RC	William & Jane Hess
Elisha (tw)	10 Jul 1854	RC	William & Jane Hess
Elizabeth C.	01 Jan 1860	LC	Isaac & Malinda Hess
Emily B.	01 Nov 1865	NG	Mathis & Pheba Hess
Henry	30 Nov 1857	RC	William & Polly Hess
Henry	05 Aug 1854	RC	Patten & Sarah Hess
Henry D.	23 Feb 1856	RC	Mathias & Phoebe Hess
Jacob	10 Mar 1861	NG	Patton & Polly Hess
Joshua	04 Sep 1859	RC	John & Jane Hess
Leah	22 Feb 1853	CS	James & Nancy Hess
Malinda C.	07 Nov 1858	RC	John(?) & Martha Hess
Martha	10 Sep 1865	RC	Levi & Susan Hess
Milly	08 Jan 1859	RC	James & Nancy Hess
Polly	20 Feb 1856	RC	Henry & Nancy Hess
Rachel	16 Sep 1860	NG	Henry & Mahala Hess
Sarah Ann	15 Jun 1855	CS	William & Polly Hess
Sylvester	10 Jun 1858	RC	John & Sarah Hess
William	18 Feb 1858	RC	Henry & Milly Hess

HIBET

Soloman S.	05 Jun 1854	RC	Charles & Amandy Hibet

HICKS

Elbert S.	17 Jun 1857	RC	George W. & Rebecca Hicks
Elihu Johnson	01 Dec 1862	RC	Jesse & Sarah Ann Hicks
Martha W.	__ Feb 1862	RC	James & Mariah Hicks
Martha W.	__ Dec 1861	RC	James & Marih Hicks
Mary Eliza	11 Sep 1853	RC	George & Rebecca Hicks
Nancy O.	26 May 1860	RC	Jesse & Sarah Hicks

HILL

Jesse	10 Oct 1855	RC	William & Mary Hill

HILLMAN

Thomas	14 Mar 1855	RC	John & Sarah Hillman

HOBBS

Eli	14 Mar 1856	RC	George & Celia Hobbs

HOGSTON

(Un/M)	28 Apr 1854	RC	Samuel & Priscilla Hogston

SOME RUSSELL COUNTY RECORDS
BIRTHS 1853-1866

Child	Date of Birth	Birth Place	Parents
HOLBROOK			
John	25 Nov 1853	RC	Robert A. & Mary E. Holbrook
HOLBROOKS			
Sarah	13 Feb 1855	RC	Squire V. & Mary M. Holbrooks
HOLEBROOK			
John	22 Nov 1854	RC	Robert A. & Mary E. Holebrook
HOLEBROOKS			
Thomas	28 Feb 1854	RC	James & Fanny Holebrooks
HOLLAND			
Samuel	06 May 1860	CS	John A. & Elizabeth Holland
HOLLEYFIELD			
Thomas	24 Jun 1853	RC	William & Elizabeth Hollyfield
HOLLY			
Elizabeth	08 Oct 1854	RC	Henry S. & Elizabeth Holly
HOLMS			
Charles M.	06 May 1860	WCo	Hezekial G.W. & Sarah Holms
HONAKER			
Biddy Jane	09 Mar 1854	RC	Henry & Rebecca Honaker
Dona M.	09 Apr 1854	RC	Henry M. & Virginia Honaker
Elizabeth C.	08 Sep 1860	NG	James & Polly Honaker
George W.	21 Dec 1856	RC	Nicholus & Nancy Honaker
Henry	12 Dec 1858	RC	Martin & Elizabeth Honaker
Josaphine	19 Jun 1860	NG	Harvey & Mahala Honaker
Lyddia	10 Sep 1858	RC	James & Polly Honaker
Martin	26 Mar 1855	NG	Nicholas & Anna Honaker
Mary W.	30 Sep 1855	RC	John W. & Lucinda Honaker
Moses	19 Jul 1854	RC	Jonathan & Latilda Honaker
Nancy E.	11 Oct 1853	RC	William P. & Eliza A. Honaker
Nancy S.	01 Sep 1859	RC	Henry M. & Elizabeth Honaker
Robert	10 May 1856	RC	Martin & Elizabeth Honaker
Sarah A.C.	__ Jul 1861	RC	Henry M & Virginia E Honaker
Vila J.	18 Sep 1860	NG	William & Martha Honaker
William	18 Apr 1856	RC	James & Mary Honaker
HOOD			
James H.	06 Sep 1862	NG	John & Maria Hood
Katy	11 Jun 1854	RC	Hanson & Mary S. Hood(?)
Nancy C.	20 Oct 1865	NG	John & Mariah Hood

SOME RUSSELL COUNTY RECORDS
BIRTHS 1853-1866

Child	Date of Birth	Birth Place	Parents
HORN			
(Un/M)[1]	09 Oct 1856	RC	Ichabud & Elizabeth Horn
Harriet E.J.	21 Jul 1862	RC	William D. & Elizabeth Horn
Juda O.	18 Sep 1853	RC	Icabod & Elizabeth Horn
Mary V.	22 Sep 1860	RC	William D. & Elizabeth Horn
Margaret	__ Jan 1861	RC	Acabud & Elizabeth Horn
Virginia V.	__ Oct 1861	RC	William D. & Elizabeth Horn
HORTON			
(Un/F)	01 Apr 1865	RC	John G. Hearnton & Angeline Horton
(Un/M)	25 Dec 1861	NG	Thomas & Vana Horton
Cleopetra	31 Aug 1857	RC	William P. & Nancy A. Horton
Elizabeth	02 Dec 1861	NG	Lewis J. & Lucinda Horton
John S.	24 Jun 1861	NG	John & Sarah Horton
John D.	03 Dec 1857	RC	Lewis J. & Lucinda Horton
John H.	10 Feb 1862	NG	Daniel & Nancy Horton
Sarah N.	22 Apr 1860	NG	Lewis J. & Lucinda Horton
HOWARD			
George C.	10 Oct 1858	RC	Hiram & Ellen Howard
William	28 Mar 1853	RV	Hiram & Ellen Howard
William H.	13 Oct 1861	NG	William H. & Polly Howard
HOWEL			
Reuben	14 Oct 1854	RC	George & Elizabeth Howel
HOWELL			
Aaron F.	24 May 1855	RC	Matison & Margaret Howell
HUBBARD			
(Un/F)	10 Dec 1861	EG	_____ & Elizabeth Hubbard
(Un/F)	10 Mar 1859	RC	James & Lucy Hubbard
(Stillborn)	27 May 1856	RC	Jessee & _____ Hubbard
HUBBORD			
George W.	05 May 1858	RC	James & Mary Hubbord
Mary	05 Jul 1860	RC	James & Lucy Hubbord
Noah L.	02 Oct 1855	RC	Jessee & Malinda Hubbord

---

1   1860 Russell County census Bickleys Mill Hh# 1458 of
Ichabod & Elizabeth Horn lists: Judith, 7; Cowan, 4; et
al.

SOME RUSSELL COUNTY RECORDS
BIRTHS 1853-1866

Child	Date of Birth	Birth Place	Parents
HUGHES			
(Un/M)	__ Dec 1861	RC	"Base"[1] & Rebecca Hughes
HUGHS			
Charles L.	25 Oct 1861	RC	William H. & Charity Hughs
William G.	17 Sep 1860	RC	William H & Charity E Hughes
HUMPHREY			
(Un/M)	27 Apr 1860	EG	Samuel & Malinda Humphrey
HUMPHREYS			
(Un/F)	18 Aug 1858	RC	Samuel & Malinda Humphreys
Mary	27 Aug 1862	EG	Samuel & Malinda Humphrey
HUNT			
Elizabeth A.	24 Sep 1855	RC	"Not known" & Nancy Hunt
Garland	28 Jul 1853	NG	Garland & Jane Hunt
Leonard L.	22 Jun 1856	RC	_____ & Ann Hunt/(Hurt ?)
Joseph	02 May 1860	EG	Henry & Louisa Hunt
Leer F.	10 Feb 1858	RC	Henry & Louisa Hunt
Lilbern	01 Mar 1858	RC	William & Mary Hunt
Martha A.	26 Jan 1856	RC	John & Polly Hunt
Robert P.	26 Jan 1866	Sm	James B. & Celia Hunt
Sarah J.	22 Apr 1853	EG	John S. & Mary Hunt
Simon N.B.	10 Mar 1861	Sm	James B & Celia Hunt
HURT			
Cyntha	01 Mar 1853	NG	Moses & Mary Hurt
Margaret	23 Oct 1854	RC	Charles & Phebe Hurt/Hunt
James	17 May 1859	RC	Moses & Mary Hurt
Josiah	11 Jun 1856	RC	Josiah & Amy E. Hurt
Leonard L.	22 Jun 1856	RC	_____ & Ann Hurt/(Hunt ?)
Mary	04 Jul 1857	RC	Moses & Mary Hurt
Mary J.	13 Feb 1862	NG	Charles & Phebea Hurt
Siras	02 May 1855	NG	Moses & Polly Hurt
HUTCHESON			
(Un/M)	29 Jul 1855	RC	Francis & Matilda Hutcheson
ISAACKS			
Emily E.	__ Nov 1859	RC	Fielden A. & Melvina Isaacks
Mary C.	10 Oct 1860	RC	Francis M & Katherine Isaacks

---

1 speculatively, born out of wedlock

SOME RUSSELL COUNTY RECORDS
BIRTHS 1853-1866

Child	Date of Birth	Birth Place	Parents
ISAACS			
Frances S.	01 Jul 1866	Gs	Fielding & Mavina Isaacs
Henry (tw)	06 Jun 1854	RC	John H. & Elizabeth Isaacs
W. Harrison	15 Jun 1862	RC	Fielding A. & Melvina Isaacs
William (tw)	06 Jun 1854	RC	John H. & Elizabeth Isaacs
JACKSON			
(Un/M)[1]	22 Dec 1856	RC	James & Susanah Jackson
(Un/M)[2]	29 Nov 1858	RC	Michall & Eunie Jackson
(Stillborn/M)[3]	15 May 1855	EG	Michael & Visa Jackson
David B.K.	11 Dec 1860	NG	Francis D. & Nancy Jackson
Elijah F.	20 Jun 1861	NG	Matison P. & Mary Jackson
James H.	10 May 1853	EG	James & Susan Jackson
James	30 Dec 1856	RC	Eli & Amanda Jackson
John E.	24 Mar 1853	EG	Michael & Eunis Jackson
Leonades	27 Dec 1861	NG	Jahial & Catherine Jackson
Leuerie	27 Jun 1859	RC	Jehial & Catherine Jackson
Louisa C.	24 Mar 1856	RC	William H. & Cyntha Jackson
Louisa L.	05 Jun 1862	NG	Francis & Nancy Jackson
Martha J.	15 Jul 1860	EG	Eli & Amanda Jackson
Monterville	04 Jun 1860	NG	William H. & Cyntha Jackson
Nancy J.	11 Jan 1858	RC	Andrew L. & Nancy Jackson
(Stillborn)	05 Jun 1856	RC	William Jackson & "Margaret Price"[4]
Susan J.	19 May 1856	RC	Michael & Eunice Jackson
Victoria	09 Jun 1859	RC	Madison & Mary Jackson
William	08 Feb 1865	RC	Jehiel & Catherine Jackson
William H.	10 Jun 1858	RC	Eli & Manda Jackson

---

1   1860 Russell County census Hendricks Mill Hh# 617 of James & Susan Jackson lists: Nancy E., 9; James H., 5; George H., 4; et al.

2   1860 Russell County census Hendricks Mill Hh# 612 of Michael & Eunice Jackson lists: Joseph M., 9; John E., 7; Susan Jane, 4; Eli H., 1; et al.

3   See Death Register

4   a possible error and off line entry with wife of William Jackson missing

SOME RUSSELL COUNTY RECORDS
BIRTHS 1853-1866

Child	Date of Birth	Birth Place	Parents
JENKS			
John W.[1]	01 Nov 1858	RC	John P. & Mary Jenks
William	20 Dec 1862	RC	John P. & Mary S. Jenks
JESSE/(Jessee)			
Beverley J. (♂)	18 Oct 1853	RC	Samuel & Jane Jesse
Cyntha E.	27 Dec 1853	RC	David & Hannah N. Jesse
David F.	24 Jul 1860	RC	Samuel & Jane Jessee
Eliza J.	25 Feb 1853	RC	Margaret Jesse
Lafayett M.	22 Oct 1853	RC	Stephen G. & Rebecca Jesse
Mary Catherine	17 Jun 1853	RC	Archer S. & Crissy Jessee
Mary	04 May 1853	RC	Joseph & Anna Jesse
(Un/child)[2]	14 Jan 1859	RC	Timothy S. & Mary Jesse
(Un/F)[3]	29 Dec 1861	RC	David Esq. & Hannah Ann Jesse
(Un/F)[4]	01 Nov 1861	RC	Elihu & Margaret Jessee
(Un/F)	16 Nov 1856	RC	George L. & Eliza Jessee.
(Un/M)[5]	09 Dec 1858	RC	Charles B. & Eliz. B. Jessee
(Un/M)	25 Aug 1866	Mo	William F. & Mary J. Jessee
(Stillborn/M)[6]	10 Dec 1857	RC	William F. & Mary J. Jessee
(Stillborn/F)	___ Nov 1862	RC	William F. & Mary Jane Jessee
(Stillborn/F)	04 Feb 1855	NG	Gabriel & Nancy S. Jessee
JESSEE/(See also: Jesse)			
Alen	___ Dec 1862	RC	Archer L. & Unis Jessee
Beverly F. (♂)	03 Jul 1854	RC	James M. & Catherine Jessee

---

1 1860 Russell County census Town of Lebanon Hh# 14 of John P. & Mary S. Jenks lists: Mary E., 6; John P., 2. John P. Jenks, Jr., died 01 Aug 1862 at age 3y 8m (See Death Register)

2 1860 Russell County census Lebanon Hh# 441 of Timothy S. & Mary Jane Jessee lists: Henry H., 5; Elizabeth E., 3; Purlina Virginia, 5/12.

3 possibly Velary Elizabeth Jessee, d. 19 Dec 1862 at age 11m 21d. See Death Register

4 died 23 Dec 1861: See Death Register

5 died 30 Dec 1858: See Death Register

6 an error: died at age 1d on 11 Dec 1857: See Death Register

SOME RUSSELL COUNTY RECORDS
BIRTHS 1853-1866

Child	Date of Birth	Birth Place	Parents
Catherine V.	03 Oct 1857	RC	Joseph H. & Mary E. Jessee
Cyntha	25 Nov 1857	RC	Joseph & Anna Jessee
David C.	03 Nov 1860	EG	Charles C. & Juda Jessee
Edward K.	29 Apr 1854	RC	William & Unice M. Jessee
Elihu	___ May 1859	RC	Noah K. & Elizabeth Jessee
Eliza C.	29 Nov 1855	RC	Joseph & Mary E. Jessee
Elizabeth	11 Jan 1857	RC	Timothy S. & Mary J. Jessee
Ellen M.	23 Jan 1856	RC	Fleming B. & Mary Jessee
Emla V.	10 Aug 1856	RC	Charles B. & Elizabeth B. Jessee
Fletcher B.	18 Sep 1856	RC	Martin C. & Catherine Jessee
Franklin P.	05 Jul 1854	RC	John & Elizabeth Jessee
George L.	14 Sep 1854	RC	Noah & Elizabeth Jessee
Harriet E.	17 Dec 1854	RC	Francis B. & Lucinda Jessee
Harriet V.	06 Nov 1862	RC	Charles B. & Elizabeth B. Jessee
Henry W.[1]	06 Nov 1859	RC	Charles B. & Elizabeth Jessee
Jefferson	22 Dec 1855	RC	Joseph & Amy Jessee
John	18 Jan 1858	RC	Fleming B. & Mary Jessee
John T.	___ Jul 1858	RC	David C. & Margaret Jessee
Joseph B.F.	08 Oct 1861	RC	Joseph & Anny Jessee
Margaret B.	01 May 1866	Cr	Martin & Mary J. Jessee
Martha E.	03 Nov 1860	RC	William L. & Elizabeth Jessee
Martha H.	10 Nov 1861	RC	Noah & Elizabeth Jessee
Martha A.	14 Nov 1859	RC	Joseph & Ann Jessee
Martha B.	20 Nov 1866	Re	Martin C. & Catherine Jessee
Mary	16 Nov 1861	RC	Martin C. & Mary C. Jessee
Mary E.	18 May 1862	RC	Samuel & Mary Jessee
Nancy C.	21 Jan 1854	RC	Stanford K. & Sarah Jessee
Nancy E.	04 Nov 1860	RC	Elihu & Margaret Jessee
Nicy	___ Apr 1860	RC	Flemming B. & Mary Jessee
Perlina K.	15 Sep 1859	RC	Elihu & Margaret Jessee
Rachel	20 Nov 1858	RC	_____ & Nancy Jessee
Rebecca E.	20 Oct 1862	EG	Charles C. & Judia Jessee
Samuel F.	12 Apr 1854	RC	George L. Jr & Elizabeth Jessee
Sarah O.	27 Dec 1860	RC	A.L. & Christiana Jessee
Sarah V.	25 Mar 1856	RC	David & Hannah Jessee
Sarah E.	___ Mar 1859	RC	Stephen G. & Rebecca Jessee
Stonewall Jackson	05 Jul 1862	RC	Martin & Mary J. Jessee

---

1 1860 Russell County census Lebanon Hh# 444 of Charles B. & Elizabeth B. Jessee lists: Emily V., 3; Henry A.W., 6/12.

SOME RUSSELL COUNTY RECORDS
BIRTHS 1853-1866

Child	Date of Birth	Birth Place	Parents
Thomas B.	12 Jul 1857	RC	Martin & Jane Jessee
Thomas J.	17 Dec 1855	RC	Stanford L. & Sarah Jessee
William G.	08 May 1858	RC	Samuel & Jane Jessee
JINKS			
Mandervile	04 Feb 1855	Le	John P. & C.E.J. Jinks/Jenks
Medra	09 May 1857	RC	John P. & Mary Jinks
JOHNSON			
(Un/M)	10 Mar 1856	RC	Walter Johnson & Mary Hutten
(Un/M)	30 Dec 1860	NG	Hugh & Matilda Johnson
(Un/M)	21 Jun 1866	Cc	Jacob & Nancy Johnson
(Stillborn male)	__ Jun 1854	RC	John & Charlotte Johnson
Beverley (♂)	11 Apr 1853	RC	Robert & Margaret E. Johnston
Clark[1]	07 Nov 1854	RC	John & Mary Johnson
Daniel	18 Jun 1855	RC	Lemuel A. & Sarah Johnson
Eliza	08 Sep 1866	Cc	J. Harvey & Margaret Johnson
Elizabeth	10 Jan 1862	RC	Lemuel A. & Sarah Johnson
Emeline	07 Oct 1853	Sa	Ancil & Polly Johnson
Florence J.	30 Jan 1861	NG	Hugh & Matilda Johnson
George W.[2]	26 Jun 1857	RC	Lemuel & Sarah Johnson
George L.	30 Oct 1862	RC	James H. & Margaret Johnson
Harvey G.	28 Mar 1859	RC	Robert Jr & Margaret E. Johnson
Hiram	09 Feb 1854	RC	Jacob & Elizabeth Johnson
Isaac F.	10 May 1859	RC	Jacob & Nancy Johnson
Jac. R.[3]	24 Aug 1862	RC	Jacob & Nancy Johnson
James B.	11 Mar 1862	NG	John & Charlotte Johnson
John F.	13 Mar 1856	RC	Hugh & Matilda Johnson
John W. Floyd	01 Jan 1862	RC	Jacob & Nancy Johnson
Josiah L.	30 Oct 1860	RC	James H. & Margaret Johnson
Leah	11 Mar 1860	NG	John & Charlotte Johnson
Lemuel J.	13 Sep 1859	RC	Lemuel A. & Sarah Johnson
Martha	21 Feb 1857	RC	Robert & Margaret Johnson
Martha	21 Feb 1857	RC	Robert & Margaret Johnson
Mary E.	05 Nov 1866	Cc	Joseph & Mary Johnson
Meriah	31 Nov 1857	RC	John & Charlott Johnson
Ranson	24 Apr 1854	RC	Samuel & Polly Johnson
William H.	29 Jan 1857	RC	Thomas S. & Jemima Johnson

---

1 died 10 Dec 1854: See Death Register

2 died 10 Jun 1862: See Death Register

3 See Death Register

SOME RUSSELL COUNTY RECORDS
BIRTHS 1853-1866

Child	Date of Birth	Birth Place	Parents
Wm. (Stillborn tw)	24 Aug 1862	RC	Jacob & Nancy Johnson
JOHNSTON			
Hiley J.[1]	20 Aug 1853	RC	William S. & Sarah Johnston
Isaac V.	02 Mar 1853	RC	Lemuel & Sary Johnston
William	17 Oct 1853	RC	Lemuel & Corneley Johnston
JONES			
(Un/F)	04 Dec 1854	RC	James V. & Elizabeth Jones
Eli	11 Apr 1859	RC	Henry & Mary Jones
John H.	21 May 1853	RC	James V. & Sarah Jones
Malisia	16 Jan 1865	NG	Soloman & Elizabeth Jones
Mary	13 May 1856	RC	Isaac & Lizy Jones
Nancy A.	03 May 1858	RC	Green B. & Parthenia Jones
JORDON			
Charles W.	19 Oct 1858	RC	Thomas & Mary Jordon
Nancy	20 Dec 1853	RC	Thomas & Mary Jordon
JUSTICE			
Isham	22 Dec 1853	RC	Hiram & Jane Justice
Preston	14 Jul 1853	RC	Jarrett/Jamett & Jane Justice
KAITH *(See also: Keeth/Keith)*			
Rebecca	22 Apr 1858	RC	Hugh D. & Phoeba Kaith
KATES			
(Un/M)	14 Jul 1861	RC	Robert B. & Katherine Kates
KEAN			
Martha J.	16 May 1854	RC	Lilburn & Susan Skean
KEATH			
Abigail	03 Feb 1860	RC	Jesse & Melvina Keath
Nancy E.	___ Feb 1860	RC	William Jr. & Milly Keath
Rachel	07 May 1861	RC	"Base" (born) & Delila Keath
KEEL			
Henry	16 Apr 1855	RC	Kelly & Nancy Keel

---

1 Highlay J. Johnston died 27 Dec 1853: See Death Register

SOME RUSSELL COUNTY RECORDS
BIRTHS 1853-1866

Child	Date of Birth	Birth Place	Parents
KEEN			
(Un/M)	20 Sep 1861	NG	Patton & Polly Keen
Lewis	30 Dec 1853	NG	William & Hester Keen
Mary P.	12 Oct 1859	RC	Patton G. & Mary Keen
Sytha A.	01 Nov 1857	RC	Patton G. & Mary Keen
KEETH			
(Un/F)	04 Sep 1857	RC	James & Catherine Keeth
Martha	03 Apr 1862	RC	Jesse & Melvina Keeth
Silbe C.	03 Jul 1855	RC	Hugh D. & Phebe Keeth
KEITH			
Cleveland	29 Aug 1866	Cw	Jesse & Melvina Keith
Fanny E.	20 Aug 1853	RC	James P. & Catherine Keith
Jesse	02 Jul 1853	RC	Hugh & Phoebe Keith
Nancy	09 Sep 1853	RC	Jesse & Viney Keith
KELLY			
(Un/M)	17 Jun 1861	Re	Peter & Polly Kelly
Beverly (♂)	01 Jul 1854	RC	Peter W. & Polly Kelly
Fletcher	09 Jul 1856	RC	James & Nancy Kelly
Floyd P. (tw)	07 Feb 1858	RC	Joseph & _____ Kelly
Henry C.	07 Feb 1859	RC	Peter & Mary Kelly
Hopkins (tw)	07 Feb 1858	RC	Joseph & _____ Kelly
Margaret	10 Jun 1860	Re	William M. & Elizabeth Kelly
Mary	14 Apr 1855	RC	Benjamine F. & Mariah Kelly
Mary J.	28 Oct 1860	Re	Charles & Martha Kelly
Sarah F.(?)	08 Aug 1861	RC	Edward D. & Luisa Kelly
Sarah	14 Jan 1854	RC	Michael & Sidney Kelly
Virginia	03 Feb 1858	RC	William N. & Elizabeth Kelly
KERNAN			
Edward O.	11 Nov 1860	RC	Thomas D. & Sophia C. Kernan
KILGORE			
Phoebe	14 Apr 1853	RC	Hiram & Anna Kilgore
KILLEN			
(Un/M)	23 Apr 1854	RC	William & Lucy Killen
KINDRICK			
(Un/M)	27 Jun 1853	RC	John & Rebecca Kindrick
Closesy J.	19 Mar 1856	RC	William & Caroline C. Stinson
Evan E.	16 Feb 1860	NG	Joseph B. & Charity Kindrick
Evitt L.	20 Sep 1856	RC	William & Melissa Kindrick
George W.	12 Jun 1866	NG	Eaven A. & Catherine Kindrick

SOME RUSSELL COUNTY RECORDS
BIRTHS   1853-1866

Child	Date of Birth	Birth Place	Parents
James T. (tw)	05 Sep 1861	NG	Evan & Catherine Kindrick
John T. (tw)	05 Sep 1861	NG	Evan & Catherine Kindrick
Malvinah	09 Apr 1859	RC	William J. & Malissa Kindrick
Nancy J.	11 Nov 1861	NG	Joseph & Charity Kindrick
William J.	18 Feb 1866	NG	John M. & Catherine Kindrick

KING

Archer Jessee	22 Oct 1862	RC	Joseph & Sarah A. King

KISER

(Un/F)	__ Nov 1860	RC	Daniel & Elizabeth Kiser
(Un/M)	27 Oct 1861	RC	Abraham & Mary Kiser
(Un/F)	__ Mar 1860	RC	Abednigo & Eliza Kiser
(Un/M)	15 Oct 1857	RC	James & Elizabeth Kiser
(Un/M)[1]	22 Dec 1856	RC	Noah & Rachel Kiser
Abraham	25 Mar 1857	RC	Nimrod & Martha Kiser
Archibald	13 Jul 1853	RC	Elihue & Jane Kiser
Augustus	26 Oct 1854	RC	John M. & Margaret Kiser
Beverly F. (♂)	25 Oct 1854	RC	Abednego & Margaret Kiser
Dale C.	01 Feb 1856	RC	Noah & Dicy Kiser
Daniel	__ Aug 1860	RC	Joseph & Mary Kiser
David	14 Feb 1854	RC	Noah & Dicy Kiser
Elihu	24 Dec 1861	RC	Daniel & Martha Kiser
Elihue	22 Jun 1853	RC	John & Silvesta Kiser
Eliza C.	26 Oct 1861	RC	Noah W. & Emaline Kiser
Elizabeth	18 Oct 1857	RC	John & Silva Kiser
Elizabeth	08 Jan 1856	RC	Abraham & Mary Kiser
Ephraigm	22 Aug 1860	RC	Noah & Rachel Kiser
Floyd	27 Jan 1861	RC	John M. & Margaret Kiser
Fullen	01 Aug 1855	RC	John & Silva Kiser
Henry T.	15 Apr 1861	RC	Elihu & Mary D. Kiser
Henry H.	__ Feb 1860	RC	Henry & Mary Kiser
Jefferson D.	__ Nov 1862	RC	Andrew A. & Martha J. Kiser
John H.L.	__ Jun 1860	RC	Abednigo & Margaret Kiser
Joseph	16 Oct 1857	RC	Noah & Dycy Kiser
Joseph	09 Oct 1862	RC	Noah S. & Rachel Kiser
Joshua	22 Dec 1859	RC	Abraham & Mary Kiser
Lilbern	27 Mar 1861	RC	George L. & Eliza Kiser
Lilburn	26 Sep 1858	RC	Andrew & Patsey J. Kiser
Margaret	24 Mar 1866	Cl	Samuel & Bethany Kiser
Martha	20 Apr 1861	RC	Joseph & Margaret Kiser

---

1   1860 Russell County census Lebanon Hh# 426 of Joseph
& Polly Kiser; Noah Kiser, 30; Rachel, 25; Robert, 3;
Polly A., 1; et al.

SOME RUSSELL COUNTY RECORDS
BIRTHS 1853–1866

Child	Date of Birth	Birth Place	Parents
Martha C.	02 Dec 1857	RC	Abednego & Margaret Kiser
Mary Allis	__ Sep 1861	RC	"Base" (born) & Malisa Kiser
Mary	16 Feb 1854	RC	Abraham & Mary Kiser
Mary J.	13 Aug 1853	RC	James & Elizabeth Kiser
Mary A.	06 Apr 1866	DC	John M. & Margaret Kiser
Nancy J.	27 Dec 1855	RC	Abednigo & Margaret Kiser
Nancy C.	13 Oct 1859	RC	Elihu & Mary Kiser
Nathaniel	15 Feb 1857	RC	Andrew A. & Patsey Kiser
Phoebe	__ Aug 1858	RC	Jas. D. & Susanna Kiser
Rachel C.	04 Sep 1861	RC	Francis M. & Elizabeth Kiser
Richard L.	14 Jan 1856	RC	Abednigo & Eliza Kiser
Sarah C.	03 Nov 1861	RC	Abednigo & Margaret Kiser
William G.	11 Jun 1859	RC	Francis M. & Elizabeth Kiser

LAFORCE

Child	Date of Birth	Birth Place	Parents
(Stillborn/M)	29 May 1862	RC	James & Dicy Laforce
Aaron	__ Dec 1858	RC	Jas. & Dicy Laforce
Almedia J.	16 Apr 1859	RC	John W. & Mary Laforce
Marala	13 Aug 1856	RC	James & Dicy Laforce
Margaret	12 Feb 1857	RC	Elijah & Pheba Laforce
Sarah L.	15 Oct 1854	RC	John W. & Mary Leforce
Susan	21 Aug 1866	DC	Elijah & Phebe Laforce

LAMBERT

Child	Date of Birth	Birth Place	Parents
Nancy	20 Aug 1854	RC	William & Matilda Lambert
Nathan[1]	02 Jan 1857	RC	William & Matilda Lambert
William C.	31 Apr 1854	RC	John P. & Abby Lambert

LAMPKIN

Child	Date of Birth	Birth Place	Parents
Alvy P.	__ Dec 1860	RC	John & Nancy Lampkin
John	10 Mar 1860	EG	John & Margaret Lampkin
Kemp	15 May 1860	EG	John W. & Nancy Lampkin

LAMPKINS

Child	Date of Birth	Birth Place	Parents
Charles	05 Jul 1855	EG	John W. & Margaret B. Lampkins

LANAHAN

Child	Date of Birth	Birth Place	Parents
(Un/M)	10 Sep 1861	NG	_____ & Jane Lanahan

---

1 died 12 Jun 1857: See Death Register

Child	Date of Birth	Birth Place	Parents
LARK			
Elizabeth[1]	09 May 1859	RC	Michael & Sarah H. Lark
George	21 Apr 1854	RC	Matthias & Elizabeth Lark
Isaac L.	12 Dec 1860	RC	Alexander & Martha J. Lark
John R.	22 Nov 1857	RC	Alexander & Martha J. Lark
Mary A.	02 Jan 1860	EG	Francis & Rachel Lark
Nancy E.	13 Mar 1858	RC	Francis & Rachel Lark
LASLEY/LASLY/LASLA			
Mary	?? Feb 1861	RC	Robert & Mary Lasley
Martha W.	___ ___ 1858	RC	Robert & Mary Lasly
Margaret A.	28 Jan 1857	RC	Robert & Mary Lassla
LAWSON			
Beverly	24 Jan 1857	RC	Umberson & Nilz Lawson
Elizabeth	05 Apr 1859	RC	John & Polly Lawson
Josephine	24 Jun 1860	EG	James W. & Sarah Lawson
Mary	10 Sep 1859	RC	William & Catherine Lawson
Rachel	11 Sep 1861	NG	John & Polly Lawson
LEE			
(Un/M twins)[2]	15 Jul 1860	NG	"Father a negro" & Nancy Lee
Abby L.	15 Feb 1866	Cw	William E. & Mary Lee
George W.L.[3]	17 Aug 1857	RC	Alexander & Eliza Lee
Georgia A.	07 Feb 1861	RC	Alexander M. & Eliza Lee
Hoteme(?) (♂)	27 May 1861	RC	"Base" (born) & Rachel Lee
LEECE			
Mary E.	16 Dec 1858	RC	William N. & Martha Leece
Virginia B.S.	03 Dec 1858	RC	Alexander M. & Eliza T. Leece
William A.	12 Dec 1861	RC	William N. & Martha M. Leece
William A.	12 Dec 1862	RC	William & Martha M. Leece

---

1 See Death Register

2 Birth register indicates a male and female and states under father's column, "Father a negro, N.P. Lee mother"; under mother's column, Nancy Lee; under column of "Deformity or Any Circumstances of Interest", "2 mulattoes at one birth from a white woman"; reported by Mid-wife, Lusa Fuller. [p43;Ln29]

3 died 31 Aug 1857: See Death Register

SOME RUSSELL COUNTY RECORDS
BIRTHS 1853-1866

Child	Date of Birth	Birth Place	Parents
LEWIS			
Alexander	12 Nov 1858	RC	William & Ann Lewis
Ira[1]	05 Feb 1853	RC	John & Narsessy Lewis
Lydia L.	08 Oct 1855	RC	John & M. Lewis
Margaret C.	20 Jun 1862	RC	John & Narcessa Lewis
Martha	04 Oct 1857	RC	John & Narcassa Lewis
LIGHT			
Andrew F.	30 Dec 1855	RC	Lazarus & Elizabeth Light
LINTICUM			
Austin B.	16 Feb 1856	RC	John C. & Helen Linticum
Louisa	27 Jul 1860	Lo	John C. & Ellen Linticum
LIPPS			
Mary	25 May 1854	RC	Morgan T. & Elizabeth Lipps
LITTON			
(Un/F)[2]	14 Nov 1859	RC	William & Nancy A. Litton
(Un/M)	20 Jun 1862	RC	William & Nancy A. Litton
(Un/F)	01 Apr 1855	EG	John W. & Lidda Litton
Aaron D.	01 Mar 1862	EG	James F. & Margaret Litton
Donaldson	17 Mar 1856	RC	John W. & Lydia Litton
Eliza Victori[3]	17 Jun 1862	RC	"O/f Wedlock" & Mary E Litton
Juda	04 May 1854	RC	George W. & Anna Litton
Mary E.	12 Jan 1862	RC	Joseph & Mary Ann Litton
Soloman L.	06 Jun 1855	EG	George W. & Obediance Litton
Vincent C.	21 Apr 1860	CS	James F. & Margaret Litton
William M.	25 May 1853	RC	William & Nancy Ann Litton
Wilson	10 Dec 1859	RC	George & Obedience Litton

---

1 Death Register states: Ira Lewis died at age 2 days on 06 Feb 1853; of Croup; in Russell County; s/o John & Norrissa Lewis; reported by father. [p2;Ln17]

2 1860 Russell County census Dickensonville Hh# 1206 of William & Nancy Litton lists: James, 12; Mary J., 11; John W., 10; William M., 7; Sarah A., 5; George B., 3; Margaret M., 7/12

3 Birth of Eliza Victori Litton reported by friend, Wesley Gilmer. [p55;Ln35]

SOME RUSSELL COUNTY RECORDS
BIRTHS 1853–1866

Child	Date of Birth	Birth Place	Parents
LOCKHART			
Disa	28 Apr 1855	NG	William & Parlee Lockhart
Melvin Lee	23 Jun 1861	NG	John E. & Margaret Lockhart
Rebecca A.	10 Mar 1860	NG	John C. & Margaret Lockhart
LOGAN			
(Stillborn/M)	10 Oct 1860	RC	Eusevius & Mary Logan
Evaline	01 Aug 1860	RC	William & Malinda Logan
Mariah	09 Nov 1853	Le	Meredith C. & Mary A. Logan
Martha H.	26 Jan 1857	RC	Merudeth & Mary A. Logan
LONG			
Andrew A.	30 Apr 1856	RC	Harvey G. & Cyntha D. Long
Charles N.	12 Jun 1866	Cl	H.G. & Cynthia Long
Clark C.	20 Feb 1853	RC	Andrew J. & Elizabeth P. Long
Eliza A.	__ Feb 1861	RC	Harvey & Cyntha D. Long
Elizabeth (tw)	07 Aug 1854	RC	J.L. & Mary J. Long
Elvina E.	15 Apr 1854	RC	Harvey G. & Cytha D. Long
John (tw)	07 Aug 1854	RC	J.L. & Mary J. Long
Louisa J.	19 Dec 1862	RC	James L. & Mary Long
Mary E.	15 Jun 1859	RC	James C. & Mary J. Long
McComas	12 May 1855	RC	Elihu J. & Malvina Long
Nancy M.	29 Aug 1855	RC	Jacob D. & Charlotte Long
William W.	29 Mar 1853	RC	Joel D. & Charlotte Long
LOVE			
Charles H.	17 Mar 1856	RC	Oscar & Mary H. Love
Elizabeth F.	11 Jan 1856	RC	_____ & Mary Elking
Samuel W.	12 Oct 1858	RC	Oscar & Mary H. Love
LOW			
Dorinda	13 May 1853	HV	John B. & Dorinda Low
Lucy	05 Apr 1853	IC	Jesse & Martha Low
LUSTER			
John[1]	29 Mar 1854	RC	William & Sarah Luster
LYNCH			
George C.	31 Jun 1862	Le	Thomas H. & Mary Lynch
James[2]	22 Apr 1858	RC	Richard H. & Sarah Lynch
Mary C.	29 Jun 1860	Le	Thomas H. & Martha Lynch

---

1 died 15 Nov 1854: See Death Register

2 died 27 Aug 1858: See Death Register

SOME RUSSELL COUNTY RECORDS
BIRTHS   1853-1866

Child	Date of Birth	Birth Place	Parents
MAGGARD			
Henry	20 Jul 1855	RC	John P. & Louisa Maggard
Louisa[1]	15 Nov 1853	RC	Samuel & Lucinda Maggard
MALICOTE			
(Stillborn/F)	15 Jul 1862	RC	Jasper N. & Laura H. Malicote
MARKUM			
George H.W.N.	20 Aug 1858	RC	Robert O. & Harriet Markum
Martin	27 Jan 1853	RC	"Unknown" & Martha Markum
Rebecca E.	11 Aug 1860	RC	Joseph & Mary A. Markum
MARSHALL			
Emba E. (♀)	19 Jan 1855	RC	Elias & Elizabeth Marshall
MARTIN			
(Un/F)[2]	15 Nov 1857	RC	John & Elizabeth Martin
(Un/M)[3]	02 Jul 1854	RC	William P. & Margaret Martin
(Un/F)	11 Jan 1861	EG	Phillip W. & Susan Martin
(Stillborn/F)	05 May 1853	HV	William P. & Margaret Martin
Elizabeth	21 Dec 1860	EG	John T. & Elizabeth Martin
Francis	03 Jul 1860	EG	A.W. & Mary A. Martin
George Washington	__ Jan 1862	RC	James & Jane Martin
James M.	02 Mar 1856	RC	Philip & Susan Martin
John A.	16 Jul 1861	EG	Andrew W. Mary F. Martin
John A.	14 Nov 1855	RC	David G. & Aneliza Martin
Nancy C.	25 Jul 1860	EG	William P. & Margaret Martin
Rebecca	01 Aug 1860	RC	George G. & Analiza Martin
Thomas W.	09 Apr 1859	RC	Andrew W. & Mary Martin
Tillitha	29 Nov 1858	RC	John & Elizabeth Martin
William M.	28 Jun 1853	RC	David G. & Ann Martin
MAY			
Johnson F.	12 Feb 1854	RC	Jessee & Nancy May
Martha A.	08 May 1860	RC	William H. & Elmiry V.A. May

---

1 Birth of Louisa Maggard was reported by grandfather, David Short. [p6;Ln3]

2 Stillborn: See Death Register

3 1860 Russell County census Lebanon Hh# 350 of William P. & Margaret Martin lists: Sarah Jane, 11; George B., 10; Isaac L., 6; Albert W., 4; Mary Ann, 2

58

SOME RUSSELL COUNTY RECORDS
BIRTHS 1853-1866

Child	Date of Birth	Birth Place	Parents
MAYS			
Lilborn	14 Dec 1853	RC	James & Mary A. Mays
Martha J.	15 Feb 1857	RC	James & Mary Mays
Rachel	12 Mar 1862	RC	James & Polly Mays
MCCLOUD			
Rachel	19 Mar 1860	EG	John & Louisa McCloud
MCCLUER			
(Stillborn/M)	14 Jul 1858	RC	Jas. & Catherine McCluer
MCCOY			
Brumfield	11 Feb 1854	RC	James & Mary McCoy
James D.	27 May 1861	RC	James & Anna McCoy
James	26 Jan 1853	RC	Robert & Malinda McCoy
Jno. M.N.	29 Jun 1853	RC	Harvey G. & Matilda McCoy
Martha	04 Mar 1859	RC	James McCoy & Ann McCoy
Mary V.L.	10 Apr 1858	RC	Harvey G. & Malinda McCoy
Sarah	04 Jul 1857	RC	James & Anna McCoy
MCFADDEN			
Margaret E.	13 Aug 1859	RC	George W & Catherine McFadden
MCFADDIN			
Abel A.	25 Jul 1860	RC	Jeremiah B. & Rachel H. McFadden
Florence G.A.	21 Oct 1862	RC	David & Louisa McFaddin
John	03 Mar 1856	RC	Thomas & Mary McFaddin
Nancy J.	02 Apr 1856	RC	George & Katy McFaddin
Sarah Isabel	16 May 1862	RC	Thomas & Mary E. McFaddin
Stanford L.	10 Jan 1862	RC	George & Catherine McFaddin
MCFADIN			
Wm. B.W.	18 Jul 1855	RC	Jeramiah & Rachel McFadin
MCFARLANE			
Eliza H.	07 Jan 1853	RC	Joseph & Sarah A. McFarlane
Joseph C.	16 Jul 1860	RC	Joseph & Sarah Ann McFarlane
Robert B.	06 Sep 1858	RC	Jas. M. & Sarah A. McFarlane
MCGLOTHLIN			
(Un/M)	15 Aug 1855	NG	Robert & Polly McGlothlin
(Stillborn/M)	12 Dec 1858	RC	Harvey & Nancy McGlothlin
John	31 Jan 1857	RC	Carrell & Lucy McGlothlin
Lafayette R.	15 Jul 1855	NG	Harvey M. & Survilda McGlothlin

59

SOME RUSSELL COUNTY RECORDS
BIRTHS 1853-1866

Child	Date of Birth	Birth Place	Parents
Martha	03 Nov 1854	RC	Robert & Rebecca Ann McGlothlin
Mary E.	02 Oct 1856	RC	Robert & Rebecca A. McGlothlin
Mary M.	30 Aug 1865	NG	Paton & Rebecca McGlothlin
Melissa T.	07 Feb 1858	RC	Daniel & Elizabeth McGlothlin
S. Lorenda	01 Mar 1860	NG	Harvey M. & Sarilda McGlothlin
William	18 May 1859	RC	Daniel & Elizabeth McGlothlin
William E.	09 Sep 1860	NG	Henderson C. & Lilly McGlothlin
William L.	10 Mar 1862	NG	Harvey M. & Susan McGlothlin

MCGRAW

Child	Date of Birth	Birth Place	Parents
(Un/M)	15 Dec 1860	NG	Thomas & Sally McGraw

MCKEE

Child	Date of Birth	Birth Place	Parents
(Stillborn/M)	15 Feb 1853	RC	Lazerus & Margaret McKee

MCKENNY

Child	Date of Birth	Birth Place	Parents
Marenda	02 Jul 1855	RC	Nathan & Nancy McKenney

MCKINNEY

Child	Date of Birth	Birth Place	Parents
Arminda K.	23 Mar 1861	NG	William & Cyntha McKinney
Calrinda	02 Aug 1862	NG	William & Cyntha McKinney
James	24 Apr 1862	NG	James & Polly "McNulty"

MCLAUGHLIN

Child	Date of Birth	Birth Place	Parents
Eliza	19 Jan 1853	RC	Israel & Elizabeth McLaughlin
Susah A.M.	27 Nov 1854	RC	Nathan & Esther McLaughlin

MCNEW

Child	Date of Birth	Birth Place	Parents
(Stillborn/F)	04 Jan 1858	RC	Alexander E. & Eliza E. McNew
Elizabeth M.[1]	04 Feb 1859	RC	Alexander E & Elizabeth McNew

MCNUTT

Child	Date of Birth	Birth Place	Parents
Samuel T.	15 Jul 1857	RC	Mitchell & Malesa McNutt

MCREYNOLDS

Child	Date of Birth	Birth Place	Parents
David	15 Feb 1854	RC	James & Sarah McReynolds
Eliza	20 Jul 1856	RC	James & Sarah McReynolds
Mary	10 May 1858	RC	Jas. & Sarah McReynolds
Susan M.	11 May 1861	RC	Soloman S & Isobel McReynolds

---

1 died Mar 1860: See Death Register

Child	Date of Birth	Birth Place	Parents
MEAD			
(Un/F)	18 Dec 1861	RC	Samuel & Martha Mead
Charles H.	11 Nov 1856	RC	Presley & Mary A. Mead
Daniel E.	08 Sep 1854	RC	Natha T. & Mary Mead
Jefferson	07 Dec 1861	RC	Nathan F. & Mary Mead
Jen. Jackson	13 Feb 1862	RC	Thos Jefferson & Elizabeth Mead
John H.D.	02 May 1861	RC	Thomas & Matilda L. Mead
Mary Jane	10 Apr 1861	EG	Henson & Lear Mead
Rebecca	26 Mar 1857	RC	Thomas & Malinda Mead
Sarah J.	05 May 1859	RC	Hanson & Leah Mead
Soloman	30 Nov 1854	RC	Richard & Luticia Mead
Thomas J.	25 Feb 1861	RC	Presley C. & Mary A. Mead
Thomas W.	24 Feb 1855	RC	Thomas & Sayer(?) Mead
MEADE			
(Un/F)	01 Sep 1866	Cc	Thomas & Matilda Meade
Andrew	20 May 1859	RC	Pressley C. & Mary A. Meade
David	06 Jun 1859	RC	Nathan & Mary Meade
Eliza G.	___ May 1859	RC	Thomas & Matilda Meade
Henry M.	26 Mar 1853	RC	James M. & Healen M. Meade
John H.[1]	10 Jul 1853	RC	Hanson & Lear Meade
Nancy M.	26 Feb 1853	RC	Thomas & Matilda Meade
William	15 May 1866	Cc	George W. & Lucinda Meade
MERCER			
(Stillborn/F)	15 Jul 1856	RC	Daniel & Emaline Mercer
MILGRIM			
(Un/F)[2]	___ Aug 1860	RC	John & Nancy Milgrim
MILLER			
(Un/M)	20 Oct 1860	Sm	Moses A. & Mary Miller
Cynthia	08 Mar 1859	RC	Valentine & Temperace Mitchel
Darthula	23 Sep 1858	RC	Moses A. & Mary Miller
Elijah C.	24 Oct 1855	RC	Jacob H.B. & Martha J. Miller
Eliza	13 Jan 1855	NG	Moses A. & Polly Miller
Elizabeth	27 Apr 1853	NG	John & Polly Miller
Elizabeth	20 Aug 1862	NG	Moses A. & Mary Miller
Elizabeth N.	15 Nov 1861	RC	Jacob & Martha J. Miller

---

1 Birth of John H. Meade was reported by grandfather, Thomas Meade. [p6;Ln37]

2 stillborn: See Death Register

SOME RUSSELL COUNTY RECORDS
BIRTHS 1853-1866

Child	Date of Birth	Birth Place	Parents
Isabel	06 Dec 1861	NG	Valentine C. & Temperance Miller
Lucinda	16 Jan 1854	RC	Jacob H. & Martha J. Miller
Mary A.	20 Apr 1856	RC	Valentine & Temperance Miller
Valentine W.D.	01 Jan 1853	NG	Moses A. & Mary Miller
William G.	10 Mar 1866	Mo	Jacob & Martha J. Miller

MILTON

Charles W.	29 Jun 1859	WY	Jas. A. & Elizabeth Milton

MINICK

Margaret Catherine[1]	28 May 1856	RC	Jacob & Sarah Minick

MINTEN

(Un/M)	04 Dec 1854	RC	Philip & Nancy Minton

MINTON

(Un/M)	01 Nov 1855	RC	Phillip & Nancy Minton
(Un/child)	29 Sep 1859	RC	Philip & Nancy Minton
Margaret	08 May 1855	RC	Franklin & Ferrenda Minton
Martha	__ May 1860	RC	Francis & Clarenden Minton
Nancy E.	10 May 1860	RC	James & Jane Minton
Sarah	11 Aug 1853	RC	Philip & Nancy Minton
Thomas P.	30 Apr 1853	RC	Samuel & Eliza Minton
Virginia	15 Oct 1861	RC	Phillip & Nancy Minton

MITCHEL

Eliza	04 Apr 1859	RC	Charles & Maria Mitchel

MITCHELL

David A.	28 Dec 1860	EG	Charles & Mariar Mitchell
James M.	26 May 1860	RC	Robert F & Martha J Mitchell
John F.	27 Jan 1860	NG	Enock & Letty Mitchell
Mary C.	06 Jul 1855	HV	Charles H. & Maria Mitchell

MONK

(Un/F)	09 Apr 1858	RC	James & Rebecca Monk
Charles	03 Aug 1853	CS	James & Rebecca Monk
Ellen	12 Jun 1857	RC	James & Eliza Monk
Emeline	04 Jun 1862	NG	Fayette & Rebecca Monk
Whitley	08 Apr 1858	RC	William & Mary Monk

---

1 died __ Sep 1859: See Death Register

SOME RUSSELL COUNTY RECORDS
BIRTHS 1853-1866

Child	Date of Birth	Birth Place	Parents
MONROE			
(Un/M)[1]	03 Aug 1853	HCo	Mordecai & Milley Monroe
MOORE			
Emaline	15 Nov 1856	RC	Elisha & Polly Moore
Fleming	22 May 1854	RC	William & Cela Moore
William R.C.	11 Mar 1861	EG	Samuel D. & Lucy J. More
MORGAN			
Mary	24 May 1857	RC	Henry & Louisa B. Morgan
MORRISON			
Mary	30 Apr 1855	EG	John W. & Elizabeth Morrison
MORTEN			
Allice L.	07 Aug 1860	RC	Thomas W. & Levisa E. Morton
MORTON			
Margaret M.	21 Nov 1862	RC	Thomas & Louisa E. Morton
MULLINS			
(Un/M)[2]	01 May 1853	RC	Andrew J. & Polly Mullins
(Un/F)	05 May 1854	RC	Bazel & Mary Mullins
(Un/child)[3]	22 May 1853	RC	Henry & Dallis Mullins
David	01 Oct 1855	RC	William & Sarah Mullins
Eliza E.	11 Aug 1853	RC	Wiley & Ludemma Mullins
Esaw	22 Nov 1853	RC	John M. & Mary Mullins
George	18 May 1855	RC	Doctor & Sarah Mullins
George W.	19 Jun 1855	RC	Wiley & Laudema Mullins
James	01 May 1854	RC	James & Sarah Mullins
James	17 May 1854	RC	John & Marier Mullins
James	20 Mar 1853	RC	Preston & Sarah Mullins
John	07 Jul 1853	RC	Wilson & Rebecca Mullins
John	25 Dec 1857	RC	Preston & Sarah Mullins.

---

1 Death Register states:[p2;Ln32] Unnamed male Monroe; died age 1 day of unknown cause in Hawkins County, TN; s/o Mordeca & Milly Monroe; reported by father.

2 Death Register states: [p3;Ln34] Unnamed female Mullins, d. 15 May 1853, age 14 days, of Hives; d/o Andrew J. & Polly Mullins; reported by father.

3 Birth of (Unnamed child) Mullins was reported by a neighbor, Charles Short. [p6;Ln11]

SOME RUSSELL COUNTY RECORDS
BIRTHS 1853–1866

Child	Date of Birth	Birth Place	Parents
Louisa	07 Sep 1857	RC	Jos. & Dils Mullens
Mary	19 Jun 1855	RC	Marshall & Eliza Mullins
Olly (♀)	04 Aug 1854	RC	Sherd & Nanny Mullins
William M.	04 Aug 1853	RC	William P & Elizabeth Mullins
William[1]	02 Jun 1853	RC	Doctor M. & Sarah Mullins

MUNCEY

Child	Date of Birth	Birth Place	Parents
Nancy M.	17 Oct 1857	RC	David & Biddy Muncey
Sarah E.	23 Mar 1855	RC	Samuel T. & Phebe Muncy
William K.	20 Jun 1862	RC	Charles D. & Rebecca Muncy

MUNSEY

Child	Date of Birth	Birth Place	Parents
Katherine	__ Apr 1861	RC	David & Bidy Ann Munsey
Margaret M.	20 May 1859	RC	Charles D. & Rebecca Munsey
Mary	20 Feb 1856	RC	David & Biddy A. Munsey

MUSIC

Child	Date of Birth	Birth Place	Parents
Beverly (♂)	08 Sep 1854	RC	Soloman & Phebe Music
Major A.	01 Jul 1857	RC	George & Martha Music
Opy Alice	02 Oct 1862	RC	Henry S. & Eliza Ann Music

MUSICK

Child	Date of Birth	Birth Place	Parents
(Stillborn/M)	11 Nov 1856	RC	Lexious & Polly Musick
Angelina	13 Feb 1858	RC	David & Sarah Musick
Brooks A.	20 Nov 1858	RC	Jessee & Ivery Musick
Eby (♂)	12 Sep 1860	NG	Jesse & Stitira Musick
Elexious	04 Oct 1853	WC	David & Sarah Musick
Fielding C.	09 May 1855	NG	William & Isabel Musick
Floyd[2]	19 Oct 1856	RC	Jacob & Vicy Musick
Granville	12 May 1858	RC	Elexious & Mary Musick
Jacob	06 Jun 1861	NG	William & Isabel Musick
Jacob	27 Jan 1854	RC	Jacob & Sarah Musick
Jos. C.	29 Aug 1859	RC	George & Martha Musick
Lydia	11 Jun 1858	RC	Jacob & Vicy Musick
Mary Ann	14 Apr 1866	WC	Henry S. & Elizabeth Musick
Richard B.	15 Mar 1859	RC	Henry S. & Eliza A. Musick
Utah	22 Dec 1859	RC	William & Jane Musick
Vistea	26 Aug 1860	WC	Jacob & Vestia Musick
William B.	08 Sep 1855	NG	David & Sarah Musick

---

1 Birth of William Mullins was reported by grandfather, William P. Mullins. [p6;Ln41]

2 See Death Register

SOME RUSSELL COUNTY RECORDS
BIRTHS 1853–1866

Child	Date of Birth	Birth Place	Parents
MUSSELLWHITE			
Alexander	10 Oct 1860	EG	William & Catherine Mussellwhite
Catherine	25 Jun 1855	EG	William & Catherine Musselwhite
MUTTER			
(Un/M)	08 Apr 1861	EG	Johnson & Mary Mutter
(Un/M)[1]	1853	EG	Johnson & Mary Mutter
(Stillborn/F)	16 Mar 1855	HV	Harvey & Eliza Mutter
Abram	02 Jan 1860	EG	William & Sarah Mutter
Charles	09 Mar 1857	RC	Roddin & Loucinda Mutter
Elizabeth J.	10 Sep 1862	EG	Res B. & Polly Mutter
George	20 May 1858	RC	William H. & Rebecca Mutter
John C.	05 Aug 1858	RC	William & Mary Mutter
John	07 Jun 1856	RC	Henry & Lizy Mutter
Mary S.	03 Mar 1857	RC	Thomas & Sarah Mutter
Nancy J.	11 Apr 1861	EG	Harvey & Elizabeth Mutter
NASH			
(Un/M)	25 Oct 1860	NG	Samuel H. & Jane Nash
Fullen	09 Jun 1855	NF	Samuel H. & Jane Nash
Mary	25 Mar 1858	RC	Samuel & Jane Nash
Samuel	08 Feb 1854	RC	Aaron H. & Catherine Nash
William	13 Apr 1853	NF	Saml. H. & Jane Nash
NECESSARY			
David N.	23 Nov 1855	RC	William J. & Nancy Necessary
George H.	28 May 1862	RC	Snead & Eliza Ann Necessary
John F.	11 Sep 1855	RC	Thomas S & Eliza A Necessary
Margaret E.	30 Nov 1857	RC	Thomas & Eliza A. Necessary
Margaret E.	12 Dec 1853	RC	Wm. J. & Nancy J. Necessary
Sarah	19 Aug 1854	RC	Joseph A. & Genetta Necessary
Talitha J.	09 Apr 1858	RC	William J & Nancy J Necessary
William H.	23 Mar 1854	RC	William P & Frances Necessary
NEWBERRY			
Martha	01 Apr 1854	RC	Tivis & Lucy Newberry
NEWCUM			
Jacob	01 Mar 1853	RC	Henry & Rebecca Newcum

---

1 1860 Russell County census Hendricks Mill Hh# 644 of
Johnson & Mary Mutter lists: Julan, 11; Joseph, 9;
George, 6; Margaret, 3; et al.

SOME RUSSELL COUNTY RECORDS
BIRTHS 1853-1866

Child	Date of Birth	Birth Place	Parents
NEWMAN			
(Un/M)	27 Oct 1861	RC	"Base"[1] & Sarah G. Newman
NIPPER			
John	09 Jul 1858	RC	Franklin C. & Nancy A. Nipper
NOONKETER			
Lena/Sena	04 Apr 1857	RC	Michael & Dilimma Noonketer
NULL			
Charles W.J.	29 May 1853	Re	Isaac N. Null & _____
ODEL			
Mary Alice[2]	25 Oct 1862	RC	O/f Wedlock & Sarah Ann Odel
John A.	27 Oct 1854	RC	James & Nancy Odle
OSBORN			
(Un/M)	22 Sep 1861	RC	David & Nancy Osborn
(Un/M)	05 Jan 1857	RC	Samuel & Eunity Osborn
Cloe V.	10 Oct 1854	RC	William & Elender Osborn
Comman	19 Sep 1857	RC	David & Nancy Osborn
Ibby C.	26 Jul 1853	RC	William & Ellen G. Osborn
John P.B.L.	18 Oct 1861	RC	William N. & Penelope Osborn
John W.	14 Jun 1855	RC	Squire & Sarah Osborn
Nicy A.	08 Feb 1854	RC	David & Unity Osborn
Samuel J.	08 Mar 1860	RC	William N. & Ellen Osborn
William A.J.	13 Jan 1856	RC	William & Ellen Osborn
William T.	01 Apr 1855	RC	David & Nancy Osborn
Charles F.[3]	16 Jul 1858	RC	Squire & Sarah Osborne
Frances S.	23 Jun 1853	RC	Soloman & Cloah Osborne
Samuel M.	__ Sep 1858	RC	William N. & Elender Osborne
OSTIN			
Thomas G.	__ Oct 1860	RC	John & Elizabeth Ostin
OWEN			
Lorenzo D.	11 Jun 1858	RC	Johnson & Zerilda Owens

---

1 Speculatively, born out of wedlock

2 Birth of Mary Nancy Odel was reported by grandfather, John Odel. [p55;Ln2]

3 Birth of Charles F. Osborne reported by Uncle, William N. Osborne. [p32;Ln26]

SOME RUSSELL COUNTY RECORDS
BIRTHS 1853-1866

Child	Date of Birth	Birth Place	Parents
OWENS			
(Un/F)	27 Sep 1861	NG	Andrew J. & Pobitha Owens
(Un/child)	10 Feb 1860	NG	Elias & Sally Owens
Albert (tw)	29 Nov 1854	RC	Andrew & Aminda Owens
Andrew (tw)	29 Nov 1854	RC	Andrew & Aminda Owens
Balfort	23 Sep 1860	NG	Johnston & Sarilda Owens
Beverly J. (♂)	14 Aug 1855	NG	Johnson & Surrelda Owens
David	28 Dec 1856	RC	Thomas & Lila Owens
David F.	10 Nov 1862	NG	Elias & Nancy Owens
Elisha M.[1]	18 Nov 1853	RC	Rufus M. & Nancy A. Owens
Eliza E.	22 Aug 1853	RC	Jacob & Hannah Owens
Hannah M.	23 Mar 1856	RC	John W. & Elizabeth Owens
Jacob H.	26 Jan 1859	RC	John W. & Elizabeth Owens
Lilburn A.	11 Jan 1853	NG	Elias & Sarah Owens
Louisa	04 Dec 1856	RC	Andy & Manda Owens
Lucinda	14 May 1865	NG	Elias & Sarah Owens
Nathan E.	03 Mar 1857	RC	Rufus & Nancy Owens
Noah	22 Aug 1857	RC	Andrew & Pheba Owens
Thomas J.	20 Jun 1853	RC	Thomas & Delila Owens
Thomas W.	10 May 1853	RC	John W. & Elizabeth Owens
PAINTER			
James Asbury	26 Mar 1862	RC	Jas. A. & Sarah Ann Painter
John M.	09 Jan 1853	RC	James & Sarah A. Painter
Mary E.	08 Sep 1857	RC	James & Sarah A. Painter
PANTER			
Rolson	05 Mar 1854	RC	James A. & Sary Panter
PARKS			
(Un/M)	22 Dec 1861	NG	_____ & Lucinda Parks
Jackson N.	11 Sep 1862	EG	Aaron & Jane Parks
Thursy J.	12 May 1860	EG	James J. & Rosa Parks
PARRIS			
John	10 Jul 1856	RC	_____ & Manda Elking
PATRICK			
Albert C.	11 Sep 1853	EG	William & Susan Patrick
George W.	15 Aug 1860	EG	William & Susan Patrick
Hannah	25 Jan 1857	RC	Hezakiah & Rachel Patrick

---

1 Elisha M. Owens died 26 Dec 1853; age 1m 8d; of Croup; in Russell County; s/o Rufus & Nancy Owens; death reported by father. [p2;Ln14].

SOME RUSSELL COUNTY RECORDS
BIRTHS 1853-1866

Child	Date of Birth	Birth Place	Parents
Helan	05 Sep 1861	EG	Hezekial & Rachel Patrick
Mary E.	19 Jul 1853	RC	John & Susannah Patrick
Philip	16 Mar 1853	EG	Hezekial & Rachel Patrick
Robert F.	25 May 1860	RC	John S. & Susanah Patrick
Sarah	__ Dec 1858	RC	Isham & Lidia M. Patrick

PATTER
Tabitha	16 Aug 1857	RC	John & Elizabeth Patter

PATTERRICK
Henry P.	22 Sep 1855	RC	John S. & Susanah Patterrick

PATTERSON
Ellen	__ Feb 1860	RC	Erasms J & Helen A Patterson
James O.	__ Oct 1862	RC	Erastus J & Helen A Patterson
Josiah J.	10 Nov 1866	Cw	Jas. T. & Celia Patterson

PATTON
Nancy Agness	24 Nov 1862	RC	Wesley S. & Mahala Patton

PECK
Thomas K.	__ Dec 1854	RC	Christopher & Isabel Peck

PERCELL
Charles H.	09 Jul 1854	RC	James & Elizabeth Percell

PERKINS
Cosby	30 Jun 1865	RC	Flemmings & Sarah Perkins
Joseph H.	21 Feb 1860	EG	Flem. & Sarah Perkins
Joseph D.	04 Mar 1859	RC	Harvey & Lucinda Perkins
Laticia C.	22 May 1861	NG	Harvey W. & Lucinda Perkins
Margaret	25 Aug 1853	EG	Fleming & Sarah Perkins
Melinda	30 Mar 1858	RC	Fleming & Sarah Perkins

PERKY
Letitia	20 Nov 1853	RC	Franklin & Catherine Perky
Louisa M.	02 Nov 1855	RC	Franklin & Catherine Perky

PERRIGIN
Caroline E.	22 Oct 1858	RC	Fermon & Jane Perrigin

PERRY
Montgomery	06 Jul 1854	RC	James & Frances Perry

PHELPS
Samuel	__ Aug 1862	WCo	William H. & Elizabeth Phelps
Samuel	01 Sep 1853	RC	Samuel & Riety Phelps

68

SOME RUSSELL COUNTY RECORDS
BIRTHS 1853-1866

Child	Date of Birth	Birth Place	Parents
PHILLIPS			
Margaret E.	21 Apr 1860	RC	Henry P. & Catherine Phillips
PHIPPS			
(Un/M)	10 Jan 1854	RC	Alexander & Sely Phipps
Columbus	18 Jun 1853	RC	Wilborn & Caroline Phipps
PINION			
(Un/M)	02 Apr 1853	NG	William & Milly Pinion
Charles M.	12 Oct 1855	NG	William A. & Milley Pinion
Milly	12 Sep 1858	RC	William & Polly Pinion
PIPPIN			
Analiza	01 Sep 1855	RC	William & Mary A. Pippin
Charles C.	25 Nov 1853	RC	Zachariah & Nancy Pippin
Elbert H.	02 Aug 1853	WCo	Robert S. & Sarah Pippin
John H.	05 Sep 1857	RC	William & Mary A. Pippin
POINDEXTER			
Samuel H.	11 Dec 1853	RC	John & Margaret Poindexter
POOL			
Elizabeth M.	01 Sep 1855	RC	Hardy & Jemima Pool
Margaret R.	16 Feb 1854	RC	Hardy & Jemima Pool
Nancy M.	___ Nov 1854	RC	Minites & Susan Pool
PORTER			
Elizabeth	___ Nov 1858	RC	Melvin L. & Susan Porter
Harriet J.	03 Jul 1866	Cc	Melvin L. & Susannah Porter
James R.D.	03 Mar 1853	RC	James R. & Lavinah Porter
James M.	17 Apr 1862	RC	Daniel M. & Malinda Porter
Jno. S.	12 Oct 1862	RC	Thomas M. & Hannah M. Porter
Joseph Floyd	01 Apr 1862	RC	Melvin S. & Susanah Porter
Karra E.	30 May 1855	RC	William & Erimica Porter
Martha	09 Jan 1857	RC	Thomas M. & Hannah M. Porter
Mary A.E.	22 May 1860	RC	Melvin L. & Susanah Porter
Mary	09 Sep 1854	RC	Thomas & Hannah Porter
Mary P.	___ Apr 1858	RC	John R. & Eliza J. Porter
Oscar	03 Mar 1857	RC	William D. & Mary C. Porter
Samuel P.	17 Jun 1860	RC	Thomas M. & Hannah M. Porter
POSTON			
Charles	06 Sep 1856	RC	Soloman & Sarah Poston
POTTER			
Levi	21 Mar 1855	RC	John & Elizabeth Potter

SOME RUSSELL COUNTY RECORDS
BIRTHS 1853-1866

Child	Date of Birth	Birth Place	Parents

POWERS

Child	Date of Birth	Birth Place	Parents
Anthony W.L.	04 Sep 1859	RC	Oliver J. & Juda Powers
Charles J.	17 Apr 1858	RC	John & Elizabeth Powers
Hiram	14 Dec 1854	RC	Jonas & Sary A. Powers
Lavisa	18 Sep 1854	RC	John & Sarah Powers
Mary H.	27 Oct 1858	RC	William H. & Helen Powers
Mary E.	20 Sep 1855	RC	John & Elizabeth Powers
Nancy V. (?)	30 Jun 1861	RC	John & Elizabeth Powers
Rhoda C.	09 Apr 1853	RC	William K. & Hellen M. Powers
Sarah C.	___ ___ 1858	RC	James & Sarah E. Powers
Sarah L.	16 Jun 1854	RC	William A. & Susannah Powers

PRATT

Child	Date of Birth	Birth Place	Parents
George W. (tw)	20 Dec 1860	RC	Richard & Susan Pratt
James J. (tw)	20 Dec 1860	RC	Richard & Susan Pratt

PRESTLEY

Child	Date of Birth	Birth Place	Parents
Evans T.	06 Apr 1857	RC	James & Susan Prestley

PRICE

Child	Date of Birth	Birth Place	Parents
(Un/M)[1]	07 Nov 1853	Lo	Thomas S. & Sarah Price
(Un/child)	24 Dec 1856	RC	Benjamine F. & Mary A. Price
(Un/F)	20 Nov 1861	EG	_____ & Eunice Price
(Un/F)	22 Feb 1860	RC	John & Rebecca Price
Aaron[2]	15 May 1862	EG	James M. & Matilda Price
David H.	10 Feb 1862	EG	_____ & Marinda Price
George W.	22 Feb 1861	RC	John & Rebecca Price
Harvey B.F.	20 Apr 1857	RC	John & Rebecca Price
Henry A.M.	14 Jun 1857	RC	William H. & Mary Price
James L.[3]	30 May 1856	RC	Samuel & Margaret Price
John B.	08 Aug 1859	RC	Samuel & Margaret Price
Louisa	01 Oct 1854	RC	William & Mary Price
Lucinda	20 Aug 1861	EG	James B.(?) & Louisa Price
Lucinda F.	06 Oct 1854	RC	Mark & Elen Price
Malinda	04 Sep 1854	RC	Daniel & Malinda Price

---

1 1860 Russell County census Hendricks Mill Hh# 529 of
Thomas S. & Sarah Price lists: Andrew, 10; Sarah Jane,
8; Benjamin, 6; Mary, 3; et al.

2 See Death Register

3 birth register is off line for mother

SOME RUSSELL COUNTY RECORDS
BIRTHS 1853-1866

Child	Date of Birth	Birth Place	Parents
Malinda[1]	03 Dec 1860	Lo	_____ & Mary A. Price
Margaret	06 Nov 1855	Lo	Richard & Sarah Price
Mary E.	29 Nov 1857	RC	Elgen & Sarah Price
Mary M.	28 Oct 1856	RC	Thomas S. & Sarah Price
Oliver	14 Nov 1854	RC	Benjamine F. & Mary Ann Price
William S.	03 Nov 1857	RC	Samuel & Margaret Price
William L.	10 Jun 1858	RC	Samuel & Margaret Price

PROFFIT

Child	Date of Birth	Birth Place	Parents
William	09 Apr 1853	NG	Austin & Viney Proffit
Elizabeth	16 Mar 1855	NG	David & Jane Proffith

PROFFITT

Child	Date of Birth	Birth Place	Parents
Henry	02 Jun 1860	NG	Samuel & Telitha Proffitt
Jacob	14 Nov 1856	RC	Preston & Patsy Proffitt
Jane	16 Feb 1861	NG	David & Jane Proffitt
Martha J.	15 Oct 1860	NG	David & Jane Proffitt

PROFITT(?)

Child	Date of Birth	Birth Place	Parents
Causby	15 Sep 1854	RC	Preston & Patsy Profitt(?)

PRUNER

Child	Date of Birth	Birth Place	Parents
George C.	10 May 1860	RC	George A. & Katherine Pruner
Joseph A.	14 Oct 1861	RC	George A. & Katherine Pruner
Margaret	10 Oct 1858	RC	George A. & Catherine Pruner

PUCKET

Child	Date of Birth	Birth Place	Parents
Margaret A.	18 Feb 1861	CR	Jeremiah & Margaret Pucket

PUCKETT

Child	Date of Birth	Birth Place	Parents
Charles	04 Jun 1857	RC	George W. & Margaret Puckett
Elender	Oct 1858	RC	George W. & Margaret Puckett
George	03 May 1858	RC	Jeremiah & Margaret Puckett
Louisa	26 Dec 1855	RC	Anthony & Hannah Puckett
Martha W.	14 Jul 1860	RC	George W. & Margaret Puckett
Martha A.	09 Mar 1858	RC	James M. & Jane Puckett
Mary	10 Oct 1855	RC	Geobel & Margaret Puckett
Richard C.	28 May 1853	RC	Anthony & Hannah Puckett
Sarah E.	19 Apr 1853	CR	Jeremiah & Margaret Puckett
Sumesstai (♂)	07 Jul 1853	RC	George W & Margaret C Puckett

---

1 Birth of Malinda Price reported by neighbor, John E.
Linticum. [p44;Ln10]

SOME RUSSELL COUNTY RECORDS
BIRTHS 1853–1866

Child	Date of Birth	Birth Place	Parents
RAINES			
William G.	16 Mar 1858	RC	George W. & Jane Raines
RAINEY			
Robert S.	10 Oct 1861	NG	_?__ay & Mary Rainey
RAMEY			
Fullen	07 Oct 1854	RC	Rainwater & Universal Ramey
William F.	28 Oct 1855	RC	James & Lucinda Ramey
RAMSEY			
Charles	30 Oct 1855	RC	Joel & Margaret Ramsey
Elbert	29 Aug 1856	RC	Rainwater & Universal Ramsey
Emla	12 Jun 1856	RC	John & Emla Ramey
Mary J.	23 Dec 1859	RC	Joel & Margaret Ramsey
Noah	10 Mar 1856	RC	John & Dicy Ramey
Sidney B. (♀)	21 Oct 1853	RC	John W. & Mary Ramsey
RAMSY			
Sebastine H.	11 Sep 1858	RC	Joel & Margaret Ramsy
RAMY			
William	22 Dec 1854	RC	James & Eliza A. Ramy
RAMZ			
Martha	27 Dec 1858	RC	George W. & Lear Ramz
RANSARD			
Arminda C.	10 Apr 1861	NG	Bechard & Temprence B Ransard
RASNAKE			
(Un/M)	10 Oct 1862	GH	Charles & Vina Rasnake
Elijah	15 Nov 1856	RC	Elijah & Elizabeth Rasnake
James	08 Sep 1856	RC	Elijah & Martha Rasnake
Mary	04 Oct 1859	RC	Bonaparte & Susan Rasnake
Thomas H.	10 Jun 1859	RC	Jasper & Matilda Rasnake
RASNICK			
Elizabeth	15 Mar 1853	WC	Elijah & Elizabeth Rasnick
George	03 Mar 1857	RC	Carrell & Vina Rasnick
Jacob	17 Feb 1855	NG	Carrell & Vina Rasnick
Mary	19 Jul 1855	NG	Elijah & Winna Rasnick
Sarah	04 Oct 1857	RC	John P. & Margaret Rasnick
William F.	01 Oct 1853	RC	Carrell & Lavina Rasnick
RATLIFF			
Alexander H.	12 Oct 1861	NG	Robert & Lavina Ratliff

SOME RUSSELL COUNTY RECORDS
BIRTHS 1853–1866

Child	Date of Birth	Birth Place	Parents
RAY			
(Un/F)[1]	01 Jun 1854	RC	James & Margaret Ray
Cyntha E.	02 Sep 1858	RC	John & Melinda Ray
Elizabeth	20 Feb 1856	RC	Ira & Mary Ray
Fleming	15 Nov 1856	RC	John & Melinda Ray
George N.(H.?)	16 Jan 1854	RC	Wilborn & Eliza A. Ray
Matison	01 Jan 1858	RC	James & Sarah Ray
Robert	28 Apr 1856	RC	James & Margaret Ray
REED			
Lucy	23 Feb 1854	RC	Hiram & Lucy Reed
REYNOLDS			
(Stillborn/F)	12 Nov 1862	RC	Reubin A. & Mary S. Reynolds
Andy. J.	12 Apr 1861	RC	William & Lucinda Reynolds
Augustin A.	28 Apr 1858	RC	Philip J. & Catherine K. Reynolds
David J.	06 Sep 1860	RC	Phillip J. & Mary J. Reynolds
Johnson	26 Apr 1861	RC	Phillip J. & Katherine Reynolds
Mary F.	22 Aug 1861	EG	Barnard & Sarah Reynolds
Mary	03 Apr 1862	EG	Isaac & Sarah Reynolds
Melvin J.	31 Aug 1860	EG	Isaac & Sarah Reynolds
Sarah V.	05 Jun 1854	RC	Philip & Elizabeth Reynolds
Victoria	05 Feb 1860	RC	Rubin A. & Kathanne Reynolds
RHEA			
Mary J.	30 Jun 1857	RC	William & Eliza Rhea
RHINOR			
Charles	05 Jan 1861	RC	George W. & Jane Rhinor
RICE			
William H.	27 Nov 1856	RC	Etter Rice & Levi Etter
RICHARDSON			
(Un/M)	22 Nov 1858	RC	Andrew & Mary Richardson
Albert	12 Nov 1856	RC	Christopher & Amanda Richardson
Charles	02 Oct 1862	Sm	Christopher & Susan Richardson
Elizabeth (tw)	13 Dec 1853	RC	Hopkins & Mary Richardson

---

1 1860 Russell County census Rose Dale Hh# 761 of James
& Margaret Ray lists: Clarin, 10; Nancy J., 8; Caroline,
6; Robert, 5; Madison, 1

73

SOME RUSSELL COUNTY RECORDS
BIRTHS 1853-1866

Child	Date of Birth	Birth Place	Parents
Elizabeth Jane	31 Mar 1861	NG	William C. & Sarah Richardson
Floyd	04 Aug 1854	RC	Christopher & Manda Richardson
French D.	09 Feb 1866	Sm	James & Cynthia Richardson
George Floyd	19 Sep 1854	RC	Thomas J. & Jane Richardson
Jas. B.	17 Jan 1858	RC	Thomas J. & Jane Richardson
John F.	22 Jul 1856	RC	Thomas J. & Jane Richardson
Mary A.	28 Nov 1862	Sm	William & Martha Richardson
Mary M. (tw)	13 Dec 1853	RC	Hopkins & Mary Richardson
Nancy	25 Mar 1866	Sm	T.J. Dickenson & Sarah J. Richardson
Robert J.	04 Mar 1861	NG	Samuel & Mary Richardson
Simeon	20 Apr 1860	Sm	Christ. & Amanda Richardson

RICHERSON
Zilpha A.	04 Jun 1855	RC	Hopkins & Mary Richerson

RICHIE
Sarah E.	12 Jun 1855	RC	James & Barcheba Richie

RICHMON
Lizzy J.	31 Jul 1856	RC	Thomas R. & Jane Richmon

RICKMAN
Henry H.	11 May 1858	RC	Thomas R. & Jane Rickman
John	27 Jan 1860	NG	Robert R. & Jane Rickman

RILEY
(Stillborn/M)	23 Jul 1857	RC	Thomas J. & Mary Riley
Caleb G.H.	10 Jun 1859	RC	Thomas J. & Martha Riley

RILY
Martha (tw)	12 Feb 1858	RC	Thomas J. & Mary J. Rily
Susan (tw)	12 Feb 1858	RC	Thomas J. & Mary J. Rily

RINER
William P.	10 Jul 1853	RC	George & Jane Riner

RING
Rachel	01 Dec 1856	RC	David & Delila Ring

RINOE
George	08 Oct 1854	RC	George W. & Jane Rinoe

RINOR
Nancy	24 Jul 1859	RC	George W. & Jane Rinor

74

SOME RUSSELL COUNTY RECORDS
BIRTHS 1853-1866

Child	Date of Birth	Birth Place	Parents
RITTENBERRY			
George H.	23 Apr 1860	RC	Armisted & Mary Ann Rittenberry
Martha E.	04 Jun 1861	RC	Rece & Elizabeth Rittenberry
Nancy Victori	30 Nov 1862	RC	Ruel & Elizabeth Rittenberry
ROBERSON			
Eliza C.	27 Apr 1860	RC	Thompson & Elizabeth Roberson
James M.	04 Dec 1855	RC	Adam & Louisa Robinson
ROBERTS			
James A.	15 Oct 1854	RC	William & Susan Roberts
ROBERTSON			
George A.	28 Oct 1860	RC	Berry & Cyntha Robinson
Lydda A.	02 Dec 1856	RC	George W. & Jane Robertson
Nancy	29 Dec 1854	RC	Mathew & Sarah Robertson
ROBINETT			
Matilda C.	28 Sep 1855	RC	Elias & July Robinett
ROBINS			
William F.	10 Jul 1858	RC	James E. & Lilly Robins
ROBINSON			
(Un/M)	04 Apr 1860	Sm	John W. & Latitia Robinson
Elijah	23 Mar 1858	RC	_____ & Manda Robinson
George	01 Sep 1861	RC	Berry & Cyntha Robinson
Hannah	04 Jun 1853	RC	Matthew & Nancy Robinson
Hanner E.	15 Apr 1862	Sm	John W. & Nancy Robinson
Hiram C.	08 May 1856	RC	James & Nancy Roberson
James M.	01 Jun 1862	RC	Thompson & Elizabeth Robinson
Jas. C.	06 Feb 1853	RC	John H. & Nancy R. Robinson
John F.	26 Dec 1866	Mo	James & Louisa Robinson
Nancy E.	08 Dec 1866	Mo	Thomas & Mary Robinson
Richard	14 Oct 1866	Cw	Thompson & Elizabeth Robinson
Thomas P.	17 Nov 1859	RC	Hiram F. & Mahala Robinson
ROBISON			
Lear	08 Jun 1857	RC	John & Susan Robison
Mary E.	18 May 1857	RC	John & Melisa Robison
ROMAN			
(Un/F)	20 Oct 1858	RC	Richard & Tempe Roman
Christopher C.	11 Jul 1859	RC	James & Elizabeth Roman
Mary A.	01 May 1862	NG	James & Elizabeth Roman

75

SOME RUSSELL COUNTY RECORDS
BIRTHS 1853-1866

Child	Date of Birth	Birth Place	Parents
ROSE			
Elizabeth	10 Mar 1854	RC	John & Charlotte Rose
Lucy J.	15 Oct 1856	SCo	Solomon T. & Martha P. Rose
Samuel	21 Dec 1854	RC	Robert & Elizabeth Rose
RULEY			
Mary E.	15 Sep 1856	RC	Thomas & Martha Ruley
RUSSELL			
Alexander	04 May 1855	RC	Absolom & Mary Russell
Drewry F.	29 Oct 1853	RC	William & Ann Russell
Sarah A.	30 Nov 1857	RC	William & Anna Russell
SALYER			
(Un/F)	27 Dec 1859	RC	John W. & Sarah Salyer
(Un/F)	01 Jan 1861	RC	Jerry & Esther Salyer
(Stillborn)	__ Aug 1859	RC	Joseph D. & Elizabeth Salyer
David	19 Dec 1860	RC	William & Margaret Salyer
Eunice S.E. (tw)	02 Aug 1859	RC	Jeremiah & Easther Salyer
George A.	10 Jun 1866	Gc	Abraham & Nancy Salyer
George M.	18 Nov 1853	RC	Henderson & Nancy Salyer
John	15 Jun 1859	RC	William & Lucinda Salyer
John H.E.	08 Feb 1858	RC	James & Elizabeth Salyer
Lucinda	30 Sep 1861	RC	William & Lucinda Salyer
Mary E.	22 Oct 1858	RC	Henderson & Nancy Salyer
Nathaniel M.	15 Jul 1860	RC	Samuel & Martha Salyers
Peter	08 Jan 1861	RC	Abraham & Nancy Salyer
Sarah E. (tw)	02 Aug 1859	RC	Jeremiah & Easther Salyer
Sarah E.	15 Apr 1859	RC	Abram & Nancy Salyer
Sarah L.	23 Nov 1866	Cc	Jasper N. & Elizabeth Salyer
William H.	16 Aug 1861	RC	John H. & Sarah Salyer
SALYERS			
(Un/M)[1]	12 Apr 1856	RC	William & Lucinda Salyers
(Un/M)[2]	28 Nov 1857	RC	Abram & Nancy Salyers
E.M.	03 Jan 1856	RC	Abraham & Nancy Salyers

---

1   1860 Russell County census Dickensonville Hh# 1175 of
William & Lucinda Salyer lists: William, 10; Nancy J.,
8; James M., 7; Hannah, 6; Shanklin, 3; John, 1; Eliza
C., 2/12

2   1860 Russell County census Dickensonville Hh# 1272 of
Abraham & Nancy Salyer lists: Alderson, 11; Elbert S.M.,
4; Lafayette Mc, 2; Sarah E., 1; et al.

SOME RUSSELL COUNTY RECORDS
BIRTHS 1853-1866

Child	Date of Birth	Birth Place	Parents
Lemuel J.	22 Jun 1853	RC	James & Elizabeth Salyers
Trigg J.	05 Dec 1857	RC	Jeramiah & Easter Salyers
SAMPER			
William H.	__ Oct 1861	RC	"Base" (born) & Mary Samper
SAMPLE			
Granville	15 Jun 1858	RC	Joshua & Margaret Sample
SAMPLES			
(Un/M)	29 _?_ 1865	NG	Larkin J. & Elizabeth Samples
(Stillborn/F)	24 Jul 1865	RC	William & Rody Samples
Catherine	10 Feb 1855	NG	Simion J. & Nancy Samples
Elbert S.	09 Jul 1853	NG	James & Elizabeth Samples
Florence	10 Oct 1860	NG	William P. & Roda Samples
Mary	01 Jul 1853	NG	Jackson & Nancy Samples
Rebecca	08 Jun 1856	RC	Stephen & Louisa Samples
Robert P.	10 Jan 1865	NG	Larkin J. Samples & Celia Hunt
William	09 Jun 1865	RC	William Samples & Lucinda Horton
SANDERS			
Catherine	09 Jun 1865	RC	Fielding & Sarah Sanders
Evan	16 Oct 1860	NG	Martin & Elizabeth Sanders
Orenia	20 Mar 1859	RC	Martin & Elizabeth Sanders
SAUNDERS			
Catherine	14 Aug 1853	NG	Martin & Elizabeth Saunders
SEE			
Martha E.	03 Apr 1855	NG	Mathias & Elizabeth See
SELF			
(Un/M)	__ Oct 1860	RC	Thomas & Elizabeth Self
Andrew J.	26 Oct 1854	RC	Thomas & Elizabeth Self
Margaret E.	25 May 1857	RC	Thomas & Elizabeth Self
Tennissee C.	23 Aug 1854	RC	William & Nancy Self
William F.	21 Jun 1858	RC	Henry M. & Sarah M. Self
SENTERZ			
Emaline	20 Dec 1854	RC	Stephen & Sarah Senterz
SERGANT			
Hugh N.	31 Jul 1857	RC	John E. & Nancy Sergant

SOME RUSSELL COUNTY RECORDS
BIRTHS 1853-1866

Child	Date of Birth	Birth Place	Parents
SESCO			
Margaret	30 Sep 1857	RC	James & Margaret Sesco
(Un/M)[1]	15 Jun 1853	SCo	James W. & Margaret Sesgo
SEXTON			
(Un/M)	___ Feb 1860	RC	Harvey & Catherine Sexton
(Stillborn)[2]	08 Dec 1855	RC	James & Mary Sexton
(unlisted tw)	16 Feb 1861	RC	Harvey & Cathsandra H. Sexton
Calvin C. (tw)	03 Nov 1861	RC	Enoch & Louisa Sexton
James R. (tw)	03 Nov 1861	RC	Enoch & Louisa Sexton
Lafayette	08 Feb 1854	RC	Charles W. & Matilda Sexton
Mary	08 Feb 1856	RC	Charles W. & Malinda Sexton
Millard F.	11 Apr 1861	ACo	William M. & Martha J. Sexton
Millerd F.	08 Oct 1856	RC	Harvey & Cathsandra Sexton
Rebecca G. (tw)	16 Feb 1861	RC	Harvey & Cathsandra H. Sexton
Virginia	19 Dec 1857	RC	Harvey & Cassandra Sexton
William	14 Apr 1858	RC	Charles W. & Matilda Sexton
SHELL			
(Un/M)[3]	05 Jul 1853	RC	Aaron & Rhoda Shell
Harvey	24 Mar 1861	RC	Isaac & Elizabeth Shell
SHELTON			
(Un/F)	10 Jun 1862	EG	_____ & Sarah Shelton
Lucinda C.	24 May 1858	RC	_____ & Sarah Shelton
SHEPHERD			
Celia	02 Apr 1862	EG	George W. & Hannar Shepherd
Henry S.	21 Apr 1854	RC	George & Hannah R. Shepherd

---

1 1860 Russell County census Hh# 1051: James W. Sisco, 33; Margaret, 44; William N.B., 5; Margaret R., 2; (et al.) *(Note: The surname Lethcoe appears in Washington County Virginia marriage register with entry of Feb 1876: William Lethcoe, 21, b. Russell County, s/o James & Margaret Lethcoe)*

2 Birth register in column "Deformity or Any Circumstances of Interest" states; "form of an elephant" [p15;Ln31]

3 Death register states:[p2;Ln37] Unnamed male Shell, died 05 Jul 1853; age 1 day; of unknown cause; in Russell County; s/o Aaron & Rhody Shell; reported by father.

SOME RUSSELL COUNTY RECORDS
BIRTHS 1853-1866

Child	Date of Birth	Birth Place	Parents
Mary	22 Feb 1860	EG	George W & Hannah R Shepherd
Robert N.	20 Jan 1856	RC	George & Hanah Shepherd
Sarah J.	09 Mar 1858	RC	George W. & Hanner Shepherd

SHOEMAKER

Child	Date of Birth	Birth Place	Parents
Isaac	18 Dec 1858	RC	Leonard & Polly Shoemaker
Layona	15 Apr 1866	NG	Benjamine & Sarah Shoemaker
Lorenzo D.	06 Feb 1862	NG	Benjamine & Idilla Shoemaker
Lucy A.	16 May 1857	RC	Reynolds & Rachel Shoemaker
Mary A.	14 Aug 1860	NG	Benjamine & Sary V. Shoemaker

SHORT

Child	Date of Birth	Birth Place	Parents
James	20 Jul 1855	RC	James & Nancy Short
Joseph	06 May 1853	RC	James & Nancy Short
Thomas	10 Mar 1856	RC	James & Elizabeth Short

SILCOX

Child	Date of Birth	Birth Place	Parents
Ambrose	01 Oct 1857	RC	William & Nancy Silcox
Jasper	04 May 1856	RC	William & Nancy Silcox

SIMERLY

Child	Date of Birth	Birth Place	Parents
Joseph C.	19 Oct 1860	RC	James & Tabitha Simerly
Mary	2? Feb 1855	RC	James & Tabitha Simerly

SKEEN

Child	Date of Birth	Birth Place	Parents
Amanda C.	15 Mar 1858	RC	George C. & Lucinda Skeen
Cyntha	__ Feb 1861	RC	Elihu & Elizabeth Skeen
Elihu	29 Jan 1860	RC	Ephraim & Eliza Skeen
Elijah	30 Oct 1855	NG	David A. & Nancy Skeen
Frances	25 Jun 1866	Cw	Jasper & Elizabeth Skeen
James H.	16 Jun 1857	RC	Jesse & Mary E. Skeen
James D.	06 Mar 1862	RC	James P. & Elizabeth Skeen
John F.	09 Jan 1854	RC	James & Winny Skeen
John W.	02 Dec 1853	NG	David A. & Nancy Skeen
John	__ Oct 1860	RC	Jesse & Mary E. Skeen
John F.	__ Jul 1858	RC	Nathaniel & Sarah Skeen
Judea L.	02 Jan 1860	CR	David & Nancy Skeen
Martha	01 Dec 1862	RC	Ephraim & Alzira Skeen
Mary	20 May 1862	RC	Nathaniel & Sarah Skeen
Pleasant M.	07 May 1856	RC	James & Winnie Skeen
Sarah R.	07 Nov 1853	RC	George C. & Lucinda Skeen
Sarah	27 Sep 1857	RC	David A. & Nancy Skeen
Sarah V.	18 May 1856	RC	Armstrong & Rebecca Skeen
Susan	18 Feb 1861	RC	James P. & Elizabeth Skeen
Tabitha E.	28 Jun 1854	RC	Henry & Matilda Skeen
William	11 Jan 1854	RC	Jesse & Elizabeth Skeen

Child	Date of Birth	Birth Place	Parents
SLAUGHTER			
John	03 Aug 1858	RC	Alfred & Elizabeth Slaughter
SMITH			
(Un/F)	___ Oct 1856	RC	George W. & Jane Smith
(Un/M)	15 Aug 1861	Le	Albert G. & Virginia Smith
(Stillborn/M)	27 Aug 1860	Le	Albert G. & Virginia B. Smith
Abraham	15 May 1854	RC	Henry & Lucinda Smith
Amanda C.	24 Jul 1860	EG	Edwin R. & Martha Smith
Annaliza	19 Sep 1857	RC	Mattison & Martha Smith
Charles C.	10 Sep 1858	RC	George Jr. & Jane Smith
Cowan	___ Jun 1860	RC	James M. & Sarah Smith
Dicy	02 Jul 1856	RC	Matison & Martha Smith
Elijah	10 Oct 1866	Cl	Joshua & Sarah Smith
Eliza	19 Nov 1853	NG	Joseph & Sarah Smith
Elizabeth	10 Apr 1856	RC	William & Matilda Smith
Flanrnoy	10 Nov 1857	RC	David & Priscilla Smith
Floyd	___ Apr 1858	RC	James M. & Sarah Smith
Fullen	02 Jun 1854	RC	James & Sarah Smith
James F.	07 Nov 1861	EG	William & Aneliza Smith
Jane P.	14 Jun 1858	RC	Edwin R. & Martha E. Smith
July Ann	18 May 1861	NG	Matison & Martha C. Smith
Mary	30 Nov 1853	TC	Madison & Martha Smith
Mary E.	10 Oct 1860	NG	James M. & Frances Smith
Mary	18 May 1856	RC	James M. & Sarah Smith
Matilda F.	06 Sep 1861	RC	John & Nancy J. Smith
Matilda	11 Jul 1854	RC	Jessee & Mahala Sutherland
Matilda	___ Aug 1858	RC	William & Matilda Smith
Nancy[1]	08 May 1862	RC	"O/f Wedlock" & Mary Smith
Peter B.H.	___ Aug 1860	RC	George Jr. & Jane Smith
Priscilla	01 Sep 1855	RC	Joshua & Sarah Smith
Rachel	14 Aug 1860	NG	Helms J. & Mary Smith
Stephen	05 Nov 1854	RC	George & Jane Smith
Sylus	05 Dec 1857	RC	Joshua & Sarah Smith
Tase C. (♂)	20 Nov 1854	RC	Gillispie J. & Letha Smith
Tivis	12 Jan 1854	RC	William & Matilda Smith
Virginia	27 Mar 1855	NG	Madison & Martha C. Smith
William B.	08 Jul 1861	NG	James L. & Margaret Smith
William	10 Apr 1865	RC	W.H. & Rebecca Smith

---

1 Birth of Nancy Smith reported by friend, R.L. Mead.
[p56;Ln31]

SOME RUSSELL COUNTY RECORDS
BIRTHS 1853-1866

Child	Date of Birth	Birth Place	Parents
SMYTH			
Christia	14 Apr 1854	RC	James W. & Jane Smith
Stephen	05 Nov 1853	RC	George W. Smyth & Ginna Smith
SNAPP			
Elihu K.	23 May 1860	RC	Elkana R.D. & Katherine Snapp
George W.	20 Jul 1855	RC	Elcenah & Catherine Snapp
Nancy E.	25 Apr 1866	Mo	Elkanah D. & Martha Snapp
Samuel L.	04 May 1858	RC	Elkana D. & Catherine Snapp
William D.	15 May 1857	RC	Elchany & Catherine Snapp
SNEAD			
(UN/M)	25 Feb 1865	NG	Napolon B. & Jane Snead
Allis	08 Jul 1862	EG	_____ & Jane Snead
Buredard	02 Aug 1861	EG	N.B. & Margaret Snead
Louisa	10 May 1857	RC	_____ & Jane Snead
Nepol B.	21 Oct 1862	EG	J.M. & Eliza J. Snead
Oliver N.	16 Jan 1860	EG	Jacob M. & Elizabeth Snead
Philip F.	16 Aug 1859	RC	_____ & Louisa Snead
SNEED			
Neple. B.	10 Jun 1862	EG	Martin & Eliza Snead
SNIDER			
Mary A.	28 Jun 1857	RC	William E. & Jerusa Snider
Robert	14 Mar 1855	RC	Jacob & Keran H. Snider
SOUTHERLAND			
(Stillborn/M)	07 Sep 1853	RC	Jesse & Mahala Southerland
Mary J.	28 Oct 1853	RC	Alexander & Mary Southerland
Squire	03 Dec 1853	RC	Vannarsalar & Seley Southerland
STAIR/STAIN			
Mary V.	29 Sep 1856	RC	Oscar & Margaret Stair/Stain
STALARAS			
Margarett	01 Dec 1862	EG	John W. & Rejina Stalars
STALARD *(also: Stallard\Staliard)*			
Rozina C.	02 Feb 1855	EG	John W. & Rozina Stalard
STALLARD			
John	15 Mar 1859	RC	John & Rosan Stallard
Mary E.	20 Oct 1853	RC	David F. & Susan Stallard

SOME RUSSELL COUNTY RECORDS
BIRTHS 1853-1866

Child	Date of Birth	Birth Place	Parents
STALIARD			
Sarah[1]	10 Mar 1853	EG	John W. & Regina Stallard
STALLIARD			
Cyris H.	29 Sep 1854	RC	Haselten & Susanah Staliard
Lucy J.	18 Nov 1854	RC	Duncan A & Elizabeth Staliard
STAMPER			
(Un/F)	__ Apr 1861	RC	Eli & Priscilla Stamper
Palina J.	03 Jul 1866	Cw	James & Cynthia Stamper
STAMPES			
Charles L.	03 Nov 1860	RC	James H. & Margaret Stampes
STANLY			
Aid(?)	10 Oct 1854	RC	John L. & Sarah Stanly
Mathias	15 Mar 1854	RC	John & Lucy Stanly
Olly (♀)	20 Jun 1854	RC	Joseph Eastep & Nancy Stanly
STAPLETON			
(Un/M)	__ Jan 1861	RC	George & Rebecca Stapleton
(Un/F)	01 Aug 1860	RC	William & Esther Stapleton
(Un/F)	__ Aug 1858	RC	William L. & Hester Stapleton
(Un/F)	15 Jul 1859	RC	William & Easter Stapleton
Abram	10 Mar 1853	RC	James & Nancy Stapleton
Martha J.[2]	10 Mar 1856	RC	William & Hester Stapleton
Mary E.	15 Jun 1853	RC	William & Easther Stapleton
Thomas	15 Oct 1854	RC	William & Easter Stapleton
STEEL			
Charles R.	02 Jun 1857	RC	Samuel & Polly Steel
Elen	19 Oct 1854	RC	Richard & Cosby Steel
Elizabeth J.	10 Dec 1858	RC	Richard & Cosby Steel
George W.	13 May 1865	NG	John W. & Malvina Steel
Mary E.	25 Dec 1859	RC	Samuel & Polly Steel
Sousannah J.	26 Dec 1855	NG	Samuel S. & Mary Steel
(Stillborn/F)	06 Mar 1861	RC	Thomas P. & Sarah Steele
George W.	15 Mar 1862	NG	Sparrell H. & Jane Steele

---

1 Birth of Sarah Staliard was reported by grandfather, Scott Deniston. [p1;Ln9]

2 1860 Russell County census Dickensonville Hh# 1296 of William & Hester Stapleton lists: Clinton, 14; Stephen, 10; Silas, 8; Mary, 6; Thomas, 5; Martha J., 3

SOME RUSSELL COUNTY RECORDS
BIRTHS 1853-1866

Child	Date of Birth	Birth Place	Parents
Jane	02 Jan 1860	Sm	Samuel S. & Polly Steele
Louisa	18 Dec 1860	NG	John W. & Malvina Steele
Melissa E.	08 Dec 1860	NG	Sparrell & Elizabeth Steele
Samuel R.	18 Sep 1861	NG	Samuel S. & Polly Steele

STEPHEN *(also: Stephens/Stephias)*

G.W. (♂)	21 Mar 1859	RC	Owen & Easter Stephen

STEPHENS

Dealpha	28 Aug 1857	RC	James H. & Pollt Stephens
Leah	15 Sep 1853	SR	Josiah & Susannah Stephens
Oiver (♂)	14 Oct 1861	NG	Owens & Easter Stephens

STEPHIAS

Easter	20 Mar 1855	NG	Owens & Elizabeth Stephias

STEVENS

Martha W.	17 May 1858	RC	Nathaniel C. & Dorothy J. Stevens

STILLWELL

(Un/M)	10 Oct 1861	NG	Evan & Jane Stillwell
William P.	26 Oct 1860	NG	Evan & Martha Stillwell

STILTNER

Angeline	30 Oct 1856	RC	Jarred & Cyntha Stiltner

STINSON

Cosby	26 Jun 1857	RC	William & Nancy Stinson
Edward D.	18 Oct 1859	RC	John & Nancy Stinson
Elisa	03 Mar 1854	RC	John & Nancy Stinson
George W.	27 Nov 1856	RC	James & Ann Stinson
Granville A.	19 Mar 1858	RC	William & Caroline Stinson
James D.	08 Jan 1860	EG	William E. & Caroline Stinson
John W.	15 Nov 1860	CR	Robert & Margaret Stinson
Malissa J.	02 Mar 1861	EG	Samuel & Amy Stinson
Margaret	28 Jun 1855	CR	William & Nancy Stinson
Martha V.	15 Jul 1861	EG	James O. & Elizabeth Stinson
Nancy	07 May 1862	CR	John & Nancy Stinson
Nancy V.	10 Apr 1854	RC	Robert & Mary Stinson
Robert	05 Dec 1856	RC	Edward & Jane Stinson
Robert	05 Dec 1855	CR	Edward & Margaret Jane Stinson
Susan	10 Feb 1862	EG	William & Nancy Stinson
Thomas R.	25 May 1865	RC	Archer & Mary Stinson

STOOTS

Eliza	01 Jan 1862	RC	Andrew & Melia Ann Stoots

SOME RUSSELL COUNTY RECORDS
BIRTHS   1853-1866

Child	Date of Birth	Birth Place	Parents
STRAW			
Thomas W.	19 Nov 1856	RC	Michael & Polly Straw
STREET			
Mary J.	02 Apr 1853	KR	Nimrod & Elizabeth Street
STROW			
Malinda	19 Apr 1860	Sm	Mike & Vertia Strow
STRUT			
(Un/M)	01 Sep 1861	NG	Simon & Rachel Strut
STUMP			
(Un/ tw)[1]	10 Apr 1860	NG	Joseph & Peggy Stump
(Un/M)[2]	13 Nov 1856	RC	Christopher & Jane Stump
(Un/M)	18 Oct 1861	NG	Joseph & Peggy Stump
Christopher	08 Mar 1859	RC	Joseph & Margaret Stump
Shadrack[3]	11 Oct 1853	NG	Joseph & Margaret Stump
SUIT			
(Un/F)	___ Oct 1861	RC	Daniel & Rhoda E. Suit
(Un/child)	05 Sep 1857	RC	Johnson & Nancy Suit
George W.	08 Nov 1861	EG	Pleasant & Mary Suit
George W.J.	08 Dec 1860	EG	Pleasant & Mary Suit
James R.	08 Nov 1855	EG	Pleasant & Mary Suit
Member A.S. (♀)	___ ___ 1858	RC	Stephen & Nancy Suit
Nancy	28 Jun 1854	RC	Ralph & Elizabeth Suit
Pleasant	___ Apr 1859	RC	Johnson & Nancy Suit
Ranson B.[4]	15 Sep 1862	RC	Stephen & Nancy Suit

---

1 A male and female twins; birth register states; "One died at birth the other one lived 5 months" [p44;Ln37]

2   1860 Russell County census New Garden Hh# 823 of Christopher & Jane Stump lists: John F., 9; Charles H., 6; James, 3.

3 Shadrack Stump: A possible error in Birth Register. Death Register [p1;Ln5] and double entry [p1;Ln 37] lists death of a Shade Stump on 01 Oct 1853, at New Garden; age 20 days; of Croup; s/o Joseph & Margaret Stump.

4 Birth of Ranson B. Suit reported by grandfather, Ranson Suit. [p56;Ln1]

84

SOME RUSSELL COUNTY RECORDS
BIRTHS 1853-1866

Child	Date of Birth	Birth Place	Parents
Sadelia	17 Jun 1853	RC	Johnston & Nancy Suit
Stephen M.	15 Sep 1859	RC	Stephen & Nancy Suit
William R.	27 May 1855	RC	Johnson & Nancy Suit

SULIVAN/SULLIVAN
Child	Date of Birth	Birth Place	Parents
James B.	04 Oct 1859	RC	John & Nancy Sullivan
Nancy	08 Jun 1855	CS	John & Nancy Sulivan

SULLIVANT
Child	Date of Birth	Birth Place	Parents
Noah B.[1]	15 Feb 1853	CS	John & Nancy Sullivant

SUTHERLAND
Child	Date of Birth	Birth Place	Parents
Daniel	10 Mar 1857	RC	William & Silva Sutherland
Elijah B.	10 Feb 1862	RC	Elijah B. & Mary Sutherland
Emaline	28 Feb 1854	RC	Samuel & Nancy Sutherland
Emily J.	09 Nov 1859	RC	Jessee & Mahala Sutherland
Ezakial	25 Mar 1854	RC	Henry & Margaret Sutherland
Frances	__ Feb 1860	RC	Elijah & Mary Sutherland
Francis	26 Feb 1859	RC	Elijah & Mary Sutherland
John	12 Mar 1853	RC	James & Nancy Sutherlin
John H.	30 Jan 1856	RC	Samuel & Nancy Sutherland
Lee Giles	22 Dec 1862	RC	John & Jane Sutherland
Mahala	29 Aug 1858	RC	Alexander & Mary Sutherland
Mary P.	__ Jun 1858	RC	Jesse & Mahala Sutherland
Orfay (♀)	12 Oct 1855	RC	James & Nancy Sutherland
Phebe	06 Sep 1856	RC	Jesse & Halley Sutherland
Phoebe	20 Feb 1858	RC	Elijah & Mary Sutherland
Sarah	03 Jun 1861	RC	Jesse & Mahaha Sutherland
Solomon	07 Dec 1856	RC	Van & Celia Sutherland
Squire	03 Dec 1854	RC	Vanranselaer & Cela Sutherland
Thomas A.	27 Oct 1866	Cl	Jesse & Mahala Sutherland

SUTTON
Child	Date of Birth	Birth Place	Parents
Eliza	31 May 1862	RC	William E. & Thursey Jane Sutton
James F.	14 Dec 1856	RC	William E. & Thursey Sutton
William R.	09 Jul 1860	RC	William E. & Thirza J. Sutton

SWORD
Child	Date of Birth	Birth Place	Parents
James M.	13 May 1855	EG	Michael & Sally Sword
Margaret	15 Jun 1858	RC	Michael & Sarah Sword

1Birth of Noah B. Sullivan was reported by grandfather, Jas. Sullivan. [p1;Ln27]

Child	Date of Birth	Birth Place	Parents
Nancy	25 Oct 1856	RC	Michael & Sarah Sword
Nathaniel	17 Dec 1853	RG	Michael & Sarah Sword

SYKES

Child	Date of Birth	Birth Place	Parents
(Un/F)	22 Oct 1855	EG	John & Causbey Sykes
(Un/M)	14 Mar 1862	NG	Samuel H. & Emma Sykes
Caldanah (male)	19 May 1857	RC	Noah & Susanah Sykes
Larkin	25 Oct 1860	Cl	John & Celia Sykes
Rachel J.	15 May 1860	Cl	Newton & Sarah Sykes
Samuel H.	23 Oct 1860	Cl	Samuel & Emely Sykes

TALBERT

Child	Date of Birth	Birth Place	Parents
John	22 Jun 1853	RC	Berry H. & Ginna Talbert
Nancy E.	10 Sep 1854	RC	Joseph T. & Nancy V. Talbert

TATE

Child	Date of Birth	Birth Place	Parents
(Un/M)	28 Jun 1861	RC	Thomas T. & Sarah A.C. Tate
(Stillborn/F)	19 Jun 1862	RC	Thomas T. & Sarah A.C. Tate
Jacob E.	03 Apr 1858	RC	James M. & Sarah J.B. Tate
Nathaniel B.	20 Mar 1860	RC	Thomas T. & Sarah A.C. Tate
Robert F.	04 Oct 1862	RC	James M. & Sarah J.B. Tate
Thomas J.	18 Sep 1855	RC	James M. & Sarah J.B. Tate
William E.	03 Apr 1860	RC	James M. & Sarah J. Tate

TAYLOR

Child	Date of Birth	Birth Place	Parents
(Un/F)[1]	24 Aug 1854	RC	Emeby & Nancy Taylor
(Un/F)	05 Dec 1853	EG	Michael & Nancy Taylor
(Un/F)	10 Jun 1861	EG	James & Nancy Taylor
(Un/M)	26 Mar 1862	NG	Harvey & Celia Taylor
(Un/F)[2]	01 Aug 1854	RC	Smith & Mary Taylor
(Un/F)	10 Oct 1857	RC	Emby & Nancy Taylor
Catherine	06 Jun 1858	RC	Willard & Margaret Taylor
Charles W.	15 Jun 1858	RC	James & Nancy Taylor
Charles	16 Jun 1865	NG	William & Lydia Taylor
Charles	10 Oct 1858	RC	Harvey & Jane Taylor
Cosby M.	15 Sep 1861	EG	Emiby & Nancy P. Taylor

---

1 1860 Russell County census Hendricks Mill Hh# 619 of Emby & Nancy P. Taylor lists: Elihu V., 14; Parris, 12; Robert W., 11; Samuel W., 9; Julia Ann E., 8; Rachael J., 5; James C., 4; Clarisa V., 2; Not-named, 4/12 male.

2 1860 Russell County census Hendricks Mill Hh# 613 of Smith & Elizabeth Taylor lists: John, 11; James H., 9; Polly Jane, 7; Hulda C., 4; Susannah, 9/12.

SOME RUSSELL COUNTY RECORDS
BIRTHS 1853-1866

Child	Date of Birth	Birth Place	Parents
Fullen H.	06 Nov 1860	EG	William P. & Margaret Taylor
Greenberry	03 Feb 1855	EG	Michael L. & Nancy Taylor
Isaac H.	09 Jun 1858	RC	Crabtree & Martha Taylor
James C.	10 Apr 1856	RC	Emby & Nancy Taylor.
Josefine	13 Apr 1856	RC	William & Margaret Taylor
Lucy A.	18 Sep 1861	NG	Harvey Jr. & Margaret Taylor
Margaret	10 Feb 1860	EG	Crabtree & Patsey Taylor
Mary E.	01 May 1853	RF	William & Jane Taylor
Mary	28 Mar 1853	HV	Crabtree & Priscilla Taylor
Rebecca	11 Oct 1855	EG	Crabtree & Priscilla Taylor
Rufus	28 Mar 1861	EG	Harvey & Celia Taylor
Samuel	10 Jul 1856	RC	Harvey & Jane Taylor
Samuel	09 May 1854	RC	Charles & Mary A. Taylor
Sarah	02 Jun 1860	NG	James & Nancy Taylor
Thomas E.	10 Jun 1857	RC	Michael & Nancy Taylor
William	10 Jun 1854	RC	Michael & Nancy Taylor

TERRY

Child	Date of Birth	Birth Place	Parents
Caldonia	23 Oct 1858	RC	James & Mary Ann A. Terry

THACKER

Child	Date of Birth	Birth Place	Parents
Calvin	28 Feb 1853	NG	Robert & Eliza Thacker
Lizy	04 Apr 1856	RC	Robert & Lizy Thacker

THOMAS

Child	Date of Birth	Birth Place	Parents
(Un/F)	08 Sep 1856	RC	Samuel & Mary Thomas
Beverly[1]	20 Jun 1853	CS	Whitley & Nancy Thomas
Evaline	28 Dec 1860	EG	Whitley & Nancy Thomas
Florence	15 Sep 1862	EG	Whitley F. & Nancy Thomas
Fullen	04 Mar 1854	RC	Rolin & Malinda Thomas
James	29 Feb 1856	RC	Eli & Elender Thomas
John P.	12 Oct 1858	RC	Thadeus P. & Sarah Thomas
Joseph A.	04 Sep 1860	RC	John V. & Virginia C. Thomas
Laura V.	20 Dec 1860	EG	T.P. & Sarah Thomas
Mary A.	25 Oct 1859	RC	Whitley & Nancy Thomas
Sarah	08 Oct 1853	Sa	Eli & Ellen Thomas
William H.	27 Sep 1857	RC	Whitley & Nancy Thomas

THOMPSON

Child	Date of Birth	Birth Place	Parents
Celia	07 Oct 1856	RC	Emory & Phoebe Thompson
Edward D.	03 Sep 1855	EG	Squire & Sousan Thompson
George C.	10 Nov 1855	NG	Jacob & Joannah Thompson
Henry	01 Apr 1865	NG	Jacob & Mariah Thompson

---

1 Birth of Beverly Thomas reported by grandfather, Abram Thomas. [p1;Ln28]

SOME RUSSELL COUNTY RECORDS
BIRTHS 1853-1866

Child	Date of Birth	Birth Place	Parents
Martha D.	05 Dec 1866	NG	Jacob & Maria Thompson
Nancy	25 Oct 1859	RC	Patton & Mary Thompson
Rachel	28 Nov 1860	NG	Emory & Phoebe Thompson
TIGNOR			
Mary	07 Jan 1855	EG	Patrick A. & Nancy Tignor
Rebecca J.	27 Feb 1853	EG	Patrick H. & Nancy Tignor
TILLER			
Shaderick W.	03 Jun 1854	RC	David & Sarah Tiller
TOAAD			
Emiline	07 Aug 1860	EG	James E. & Elizabeth Toaad
TOD			
Robert E.	09 Sep 1862	EG	James E. & Elizabeth Todd
TOLBERT			
H. (♂)	10 Jun 1855	NG	Increase S. Judd & _____
TOOD			
Albert F.	05 Mar 1858	RC	James E. & Elizabeth Tood
TRENT			
Margaret M.	08 Aug 1858	RC	Hardy J. & Eliza C. Trent
TUNNEL			
(Un/F)	10 Feb 1854	RC	Marcus L. & Margaret Tunnel
TURLEY			
Catherine	08 Oct 1860	EG	James E. & Mary Ann Turley
TURNER			
Floyd	17 Apr 1856	RC	Darrestus & Mary J. Turner
Lucinda	25 Apr 1854	RC	Charles & Elizabeth Turner
Mieageon (♂)	11 Aug 1853	RC	James & Catherine Turner
Sylverster	__ Jan 1859	RC	Dorester & Mary J. Turner
UNDERWOOD			
Sarah[1]	03 Oct 1859	RC	Thomas & Martha Underwood

---

1 Birth of Sarah Underwood reported by grandfather, Thomas Underwood. [p37;Ln38]

SOME RUSSELL COUNTY RECORDS
BIRTHS 1853-1866

Child	Date of Birth	Birth Place	Parents
VANCE			
(Stillborn/M)	05 Feb 1854	RC	David & Elizabeth Vance
Martha A.	03 Mar 1855	RC	Absolom & Nancy Vance
VANDERPOOL			
(Un/F)	03 Dec 1862	RC	Jno. A. & Melvina Vanderpool
VANOVER			
Alen	19 May 1854	RC	William & Elizabeth Vanover
Allen	19 Apr 1855	RC	William & Elizabeth Vanover
Alva	09 Jun 1855	RC	John & Kisvra Vanover
Harvey[1]	07 Jul 1853	RC	_____ & Elizabeth Vanover
Joseph A.	12 Feb 1853	RC	Henry A. & Rhoda Vanover
Martha J.	27 Aug 1855	RC	Eli & Olle Vanover
Mary J.	01 May 1854	RC	Cornelious & Margaret Vanover
Sarah J.	30 Aug 1855	RC	Henry & Roda Vanover
VAUGHAN			
Matilda E.	04 Oct 1858	RC	Lorenzo D & Matilda S Vaughan
VAUGHN			
Charles, Walker	__ Aug 1862	RC	L.D. & Matilda Vaughn
James W.	25 Apr 1857	RC	L.D. & Malinda Vaughn
VENCIL			
Henry	12 Mar 1860	NG	Henry & Sarah Vencil
VENCILL			
Jane	10 Mar 1859	RC	William & Margaret Vencill
VENTERS			
Helen	20 Jan 1854	RC	Martin & Susan Venters
Louisa	30 Jul 1855	RC	James & Emaline Venters
VERMILLION			
(Un/M)	20 Jul 1862	EG	Elihu & Eliza Vermillion
Mary	13 Feb 1860	NG	B.F. & Mary Vermillion
Rachel (died)	15 Sep 1865	NG	Lihugh & Mary Vermillion
Robert H.	23 Jan 1853	EG	George & Martha J. Vermillion
Sarah E.	20 Mar 1857	RC	John M. & Caty F. Vermillion
VIARS			
Malinda	02 May 1856	RC	Lewis & Mary Viars

---

1 Birth of Harvey Vanover was reported by grandfather,
Cornelius Vanover. [p5;Ln11]

SOME RUSSELL COUNTY RECORDS
BIRTHS 1853-1866

Child	Date of Birth	Birth Place	Parents
VICARS			
(Un/F)	28 Oct 1860	RC	John & Sarah Vicars
Elbert S.	01 Jan 1856	RC	Robert B. & Phebe E. Vicars
Elen K.	01 Nov 1858	RC	William & Susan No Vicars
James	25 Jul 1856	RC	Robert P. & Unity Vicars
Joel B.	26 Mar 1860	RC	Paul B. & Lucinda Vicars
John	20 Dec 1857	RC	John & Sarah Vicars
Martha A.J.	06 Mar 1859	RC	Robert B. & Phoebe Vicars
Martha	05 Jun 1856	RC	William & Susanah Vicars
Peter	18 Feb 1856	RC	John & Sarah Vicars
Samuel	30 Jun 1854	RC	Samuel & Susan Vicars
Sarah L.	27 Dec 1861	RC	James B. & Margaret Vicars
William J.	12 Feb 1858	RC	Paul & Lucinda Vicars
VICKERS			
(Un/M)	06 Feb 1853	RC	Robert B. & Phoebe E. Vickers
Louisa	21 Apr 1853	RC	David C. & Senith Vickers
VINCEL			
George H.	16 Dec 1861	EG	William & Margaret Vincel
John M.	15 Dec 1853	RV	Lewis & Ann Vincel
John H.	09 Nov 1861	EG	George & Christine Vincel
VIPPERMAN			
(Un/M)	22 Aug 1860	NG	John W. & Malinda Vipperman
William R.	29 Jun 1865	NG	George & Martha J. Vipperman
WAGONER			
John V.	15 May 1853	RC	William & Nancy Wagoner
Nancy E.	__ Jun 1858	RC	William D. & Nancy Wagoner
WALDEN			
(Un/M)	25 Mar 1855	EG	Richard & Ann Walden
Abigal	01 May 1856	RC	Richard & Ann Walden
Ballard[1]	04 Sep 1861	EG	_____ & Jane Walden
WALKER			
Elbert G.	11 Aug 1860	RC	Robert & Isabella Walker
WALLIS			
(Un/M twins)	05 Nov 1861	NG	Howard & Nancy Wallis
Armind (♀)	03 Apr 1856	RC	James W. & Jane Wallis

---

1 Birth of Ballard Walden reported by "An Walden"
(relationship not stated in register) [p51;Ln12]

SOME RUSSELL COUNTY RECORDS
BIRTHS   1853-1866

Child	Date of Birth	Birth Place	Parents
Caroline	01 Jun 1855	NG	Major J. & Elender Wallis
George W.	25 Feb 1855	NG	Aaron & Catherine Wallis
James M.	06 Apr 1859	RC	Howard & Nancy E. Wallis
John C.	10 Feb 1862	Ha	_____ & Sarah Wallis
Louisa	28 Nov 1855	RC	Thomas & Elizabeth Wallis
Mary M.	01 Feb 1854	RC	James W. & Jane Wallis
Melvina	23 Mar 1853	CM	Aaron & Catherine Wallis
Thomas R.	18 Mar 1853	RC	William & Elizabeth Wallis
WAMPLER			
George H.	05 Jan 1854	RC	Jessee & Talitha Wampler
Thomas J.	07 May 1856	RC	Jesse & Tabitha P. Wampler
WARD			
Letty	05 May 1853	NG	William T. & Mary Ward
William F.	25 May 1860	NG	William T. & Polly Ward
WARRICK			
Mary L.	23 Feb 1855	RC	James & Cyntha Warrick
William W.	03 Dec 1854	RC	Felden & Roda Warrick
WEBB			
Levisa	30 Dec 1856	RC	Elijah & Juliar Webb
WEDDLE			
(Un/M)	27 Sep 1856	RC	John C. & Mary A. Weddle
Samuel H.	29 Mar 1855	RC	Josephus & Elizabeth Weddle
WELLS			
Lucinda J.	02 Mar 1853	RC	Zachariah & Marittia Ann Wells
WHEATLEY			
John	17 Jan 1853	RC	Arthur & Nancy Wheatley
WHEELER			
David	__ Apr 1860	RC	Pleasant H. & Anny Wheeler
Eliza A.	03 May 1858	RC	Jas. C. & Matilda Wheeler
Frances M.	21 Apr 1854	RC	Pleasant & Anny Wheeler
James H.	__ Dec 1860	RC	James C & Millissa F Wheeler
Mary Jane	12 Mar 1853	RC	James C. & Malicia Wheeler
WHETSEL/WHETZEL			
Betty H.	22 Feb 1859	RC	Benjamine & Elizabeth Whetsel
Margaret L.	27 Oct 1855	RC	Benjamine & Elizabeth D Whetzel

SOME RUSSELL COUNTY RECORDS
BIRTHS   1853-1866

Child	Date of Birth	Birth Place	Parents
WHITE			
(Un/F)	06 Sep 1860	EG	John B. & Rachel White
Darthula	03 Apr 1860	EG	Robert A. & Darthuly White
Eliza J.	08 Jun 1858	RC	John & Rachel White
Joseph H.	18 May 1860	RC	Preston & Julia White
Lawsen	12 Aug 1861	EG	Robert & Darthula White
Louisa	07 Jun 1856	RC	_____ & Manervy White
Margaret S.	19 May 1866	Cc	David & Delila White
Sarah E.	22 Nov 1855	RC	David & Delila White
William E.	17 Jun 1856	RC	John & Rachel White
WHITED			
Mary J.	14 Jul 1860	NG	Robert M. & Ann Whited
WHITEHEAD			
John T.	11 May 1857	RC	Robert M. & Anna Whitehead
WHITESIDE			
Eliza Thomas	25 Nov 1854	RC	Robert M. & Sarah Whiteside
WHITLY			
Clamda	15 Sep 1854	RC	Arthur & Nancy Wheatley
WHITT			
Angeline	22 Oct 1859	RC	John Jr. & Mary Whitt
Cely E.	03 Jan 1853	NG	John & Mary Whitt
Sarah L.	16 Aug 1853	HV	John B. & Rachel B. Whitt
Thomas	02 May 1855	EG	John & Mary Whitt
WIATT			
Mary A.	29 Jan 1860	EG	John & Margaret Wiatt
WILLEY			
Cowan	__ Aug 1862	RC	Andrew & Elizabeth Willey
Wilbern	19 Jan 1861	RC	Andy & Elizabeth Willey
WILLIAMS			
(Un/M)	10 Mar 1862	EG	George W. & Charity Williams
(Un/M)[1]	19 Apr 1853	RC	John D. & Elizabeth Williams
(Stillborn/F)	18 Mar 1853	RC	Andrew & Nancy Williams

---

1 Death register states:[p2;N27] (Unnamed male)
Williams, died age 1 day from measles in Russell County;
s/o John & Elizabeth Williams; reported by father who
also reported death of wife, Elizabeth, 10 days later,
also from measles.

SOME RUSSELL COUNTY RECORDS
BIRTHS 1853–1866

Child	Date of Birth	Birth Place	Parents
Beverly (♂)	22 Dec 1854	RC	James B. & Lidda Williams
Elizy (tw)	21 Apr 1857	RC	Daniel & Mary Williams
Emaline	07 Mar 1861	RC	Daniel & Mary Williams
Emmett	22 Jul 1860	CR	James D. & Elizabeth Williams
George H.	09 Oct 1855	RC	James B. & Lydda Williams
Hugh A.	11 Jan 1853	RC	James B. & Lydia M. Williams
James H. (tw)	21 Apr 1857	RC	Daniel & Mary Williams
John H.	11 Jan 1856	RC	Andrew & Elizabeth Williams
John N.	23 Feb 1857	RC	James & Elizabeth Williams
Lafayette	28 May 1858	RC	George Jr. & Charity Williams
Marion	28 Sep 1857	RC	_____ & Hanner Williams
Martin	10 May 1860	RC	Harden B. & Ova Williams
Mary E.	08 May 1859	RC	Andrew & Elizabeth Williams
Nancy E.	23 Dec 1860	RC	Andrew J. & Susan D. Williams
Richard	29 Oct 1858	RC	Daniel & Mary Williams
Stephen A.	02 Jan 1858	RC	Lemuel & Margaret Williams
Thomas	20 Dec 1859	RC	Daniel & Polly Williams

WILLIS

Child	Date of Birth	Birth Place	Parents
David J.	31 Jun 1857	RC	Richard & Martha Willis
Jonah	15 May 1866	CC	Richard & Martha Willis

WILMINGSON

Child	Date of Birth	Birth Place	Parents
Mitchell A.	19 Feb 1856	RC	Mitchell & Elizabeth Wilmingson

WILSON

Child	Date of Birth	Birth Place	Parents
Edith C.	12 Nov 1853	RC	Joab & Dready Wilson

WISE

Child	Date of Birth	Birth Place	Parents
(Un/F)	30 Apr 1862	Le	John & Margarett Wise
Martha	14 Jan 1860	RC	James D. & Nancy Wise
Susan Virginia[1]	08 Feb 1862	RC	William & Rachel Wise

WISON

Child	Date of Birth	Birth Place	Parents
Beverley (died)	31 Jan 1856	RC	William & _____ Wison

WISOR

Child	Date of Birth	Birth Place	Parents
Noria	20 Jun 1854	RC	William & Catherine Wisor

---

1 Birth of Susan Virginia Wise was reported by friend, Wilson Harmon. [p56;Ln24]

SOME RUSSELL COUNTY RECORDS
BIRTHS 1853-1866

Child	Date of Birth	Birth Place	Parents
WITT			
James A.[1]	08 Aug 1860	EG	John & Catherine Witt
WOLF			
Sarah	01 Sep 1856	RC	Malon & Margaret Wolf
Thomas	15 Feb 1854	RC	John & Elizabeth Wolf
Virginia	10 Dec 1857	RC	John & Elizabeth Wolf
Washing[2]	05 May 1854	RC	Mellen & Margaret Wolf
WOOD			
(Un/child)	25 Dec 1855	RC	Beary & Abigal Wood
(Stillborn)	__ Dec 1853	Sa	Samuel & Elizabeth Wood
WOODDY			
Caldonie	15 Oct 1860	NG	Jacob & Judia Wooddy
WRIGHT			
(Un/M)	14 Nov 1853	RC	Parris & Mary Wright
David C.	20 Jul 1857	RC	John B. & Nancy Wright
Harriet J.	19 Sep 1854	RC	John & Susan Wright
Martha J.	29 Oct 1854	RC	Aaron & Ezabel Wright
Meredith	01 Oct 1853	RC	Robert & Sarah Wright
Nancy E.	20 Jun 1854	RC	Alexander & Susan Wright
Thomas	26 Jul 1854	RC	William & Caroline Wright
WYATT			
Josephine[3]	13 Apr 1860	EG	_____ & Elizabeth Wyatt
Louisa E.	15 Mar 1862	EG	John & Margarett Wyatt
YATES			
Olle (♀)	22 Nov 1855	RC	Jacob & Haizy Yates
Sindesty	22 Aug 1857	RC	Jeramiah & Mary A. Yates
YOUNG			
James Patton	16 Sep 1862	RC	Harvey B. & Catherine Young

---

1 Birth of James Whitt was reported by neighbor, C.A. Smith. [p45;Ln10]

2 Birth of Washing Wolf was reported by "g. father", Benjamine Wolf. [p12;Ln37]

3 Birth of Josephine Wyatt was reported by neighbor, C.A. Smith. [p45;Ln9]

SOME RUSSELL COUNTY RECORDS
Slave Births   1853-1866

Able Alderson, Owner:
Sarah, d/o Queen   01 Dec 1857 Russell County

John D. Alderson, Owner:
Demoris, s/o Hannah   __ Jul 1862 Russell County

T.C.M. Alderson, Owner:
Sally Ann   __ Apr 1861 Russell County
Bob, s/o Rhoda   __ Jul 1861 Russell County

John Alexander, Owner:
    Nancy, d/o Sarah   21 May 1856 Russell County
    Mary M.M.C., d/o Rachel   24 Dec 1858 Russell County

M. Alexander, Owner:
William s/o Sarah   29 Oct 1853 Russell County

Thomas J. Baley, Owner:
Bob   01 Oct 1861 New Garden

Stephen Banner, Owner:
Mary, d/o Eliza   30 Oct 1856 Russell County
(Un/M), s/o Eliza   01 Apr 1861 Russell County
George, s/o Queen   27 Apr 1861 Russell County
Elizabeth, d/o Queen   27 Apr 1861 Russell County

Edwin R. Baylor, Owner:
Floyd, s/o Ann   26 May 1860 Russell County

John Bickley, Owner:
(Un/M), s/o Helen   28 Oct 1854 Russell County
Charles, s/o Helan   09 Jan 1856 Russell County
James, s/o Helin   19 Aug 1860 Russell County
Henry, s/o Helen   __ Mar 1862 Russell County

Robert Boyd, Owner:
James Hopkins Boyd   __ Aug 1862 Russell County

John Browning, Owner:
Andy, s/o Nelly   05 Jul 1857 Russell County
(Un/F), d/o Amy   01 Mar 1860 Russell County
Mary, d/o Darcus   10 Oct 1861 Elk Garden

Vincent Browning, Owner:
(Un/F), d/o Diner   11 Mar 1860 Russell County
Res, s/o Milly   11 Aug 1861 Elk Garden

Ezekiel Burdine, Owner:
Mary E., d/o Mary   19 May 1859 Russell County
Louisa V., d/o Sarah   03 Jun 1859 Russell County

SOME RUSSELL COUNTY RECORDS
Slave Births   1853-1866

Nathan E. Burdine, Owner:

George, s/o Fanny	10 Feb 1853 Russell County
James, s/o Roena	07 Jun 1854 Russell County
Thomas, s/o Roena	01 Jul 1857 Russell County
Hannah, d/o Fanny	04 Jul 1857 Russell County
Emily	14 Apr 1860 Russell County
Nancy	26 Oct 1860 Russell County
(Un/child) of Margaret	17 Feb 1862 Russell County

Sarah Burdine, Owner:

Caroline Jane	07 Feb 1853 Russell County

Wilson E. Campbell, Owner:

Emmaline, d/o Betty	15 May 1860 Russell County
(Un/M)	15 Aug 1861 New Garden

Charles Carrell, Owner:

Cass Carrell	__ ___ 1853 Lebanon
(Un/M), s/o Nan	01 Dec 1861 Russell County

Dale Carter, Owner:

Homy s/o Nancy	04 Aug 1853 Russell County
Maria d/o Ibby	07 Aug 1853 Russell County
Rachel	10 May 1853 Russell County
Mary, d/o Ibbee	21 Feb 1855 Russell County
Fletcher, s/o Lott	12 May 1860 Russell County
Ellen, d/o Ibby	23 Mar 1861 Russell County

Joseph Combs, Owner:

Stephen, s/o Sophia	04 Jul 1857 Russell County
(Un/M), s/o Mary	__ Jan 1861 Russell County

George Cowan, Owner:

(Un/M)	10 Aug 1861 Elk Garden

John C., Owner:

Henry J., s/o Amond	10 Jan 1856 Russell County

Charles C. Dickenson, Owner:

Diner, d/o Ama	02 Aug 1857 Russell County
Ross, s/o Amy	11 Sep 1859 Russell County

James H. Dickenson, Owner:

Caroline, d/o Mininy	15 Jun 1853 Russell County
(Un/F), d/o Milly	07 Jun 1854 Russell County
Sarah A., d/o Margaret	__ Mar 1859 Russell County
Nelson, s/o Jane	__ Aug 1860 Russell County
John, s/o Mary	__ Aug 1861 Russell County

John Dickenson, Owner:

SOME RUSSELL COUNTY RECORDS
Slave Births   1853-1866

Sarah, d/o Queen   17 Apr 1854 Russell County
Mattan, s/o Harriet   10 Apr 1855 Russell County
Silvester, s/o Franceus   01 Sep 1855 Russell County
Mary, d/o Queen   12 Jul 1857 Russell County
Nancy, d/o Harriet   19 Apr 1858 Russell County
Sarah, d/o Mary   __ Dec 1860 Russell County

Henry P. Dickenson, Owner:
Henry P., s/o Elvira   09 Jan 1861 Russell County
Samuel, s/o Temperance   __ Dec 1861 Russell County

Thomas F. Dickenson, Owner:
Sarah, d/o Rhoda   __ Dec 1860 Russell County

Jacob Dorton, Owner:
Ferrell, s/o Rosia   __ Aug 1859 Russell County
Washington, s/o Rocey   __ Aug 1860 Russell County

Andrew Ferguson, Owner:
Floyd   07 Mar 1854 Russell County
Jane, d/o Emily   15 Nov 1857 Russell County
(Un/M)   10 Jan 1861 Elk Garden

Anthony M. Ferguson, Owner:
William   09 Dec 1853 Cedar Creek

Granville Ferguson, Owner:
Rees   15 Aug 1861 Elk Garden

John C. Ferguson, Owner:
(Un/F)   05 May 1854 Russell County
(Un/F)   01 Sep 1854 Russell County
Robert   15 Jan 1855 Russell County
Francis   18 Jan 1855 Russell County
(Un/M), s/o Manar(?)   28 May 1860 Russell County

E. Ferrell, Owner:
Bob, s/o Balinda   22 Jun 1861 New Garden

Major A. Fletcher, Owner:
(Un/F), d/o Jane   10 Mar 1861 New Garden

William Frick, Owner:
Catherine   10 Aug 1853 Russell County

Robert Fugate, Owner:
James s/o Jane   17 May 1853 Russell County
Joseph, s/o Sarah   30 Aug 1860 Russell County

Samuel B. Fugate, Owner:

SOME RUSSELL COUNTY RECORDS
Slave Births 1853-1866

Flora, d/o Nancy   17 Dec 1853 Russell County
George, s/o Nancy   15 Mar 1855 Russell County

Hiram Fullen, Owner:
Harvey, s/o Mary Hubbord   28 Mar 1856 Russell County
(Un/M)   13 Apr 1861 Elk Garden

Zadock N. Gardner, Owner:
Floyd Gardner   10 Apr 1853 New Garden
Bauregard   20 Jan 1861 New Garden
(Un/M)   28 Jan 1861 New Garden

Ezkiel B. Garrett, Owner:
Dock, s/o Susun   16 Nov 1860 Elk Garden

Thomas H. Garrett, Owner:
Casline   01 May 1854 Russell County
(Un/M), s/o Fan   10 Dec 1861 Elk Garden

Thomas Gibson, Owner:
Charles W., s/o Isabella   20 Jan 1856 Russell County

John C. Gillespie, Owner:
(Un/M), s/o Mima   10 Apr 1860 Richlands
(Un/M), s/o Mima   10 Sep 1862 New Garden

Cummings Gilmer, Owner:
Bob   16 Mar 1861 Cedar Creek

Samuel E. Gilmer, Owner:
(Un/M), s/o Aisly   15 Aug 1856 Russell County
Florence, d/o Sara   01 Sep 1860 Russell County
Richard, s/o Martha   01 Nov 1860 Russell County

George Gose, Owner:
Aaron, s/o Sidney   __ Jul 1858 Russell County

Harvey Gray, Owner:
Ibby Gray, d/o Mary   01 Oct 1853 Russell County

Jos. Hackney, Owner:
Mary J., d/o Sarah   09 Mar 1861 Russell County

James M. Hanson, Owner:
Elizabeth, d/o Silva   10 Oct 1856 Russell County
George, s/o Sylva   __ ___ 1858 Russell County

William Hargiss, Owner:
John Hargess   29 Jul 1853 Corner Settlement

SOME RUSSELL COUNTY RECORDS
Slave Births   1853–1866

Caleb Hawkins, Owner:
George, s/o Rachel   02 Mar 1854 Russell County

Andy F. Hendricks, Owner:
(Un/F), d/o Melisa   04 Apr 1858 Russell County
Sarah, d/o Philliss(?)   09 May 1858 Russell County
(Un/M)   15 Sep 1860 Elk Garden
(Un/M)   12 Oct 1860 Elk Garden
(Stillborn 3 females)   10 Oct 1861 Elk Garden

Aaron L. Hendricks, Owner:
(Un/child)   ___ Mar 1853 Elk Garden
(Un/child)   ___ Mar 1853 Elk Garden
(Un/child)   ___ Sep 1853 Elk Garden
Peter, s/o Diley   15 Apr 1857 Russell County
(Stillborn/M), s/o Diley   ___ ___ 1857 Russell County
Hannah, d/o Matilda   20 Sep 1859 Russell County
Jeff   16 Mar 1860 Elk Garden
Emeline   01 Jun 1860 Elk Garden
Askew, s/o Sarah   25 Nov 1862 Elk Garden
Lucinda, d/o Darcus   25 Mar 1862 Elk Garden

James W. Hendricks, Owner:
(Un/child)   15 Aug 1853 Elk Garden
(Stillborn/M), s/o Rachel   18 Mar 1857 Russell County
Ellen M., d/o Nani   01 May 1858 Russell County
Matilda, d/o Mary   23 May 1858 Russell County
Andy C.   26 Feb 1860 Elk Garden
Martha   07 Sep 1860 Elk Garden
George   03 Dec 1860 Elk Garden
Lear   15 Nov 1861 Elk Garden
(Un/M), s/o Lucy   10 Feb 1862 Elk Garden

Milissa Hendricks, Owner:
Andy, s/o Ann   15 Sep 1862 Elk Garden

Pleasant Horn, Owner:
Harry, s/o Mary   11 Jan 1855 Russell County
Margaret, d/o Mary   04 Mar 1861 Russell County

Lewis Horton Sr., Owner:
(Un/M), s/o Sarah   10 Nov 1862 New Garden

John T. Howard, Owner:
Oliver, s/o Pruda   22 Jan 1854 Russell County
Ellen, d/o Nancy   06 Apr 1860 New Garden

Johnson Howard, Owner:
(Un/F), d/o Harriet   10 Apr 1862 Elk Garden

SOME RUSSELL COUNTY RECORDS
Slave Births   1853-1866

William Howard, Owner:
Elizabeth, d/o Sarah H.   20 Aug 1856 Russell County

James Gent/Jent, Owner:
Isaac, s/o Mary   __ ___ 1854 Russell County
Osten, s/o Lydda   07 Feb 1857 Russell County

Jefferson Jessee, Owner:
Patton, s/o Temperance   15 Mar 1855 Russell County
Caroline, d/o Tempe   11 Apr 1857 Russell County

Elizabeth Johnson, Owner:
Robert, s/o Amanda   01 Dec 1859 Russell County
Melissa   24 Dec 1860 Loop
(Un/M)   11 Feb 1861 Elk Garden
Thomas S., s/o Ann   04 Sep 1862 Elk Garden

Andrew Kiser, Owner:
Fanny, d/o Mary   __ Dec 1860 Russell County

John W. Lampkin, Owner:
(Un/F)   09 Jun 1854 Russell County
Kemp, s/o Nancy   15 May 1860 Elk Garden
John, s/o Margaret   10 Mar 1860 Elk Garden
Sally, d/o Lilly   04 Aug 1862 Elk Garden

Alexander M. Lee, Owner:
Hamit, s/o Manah   01 Nov 1860 Russell County

Samuel Leece, Owner:
Josephine L., d/o Mary L.   01 Jul 1854 Russell County
Fletcher L., s/o Mariah L.   02 Feb 1854 Russell County
Harriet L., d/o Mariah L.   05 Feb 1854 Russell County

William N. Leece, Owner:
(Un/M)   26 May 1854 Russell County
Alice, d/o Pricca   17 Feb 1862 Russell County

John W. Litton, Owner:
Eliza   24 Mar 1853 Elk Garden
Adaline, d/o Adaline   04 Feb 1856 Russell County
Samuel, s/o Lydda   10 Mar 1858 Russell County

James Mullens, Owner:
Pheba, d/o Lilly   10 Oct 1854 Russell County
Thomas, s/o Dilce   22 Jul 1854 Russell County
Dam, d/o Harret   06 Apr 1854 Russell County

Isaac Muncy, Owner:
Samuel, s/o July   15 Mar 1854 Russell County

SOME RUSSELL COUNTY RECORDS
Slave Births   1853-1866

Eliza, d/o Juley   03 Aug 1855 Russell County

Aaron H. Nash, Owner:
(Un/M), s/o Sary   15 Mar 1854 Russell County
George W., s/o Remer   27 Jan 1856 Russell County
Margaret, d/o Lasy   17 May 1856 Russell County
James E., s/o Ariener(?)   19 Sep 1859 Russell County
Amanda, d/o Harriet   __ Mar 1859 Russell County
Mary, d/o Sarra(?)   __ May 1860 Russell County

Chloe Osborn, Owner:
Mary, d/o Sylvia   14 Jul 1858 Russell County
Unamed of Sylvesta   __ Feb 1859 Russell County
Patten, s/o Isabel   __ Jun 1861 Russell County
William, s/o Silva   __ Jun 1861 Russell County

Solomon Osborn, Owner:
George, s/o Isibella   01 Nov 1855 Russell County
George, s/o Celia   10 Nov 1856 Russell County

George A. Pruner, Owner:
Charles, s/o Margaret   __ Jan 1860 Russell County

Nancy Samples, Owner:
William   15 Jun 1855 New Garden

Albert G. Smith, Owner:
Susannah   06 Nov 1853 New Garden
(Un/F)   08 Sep 1855 New Garden
James   31 Mar 1856 Russell County
(Un/M)   10 Apr 1860 Lebanon
(Un/M)   15 Dec 1861 Lebanon

Charles A. Smith, Owner:
Iseral   10 May 1853 Clifton
Emeline   __ Dec 1853 Clifton
(Un/M)   ____ 1855 Elk Garden
Sam   27 Aug 1860 Little River
(Un/M)   20 Apr 1860 Little River
Any, d/o Sarah   10 Mar 1862 Clifton
Mary, d/o Darcus   08 Jun 1862 Clifton
Henry, s/o Lydia   04 Sep 1862 Clifton

John T. Smith, Owner:
Florance   10 Jan 1861 Elk Garden

John W. Smith, Owner:
Ida   03 Jul 1860 New Garden

Mary D. Smith, Owner:

SOME RUSSELL COUNTY RECORDS
Slave Births   1853–1866

(Un/F), d/o Sarah   10 Nov 1862 Elk Garden

James Sykes, Owner:
Lennick   16 Apr 1853 Reeds Valley

T.P. Thomas, Owner:
David   21 Jun 1860 Elk Garden

Patrick A. Tignor, Owner:
(Un/M)   30 Jan 1855 Elk Garden

Jesse Vermillion, Owner:
Harvey, s/o Priscilla   03 Jul 1853 Russell County
Sarah, d/o Priscilla   01 Sep 1855 Russell County

Elijah Webb, Owner:
Julia Ann   18 Mar 1855 Elk Garden

William H.B. White, Owner:
Henry, s/o Matilda   10 May 1862 Elk Garden

Some Russell County Records
Deaths   1853 — 1866

The following death records appear in alphabetical order by surname and contain the following:

Surname, name; date of death; age at death; cause of death; place of death; parents; place of birth; occupation; spouse. [page and Line number of entry] *Compiler's notes and comments appear in ( ) and in italics*

The many off-line entries and various mistakes found indicates documentation of listed names should be verified by additional sources.

SOME RUSSELL COUNTY RECORDS
Deaths 1853 — 1866

Addison, (male); 15 Jul 1865; 3m 15d; (cause of death not given); Elk Garden; s/o Rodden & Arminda Addison; b. Russell County. [p19:Ln3]

Alexander, John; 04 Oct 1862; 95y 5m; Debility; Russell County; s/o- _____ & Ann Alexander; b. Ireland; a Farmer; consort of Mary Alexander; reported by "consort". [p17;Ln1]

Amburgy, Martha Alice; 17 Aug 1866; 2y 8m; Worms; Russell County; d/o William & Chnah*(Syntha)* Amburgy; b. Russell County; reported by grandfather, John M. Amburgy. [p20;Ln1]

Artrip, Fredrick; 06 May 1853; 5m; Flux; New Garden; s/o Jas. & Sarah Artrip; b. New Garden; reported by father, James Artrip.[p1;Ln33]

Artrip, James; 12 Nov 1857; 9m; cause not given; Russell County; s/o Mary & William Artrip; reported by father. [p9;Ln25]

Artrip, Martha L.(?); 10 Jul 1861; 2y 6m 10d; Flux; New Garden; d/o Joseph Artrip; b. New Garden; consort(sic) of Martha Artrip *(obviously refers to Joseph Artrip)*; reported by father. [p14;Ln28]

Artrip, Mary; __ Aug 1861; 6y; Flux; Russell County; d/o William & Mary Artrip; b. Russell County; reported by William Artrip. [p14;Ln27]

Artrip, Susan; 01 Sep 1853; 2y 6m 10d; Flux; New Garden; d/o Jas. & Sarah Artrip; b. New Garden; reported by father, James Artrip.

Aston, Mary; 11 Jul 1862; 37y; Typhoid Fever; Russell County; d/o Robert & Elen Bailey; b. Ireland; a Housekeeper; consort of Samuel Aston, dec'd.; reported by son, Robert Aston. [p17;Ln2]

Austin, Flemming; 06 Jul 1860; 6m; "Irresipilus"; Russell County; s/o Thomas Austin Jr.; reported by mother, Jane Austin. [p12;Ln32]

Austin, Robert; 04 Nov 1862; 1y 5m; Croup; Russell County; s/o John & Elizabeth Austin; b. Russell County; reported by father. [p17;Ln3]

Ayers, (female); 05 Oct 1865; 1m 25d; Elk Garden; d/o George & Elizabeth Ayers; b. Russell County. [p19;Ln4] *Identified by birth register as Unnamed Female Ayers, born 05 Oct 1865, New Garden; d/o George & Elizabeth Ayers).*

Baker, (male)[1]; ___ Nov 1861; 14d; Cause Unknown; Russell County; s/o George A. & Lulian/*(Julia)* Baker; b. Russell County; reported by father. [p14;Ln21]

Baker, Caroline E.; ___ Dec 1861; 1y 4m; Bold hives; Russell County; d/o John H. Baker; b. Russell County; reported by father. [p14;Ln1]

Baker, Frances Helen; 14 Feb 1862; 9m; Cause Unknown; Russell County; d/o William C. & Edith Barker; b. Russell County; reported by father. [p17;Ln11]

Baker, George J.; 06 Apr 1853; 6y 28d; Flux; Russell County; s/o Jas & Highley Baker; b. Russell County; reported by father, James Baker. [p3;Ln17]

Ball, Henry; 22 Oct 1860; 1y 1m; Flux; Weavers creek; s/o Cornelius & Nancy Ball; b. Weavers Creek; reported by father. [p13;Ln1]

Ball, John T.; 24 Nov 1859; 6y 10m; Fever; Russell County; s/o Moses & Mary Ball; reported by father. [p11;Ln34]

Ball, Louisa; 01 Aug 1859; 1y 2m; Croup; Russell County; d/o Robert & Cynthia Ball; reported by father. [p11;Ln33]

Banion, Helen E.; 28 Dec 1853; 1y 11m; Measles; Russell County; d/o Thomas & Artaminta Banion; b. Russell County; reported by father. [p3;Ln2]

Banion, Margaret; 14 Mar 1854; 25y 5m 6d; Fever; Russell County; d/o Jefferson & Anny Banyon; b. Tennessee; unmarried; reported by father, Jesse Banion. [p6;Ln4]

Banner, Elizabeth; 08 May 1860; 70y 8m 15d; "Inf. of Bladder"; Russell County; d/o Stephen Gose, Dec'd; a Housekeeper; consort of John Banner, Dec'd; reported by her son, John Banner. [p12;Ln18]

Banner, James; 08 Jul 1853; 3m; Flux; Russell County; s/o Eliza Ann Banner; b. Russell County; reported by mother. [p5;Ln6]

---

[1] 1860 Russell County census Bickleys Mill Hh# 1432; George A. Baker, 23; Julia A., 21; John S., 1/12. Birth register indicates this child was an unnamed female

SOME RUSSELL COUNTY RECORDS
Deaths 1853 — 1866

Banner, John T.; 15 Feb 1860; 5y 7m 2d; "Inf. of Bladder"; Russell County; s/o George Banner; reported by George Banner. [p12;Ln17] *(Birth register lists a John T. Banner, born 13 Jul 1854 in Russell County; s/o George & Priscilla Banner).*

Banner, Margaret E.; 05 Jul 1853; 2y 11m; Flux; Russell County; d/o Stephen & Sarah Banner; b. Russell County; reported by father. [p5;Ln5]

Barker, James; 16 Jun 1854; 9m 12; "Scrofulous"; Russell County; s/o Robert & Sarah Barker; b. Russell County; reported by father. [p6;Ln9]

Bartley, Andrew; 19 dec 1853; 16y 7m 8d; Cause Unknown; Russell County; s/o Jesse & Jemima Bartley; b. Russell County; a farmer; reported by father. [p3;Ln39]

Bartly, Ludema; 11 Mar 1854; 1y 7d; Cause Unknown; Russell County; d/o Isaac & Burthy Bartly; b. Russell County; reported by father. [p6;Ln14]

Barton, (male); 10 Jul 1859; 1m 15d; Cause Unknown; Russell County; s/o Washington & Elizabeth Barton; reported by father. [p11;Ln31]

Barton, (male); 02 Oct 1861; 1m 12d; Flux; New Garden; s/o William Barton; consort(sic) of Margaret Barton *(obviously refers to William Barton)*; b. New Garden; reported by father. [p14;Ln30]

Belcher, Erastus; 02 Dec 1853; 4y; measles; Elk Garden; s/o Lucy Belcher; b. Little River; reported by grandfather, John Belcher. [p1;Ln15]

Berry, William; 20 Mar 1859; 60y; "Chronic"; Russell County; parents not given; b. Montgomery County; a Shoemaker; reported by friend, Ichabod Horn. [p11;Ln2]

Beverley, Mary; 02 Jul 1853; 3y 3m; Quincy; Russell County; d/o Elijah & Nancy Beverly; b. Russell County; reported by father. [p4;Ln21]

Beverly, Sarah E.; 01 May 1855; 2y 11m; Croup; Russell County; d/o William & R. Beverley; reported by father. [p7;Ln19]

Bickley, George A.; 20 Nov 1853; 6y 1m; Scarlet Fever; Russell County; s/o William C. & Harriet B. Bickley; b. Russell County; reported by father. [p4;Ln15]

Bickley, Henry D.; 01 Aug 1853; 6m; Flux; Russell County; s/o Marion
T. & Martha Bickley; b. Russell County; reported by grandfather,
Charles Bickley. [p4;Ln32] (*Birth register states: born 23 Jan
1853, s/o Marion T. & Martha B. Bickley*) (*also see double entry
information reported by father*)

Bickley, Henry D.; 21 Aug 1853; 9m; Flux; Russell County; s/o Marion
& Martha B. Bickley; b. Russell County; reported by father.
[p4;Ln38]

Bickley, John R.; 22 Oct 1853; 1y 1m 6d; Croup; Russell County; s/o
William C. & Harriet Bickley; b. Russell County; reported by
father. [p4;Ln16]

Bickley, Martha B.; 09 Apr 1853; 26y 8m 14d; Typhoid Fever; Russell
County; d/o Henry & Eliz. Dickenson; b. Russell County; consort
of Marion T. Bickley; reported by husband. [p4;Ln36]

Black, Mary E.; __ Jan 1862; 31y; Fever; Russell County; d/o Susan
_____; a Housekeeper; Unmarried; reported by friend, James
Painter. [p17;Ln7]

Blessing, (male); 20 Apr 1853; 1d; Cause Unknown; Russell County;
s/o Crockett & Mary Blessing; b. Russell County; reported by
grandfather, Jeremiah Fields. [p2;Ln28]

Blizzard, Elihu; 25 Aug 1857; 2m 9d; Fever; Russell County; s/o Ruth
& Sidner Blizzard; b. Russell County; reported by father.
[p9;Ln2]

Blizzard, James E.; 25 Apr 1860; 10d; Cause Unknown; Russell County;
s/o Sidner Blizzard; reported by Sidner Blizzard. [p12;Ln30]

Blizzard, Mary E.; 08 Aug 1856; 24d; cause not given; Russell
County; d/o Sidney & Lucy (Blizzard); b. Russell County;
reported by father. [p8;Ln12]

Blizzard, Nancy K.; 15 Apr 1860; 1y 7m; Croup; Russell County; d/o
Sidner Blizzard; reported by Sidner Blizzard. [p12;Ln29]

Boggs, Able; 22 Jan 1853; 1m 21d; Hives; Russell County; s/o William
& Rebecca Boggs; b. Lee County; reported by mother. [p3;Ln30]
(*See also: Ln 31; William Boggs*)

Boggs, William; 18 Jul 1853; 30y 2m; Measles & Flux; Russell County;
s/o Eli & Mary Boggs; b. Lee County; a Farmer; consort of
Rebecca Boggs; reported by wife. [p3;Ln31]

SOME RUSSELL COUNTY RECORDS
Deaths 1853 – 1866

Bond, (male)[1]; 03 Dec 1855; 4d*(sic)*; cause not given; Russell County; s/o Charles F. & Mary J. Bond; b. Russell County; reported by father. [p7;Ln21]

Boothe, Rebecca Bertha; 08 Jun 1854; 13y; cause not given; Elk Garden; d/o John Boothe; b. Russell County; reported by father. [p6:Ln29]

Boswell, Thomas P.; 02 Aug 1866; 8y; Flux; Russell County; s/o William T. & Hannah Boswell; b. Russell County; reported by mother. [p20;Ln7]

Bough, James Harvey; 01 Jul 1853; 11m; Flux; Russell County; s/o John J. & Louisa Baugh; b. Russell County; reported by father. [p2;Ln40]

Bowman, James E.; 24 Feb 1860; 19d; Hives; Russell County; s/o Peter Bowman; b. Russell County; reported by father. [p12;Ln10]

Bowman, John; 05 Oct 1853; 55y 1m 20d; Consumption; Russell County; s/o Peter & Nancy Bowman; b. Washington County, TN; reported by son, Peter Bowman. [p2;Ln38]

Bowman, William H.; 22 Jan 1862; 23y 4m 7d; Fever; "Henry & Emory Hospital"; s/o John & Elizabeth Bowman; b. Tennessee; a Soldier; Unmarried; reported by mother. [p17;Ln4]

Boyd, (male); 05 Jul 1853; 1 day; cause unknown; New Garden; s/o Jonathan & Mary Boyd; b. New Garden; reported by father. [p1;Ln4] *(Note: a double listing [p1;Ln 36] shows same information).*

Boyd, Albert; __ ___ 1862; 19y; "by Wound"; Staunton, Va.; s/o John H. Boyd; b. Russell County; a Farmer; Unmarried; reported by father. [p15;Ln2]

Boyd, Celia E.; 03 Jun 1860; 8y; "Burnt to death"; New Garden; d/o Jas. & Prissilla Boyd; b. New Garden; reported by father. [p13;Ln2]

Boyd, Isaac M.; 17 Sep 1862; 3y 6m 27d; "Dyptherea"; Russell County; s/o Charles P. & Martha Boyd; b. Russell County; reported by father. [p17;Ln10]

---

[1] Birth register lists an Unnamed Male Bond, b. 23 Aug 1855. Speculatively, this child died at age 4 months.

SOME RUSSELL COUNTY RECORDS
Deaths 1853 — 1866

Boyd, John D.; 18 Sep 1866; 1y 9m; Flux; Russell County; s/o Charles & Martha Boyd; b. Russell County; reported by father, Charles D. Boyd. [p20;Ln2]

Boyd, Julia Ann; 29 Oct 1862; 1y 6m; Swords Creek; d/o Robert A. Boyd; b. Russell County; reported by father. [p15:Ln1].

Boyd, Margaret A.; 02 Oct 1866; 4y 3m; Flux; Russell County; d/o Charles & Martha Boyd; b. Russell County; reported by father, Charles D. Boyd. [p20;Ln3]

Bradley, Edward; 20 Apr 1862; 3y; Croup; Russell County; s/o Clary Bradley; b. Scott County, Va.; reported by grandfather, Ephraim Bradley. [p17;Ln6]

Bradshaw, (female); 01 Apr 1854; 7m; cause not given; Elk Garden; d/o John Bradshaw; b. Russell County; reported by father. [p6;Ln28]

Bradshaw, Elisa J.; 01 Apr 1855; 1y; cause unknown; Horton Valley; d/o John Bradshaw; b. Russell County. [p8;Ln6]

Bradshaw, John; 14 Jun 1859; 25y; Fever; Russell County; s/o John & Jane Bradshaw; Unmarried; reported by father. [p11;Ln32]

Bradshaw, Mary M.; 05 May 1853; 10y; Cause Unknown; Hortons Valley; d/o William & Jane Bradshaw; b. Hortons Valley; reported by father. [p1:Ln13].

Breeding, Elizabeth; 01 Nov 1854; 5m; Croup; Russell County; d/o William & Elizabeth Breeding; b. Russell County; reported by father. [p5;Ln1]

Breeding, John William H.; 06 Apr 1862; 20y 7m 28d; Pneumonia; Petersburg, Va.; s/o William & Elizabeth Breeding; b. Russell County; a Soldier; Unmarried; reported by father. [p17;Ln5]

Browning, Fairman P.; 13 Aug 1853; 4y 11m 25d; Fever; Russell County; s/o William McR & Susan Browning; b. Russell County; reported by father. [p2;Ln29]

Browning, Mary C.; 17 Aug 1859; 6y 9m 4d; Fever; Russell County; d/o J.C. & Elizabeth Browning; b. Russell County; reported by father, Jno. C. Browning. [p11;Ln3]

Browning, Rachel; 12 Aug 1866; 72y; Flux; Elk Garden; b. Russell County*; Married; reported by J.J. Bays [p19;Ln11] (*1850 Russell census indicates born in Maryland; 1860 Russell County census household #96 lists: John Browning, 66; _Rachael_, 65; et al.)

SOME RUSSELL COUNTY RECORDS
Deaths 1853 — 1866

Buchanan, Delphia; 25 Jan 1853; 45y 4m 13d; Cause Unknown; Russell County; d/o Andrew & Elizabeth Davis; b. North Carolina; consort of Jno.V. Buchanan; reported by husband. [p3;Ln28]

Bumgarner, Sarah J.; 19 Sep 1862; 15y; "Dyptherea": Russell County; d/o William & Elizabeth Bumgarner; b. Wilkes Co., NC; Unmarried; reported by father, W.S. Bumgarner. [p17;Ln8]

Bumgarner, Vanlanding___; 11 Oct 1862; 3m; Croup; Russell County; s/o William & Elizabeth Bumgarner; b. Wilkes Co., NC; reported by father, W.S. Bumgarner. [p17;Ln9]

Bundy, Lilburn H.; 09 Jul 1858; 1y 9m 12d; "Dierhea"; Russell County; s/o Daniel & Rebecca Bundy; b. Russell County; reported by father. [p10;Ln17]

Bundy, Sarah E.; __ May 1859; 6m; Fever; Russell County; d/o Daniel & Rebecca Bundy; b. Russell County; reported by father. [p11;Ln4]

Bundy, William F.; 10 Jan 1858; 3y 7m; Croup; Russell County; s/o S. & Sarah Bundy; b. Russell County; reported by father, Sampson Bundy. [p10;Ln16]

Burk, George L.; 11 Aug 1853; 14y 3d; Flux; Russell County; s/o Isaiah & Martha Burk; b. Russell County; reported by father. [p3;Ln20]

Burk, Isaac; 24 Jul 1853; 9m 21d; "Quinsey"; Russell County; s/o John & Nancy Burk; b. Russell County; reported by mother. [3;Ln13]

Burk, Jerome C.; 30 Aug 1861; 1m 10d; Flux; Elk Garden; d/o William Burk; b. Elk Garden; consort of Mary Burk (probably meant to be wife of William Burk); reported by father. [p14;Ln29]

Burk, William; 15 Oct 1865; 15d; Elk Garden; cause not given; s/o Winton & Dorcas Burk; b. Russell County. [p19;Ln2]

Bush, Josiah; 22 Mar 1854; 30y; Fever; Russell County; s/o Austin & Nancy Bush; b. Russell County; a Farmer; unmarried; reported by sister, Nancy Tolbert. [p5;Ln9]

Campbell, Almira; 28 Mar 1860; 1y 4m 26d; Whooping cough; Elk Garden; d/o Jas. & Mahala J. Campbell; b. Elk Garden; reported by mother. [p13;Ln6]

Campbell, Emeline; 08 Sep 1859; 11y 6m; Fever; Russell County; d/o Henry & Milly Campbell; reported by father. [p11;Ln35]

Campbell, Joel; 02 Aug 1862; 21y 11m 5d; "Fever or wound"; "In the Army"; s/o Henry Campbell; b. Russell County; a Soldier; reported by father. [p15;Ln10]

Candler, William R.; 19 Sep 1862; 23y 6d; Wounded; "State of Maryland"; s/o Singleton & Adaline H. Candler; b. Russell County; In the Army; reported by father. [p17;Ln12]

Carrell, Mary Ann; 11 Aug 1853; 2y; Flux; Russell County; d/o Thomas & Jane Carrell; b. Russell County; reported by father. [p2;Ln46] *(Note: speculatively Ln45 was, grandmother, Elizabeth Cross)*

Carrell, Robert H.J.; 07 Nov 1853; 13y 2m 7d; Flux; Russell County; s/o Jas. & Lila Carrell; b. Russell County; reported by father, James P. Carrell. [p4;Ln3]

Cartey, Henry C.; 15 Sep 1853; 10y 8m; Flux; Russell County; s/o John & Nancy Cartey; b. Russell County; reported by father, John P. Cartey. [p2;Ln22]

Carty, Elbert J.; 13 Dec 1858; 4y 6m; Croup; Russell County; s/o Thomas & Caroline Carty; b. Russell County; reported by father, Thomas J. Carty. [p10;Ln18]

Carty, James L.'; __ Apr 1862; 21d; Croup; Russell County; s/o G.S.G.W. & Mary Carty; b. Russell County; reported by father, S.G.W. Carty. [p17;Ln13]

Carty, Joseph; 14 Sep 1861; 7d; Croup; Russell County; s/o John B. & Delila Carty; b. Russell County; reported by father. [p14;Ln14]

Castle, (female); __ May 1860; 5d; Cause Unknown; Russell County; d/o Ralph S. Castle; reported by Ralph S. Castle. [p12;Ln28]

Castle, (male); 07 Mar 1853; 1d; Cause Unknown; Russell County; s/o Ralph & Sarah Castle; b. Russell County; reported by father. [p2;Ln36]

Castle, Catherine; 21 Aug 1856; 60y; "Paulsey"; Russell County; d/o Joshua & Anna Pennick; b. Scott County; consort of Zachariah Castle; reported by husband. [p8;Ln8]

Castle, Sarah; 28 Jun 1853; 49y; Consumption; Russell County; d/o Ralph & Nancy Suit; b. North Carolina; consort of Elijah Castle; reported by husband. [p2;Ln15]

---

[1] See Birth Register; James L., s/o Samuel G.W. & Mary Carty

SOME RUSSELL COUNTY RECORDS
Deaths 1853 – 1866

Chafin, Elizabeth; 03 Jun 1857; 3m; cause not given; Russell County; d/o Rebecca & Oliver Chafin; b. Russell County; reported by father. [p9;Ln11]

Chapman, (male); 16 Oct 1862; 19d; "Diptherea"; Russell County; s/o B.F. & Charity Chapman; b. Russell County; reported by "his grandmother"(sic), Wm. Chapman. [p16;Ln2]

Chapman, Margaret A.; 30 Dec 1862; 2y 3m 26d; "Diptherea"; Russell County; d/o B.F. & Charity Chapman; b. Russell County; reported by "his grandmother(sic), Wm. Chapman. [p16;Ln3]

Chatron, Joseph C.; 15 Jul 1853; 7y 4m; Flux; Russell County; s/o William & Lucinda Chatron; b. Russell County; reported by father. [p5;Ln4]

Childers, Osy; 08 May 1866; 9m; Croup; Castlewoods; d/o David & Martha Childers; b. Russell County; reported by father. [p20;Ln12]

Clark, (male); 23 Jul 1860; 12d; Flux; New Garden; s/o Daniel & Leah Clark; b. New Garden; reported by father. [p13;Ln7]

Clark, (male); 01 Aug 1860; 5m 27d; Flux; New Garden; s/o Patrick & Eliza Clark; b. New Garden; reported by father. [p13;Ln4]

Clark, Floyd G.; 28 Jul 1860; 5y; Flux; New Garden; s/o Patrick & Eliza Clark; b. New Garden; reported by father. [p13;Ln3]

Clark, Mary; 15 Aug 1854; 33y 2m 18d; Bronchitis; Russell County; d/o Daniel & Darky Hartsock; b. Scott County; reported by husband, Robert Clark. [p5;Ln15]

Clark, Sarah A.J.; 28 Aug 1860; 2y 9m; Flux; New Garden; d/o J.P. & Elizabeth Clark; b. New Garden; reported by father. [p13;Ln5]

Claypole, (male); 11 May 1862; 1d; Cause Unknown; New Garden; s/o James Claypole; b. Russell County; reported by father. [p15;Ln6]

Claypool, Charity; 10 Jul 1862; 4y 10d; "Dypotherea"; New Garden; d/o James N. & Chirty Claypool; b. Tazewell, Va.; reported by father. [p15;Ln9] (Note: James N. was possibly James V. Claypool).

Claypool, Jeremiah M.; 11 Aug 1862; 7y 1m 6d; Fever; New Garden; s/o James N. & Chairty Claypool; b. Tazewell, Va.; reported by father. [p15;Ln8] (Note: James N. was possibly James V. Claypool).

SOME RUSSELL COUNTY RECORDS
Deaths 1853 — 1866

Claypoole, James; 28 Jul 1862; 87y 10m 20d; Old Age; New Garden; a Farmer; Unmarried; reported by nephew, John Claypoole. [p15;Ln7]

Clifton, Susanna; 06 Jun 1856; 45y 7m; cause not given; Russell County; parents not given; consort of Martin J. Clifton; reported by husband. [p8;Ln14]

Cloud, (male); 20 Apr 1865; 1y 10m; cause not given; Elk Garden; s/o John Cloud. [p19;Ln6] (Note: Death register multiple line ditto indicates name of William Burk. *(Identified by Birth register as Unnamed Male Cloud (stillborn), born 20 Apr 1865, Russell County; s/o John & Sussa Cloud)*

Cockran, Frances T.; 29 Jul 1860; 1y 4m; Flux; New Garden; d/o Marvell Cockran; b. New garden; reported by father. [p13;Ln8]

Cockran, Lucinda; 09 Nov 1856; 41y 11m 24d; "Childbed"; Russell County; parents not named; b. Franklin County; consort of Marvel Cockran; reported by Jackson Mutter. [p8;Ln2]

Coleman, Joshua; 30 Nov 1853; (age not given); Scarlet Fever; Sandy; s/o Jas. & Mary Coleman; reported by father, James Coleman [p2;Ln10] *(a Joshua Coleman, age 7/12, is listed in 1850 census household #1673 of James & Mary Coleman)*

Colley, Hugh Harry; 26 Feb 1853; 2y; Cause Unknown; Russell County; s/o John & Ann Colley; b. Russell County; reported by father, John Colley. [p3;Ln44] *(Note: name listed as Hugh Harry without Colley surname). (See also double listing)*
Coly, Hugh; 26 Feb 1854; 3y 4m 2d; Croup; Russell County; s/o John & Anny Colly; b. Russell County; reported by father. [p6;Ln13]

Colley, John; 01 Sep 1853; 2y; Cause Unknown; Russell County; s/o Joshua & Didama Colley; b. Russell County; reported by father. [p3;Ln45]

Collins, Nathan E.; ___ Feb 1862; 6m; Croup; Russell County; s/o William H. & Mary Collins; b. Russell County; reported by father. [p17;Ln14]

Colly, Christiner; 06 Dec 1855; 61y 11m 25d; cause not given; Russell County; d/o John & Margaret Counts; consort of Richard Colley; reported by husband. [p7;Ln27]

Combs, Alexander; 05 May 1866; 20y; "Shot as a Robber"; "Car's Creek"; s/o Alexander & D. Combs; b. Russell County; a Farmer; Unmarried; reported by father. [p20;Ln10]

Combs, Elbert; 06 Jul 1861; 6y 1m 10d; Flux; New Garden; s/o William Combs "consort of A_na_ Combs; b. New Garden; reported by father. [p14;Ln34]

Combs, Octava; 07 Aug 1861; 5m 25d; New Garden; d/o Cullin Combs Jr.; "consort of Desty Combs"; b. New Garden; reported by father. [p14;Ln32]

Combs, Samuel; 09 Aug 1862; 26y; "Wounded in Action"; "In southern Army"; s/o Thompson Combs; a Soldier; Married; reported by father-in-law, James Gent. [p16;Ln20]

Combs, Rachel; 30 Apr 1857; 16d; Croup; Russell County; d/o Feeling & Sarah Combs; b. Russell County. [p9;Ln40]

Compton, Sarah; 12 Oct 1853; 5y; Sore Throat; New Garden; d/o Jerry & Martha Compton; b. New Garden; reported by father. [p2;Ln1]

Cooper, (female); 27 Mar 1866; 20d; Cause Unknown; Castlewoods; d/o William P. & Tabitha Cooper; b. Russell County; reported by father. [p20;Ln13]

Cooper, Susan P.; __ Dec 1858; 4m; Hives; Russell County; d/o William & R. Cooper; b. Russell County; reported by father. [p10;Ln21]

Corvin, George G.; 03 Aug 1853; 6y 2m 14d; Flux; Russell County; s/o John & Melvina Corvin; b. Wythe County; reported by father. [p3;Ln15]

Couch, David; 11 Aug 1853; 8y 2m; Flux; Russell County; s/o John & Fanny Couch; b. Russell County; reported by father. [p4;Ln13]

Couch, Henry; 19 Aug 1861; 21y; "Burnt by Powder"; Russell County; s/o Jeremiah & Peggy Couch; b. Russell County; a Farmer; Unmarried; reported by father. [p14;Ln16]

Couch, Hezekial; 14 Jul 1853; 13y 11m; Flux; Russell County; s/o John & Fanny Couch; b. Russell County; reported by father. [p4;Ln11]

Couch, John C.; 14 Jul 1853; 11y 10m; Flux; Russell County; s/o John & Fanny Couch; b. Russell County; reported by father. [p4;Ln12]

Couch, John; 22 Aug 1853; 1y; Flux; Russell County; s/o Jeremiah & Margaret Couch; b. Russell County; reported by father. [p4;Ln7]

Couch, Mary Eliz.; 29 Apr 1853; 11m 20d; Croup; Russell County; d/o John Eliz. Couch; b. Russell County; reported by father. [p5;Ln3]

SOME RUSSELL COUNTY RECORDS
Deaths 1853 - 1866

Couch, Mary; 15 Aug 1853; 21y 11m; Flux; Russell County; d/o John & Fanny Couch; b. Russell County; reported by father. [p4;Ln10]

Couch, Susan; 09 Jul 1853; 5y 2m; Flux; Russell County; d/o Jeremiah & Margaret Couch; b. Russell County; reported by father [p4;Ln6]

Counts, (female); 13 May 1857; 1d; cause not given; Russell County; d/o Patsey & W. Counts; b. Russell County; reported by father, William Counts. [p9;Ln24]

Counts, (female); 08 Aug 1859; 12d; Fever; Russell County; d/o David & Nancy Counts; reported by father. [p11;Ln36]

Counts, Eliza A.; 10 Oct 1859; 23y; Cause Unknown; Russell County; parents and place of birth not given; consort of John J. Counts; reported by husband. [p11;Ln5]

Counts, Harriet; 07 Jan 1862; 10m; Croup; Russell County; d/o John W. & Elizabeth Counts; b. Russell County; reported by father. [p17;Ln17]

Counts, Joshua F.; 17 Jan 1859; 23y 2m 25d; "Chronic"; Russell County; s/o Joshua & Martha Counts; a Farmer; Unmarried; reported by father. [p11;Ln7]

Counts, Martha; __ Apr 1860; 25y; Consumption; Russell County; d/o Rubin Finney; b. Russell County; consort of Joshua Counts. [p12;Ln1]

Counts, Phebe; 17 Feb 1861; 64y; "Sudden"; Russell County; parents not named; b. Russell County; a Housekeeper; consort of John Counts Sr.; reported by John Counts Sr. [p14;Ln15]

Counts, Priscilla; 07 Oct 1859; 3m; Cause Unknown; Russell County; d/o John J. & Eliza A. Counts; reported by father. [p11;Ln6]

Counts, Soloman; 01 Nov 1853; 3y; Fever; Russell County; s/o Canaan & Ann Counts; b. Russell County; reported by father. [p3;Ln36]

Cowan, Bolivar; __ __ 1862; 27y; Camp fever; Bath, Morgan Co.; s/o George Cowan; b. Russell County; a Farmer; reported by father. [p15;Ln5]

Cowan, John T.; __ __ 1862; 37y; "by Wound"; Russell County; s/o George Cowan; b. Russell County; a Farmer; Unmarried; reported by father. [p15;Ln4]

Cowan, Robert E.; __ __ 1862; 31y; "by Wound"; Staunton, Va.; s/o George Cowan; b. Russell County; a Farmer; Unmarried; reported by father. [p15;Ln3]

SOME RUSSELL COUNTY RECORDS
Deaths 1853 — 1866

Cox, John; 12 Apr 1861; 5y 9m 15d; New Garden; Flux; s/o John Cox "consort of Mary Cox"; b. New Garden; reported by father [p14;Ln33]

Crismon, John J.; 30 Dec 1853; 3m 2d; Measles; Russell County; s/o Thomas & Artaminta Banion; b. Russell County; reported by father, Thomas Banion. [p3;Ln3]

Crook, Rhoda A.; 31 Aug 1853; 27y; Cold; Russell County; d/o David & Nancy Crook; b. Russell County; reported by father. [p3;Ln37]

Cross, David S.; 19 Jun 1858; 2y 2m 3d; Flux; Russell County; s/o M. & Jane Cross; b. Russell County; reported by father, Modecai Cross. [p10;Ln20]

Cross, Elizabeth; 18 Mar 1853; 45y; "From wond on the knee"; Russell County; d/o Aell(?) & Mary Ann Cross; b. "Shenadore Co."; Unmarried; reported by son-in-law, Thomas Carrell. [p2;Ln45]

Cross, Felix J.; 19 Jun 1858; 7y 17d; Flux; Russell County; s/o M. & Jane Cross; b. Russell County; reported by father, Modecai Cross. [p10;Ln19]

Culbertson, James M.; 25 Apr 1862; 29y 4m 21d; Wounded; near Richmond; s/o Tyre & Martha Culbertson; b. Russell County; In the Army; Unmarried; reported by father. [p17;Ln16]

Culbertson, William R.; 12 Aug 1862; 23y; Wounded; near Richmond; s/o Tyre & Martha Culbertson; b. Russell County; In the Army; Unmarried; reported by father. [p17;Ln15]

Culverson, Matty; 18 Jun 1862; 2y 3m 10d; "Diptherea"; Lebanon, Va.; d/o E.J. & Matty Culverson; b. Lebanon, Va.; reported by mother. [p16;Ln1]

Cumbo, Sarah C.; 04 Sep 1859; 14y 1m 18d; Fever; Russell County; d/o William & Eliza A. Cumbo; reported by father. [p11;Ln8]

Cumbow, Charles; 01 Sep 1866; 25y; Flux; Cedar Creek, Russell County; s/o Isaiah & Mary Cumbow; b. Russell County; a Farmer; consort of Darthula Cumbow; reported by "mother"(*sic; wife*), Darthula Cumbow". [p21;Ln51] *(Identified by 1860 Russell County census as Charles Cumbo, age 16; living in household of Isaiah & Mary A. Cumbo)*

Cumbow, Mary E.; 06 Sep 1866; 1y 8m; Flux; Cedar Creek, Russell County; d/o Charles & Darthula Cumbow; b. Russell County; reported by "father"(*sic; mother, as indicated in the above entry, her father died 5 days before*). [p21;Ln52]

SOME RUSSELL COUNTY RECORDS
Deaths 1853 — 1866

Cunningham, Harvy S.; 10 Jan 1857; 2y 4m; cause not given; Russell County; s/o Louisa & T. Cunningham; b. Russell County; reported by father, Thomas Cunningham. [p9;Ln16]

Cunningham, Mary; 03 Mar 1853; 7y 11m 3d; "Eracipalus" (Erysipelas); Russell County; d/o Thomas & Louisa Cunningham; b. Russell County; reported by father. [p2;Ln33]

Dale, Doctor; 05 Feb 1853; 10d; Cause Unknown; Russell County; s/o Hayman & Eliza D. Dale; b. Russell County; reported by father, Hayman Dale [p5;Ln7] *(Birth register lists: Doctor P. Dale, b. 23 May 1853, Russell County, s/o Hiram & Elizabeth D. Dale).*

Dale, Fanny G.; 22 Jun 1866; 5y 6m; Fever; "Grinip Co., Ky"*(Greenup Co.)*; d/o Hiram & Fanny Dale; b. Russell County; reported by father. [p20;Ln14]

Darnold, Morgan; 01 Jun 1853; 9m; Cause Unknown; Russell County; s/o Mary Darnold; b. Russell County; reported by mother. [p3;Ln47]

Davis, (male); 08 Sep 1854; 5y; cause not given; New Garden; s/o Thomas Davis; b. Russell County; reported by father. [p6;Ln46]

Davis, Charles M.; 24 Oct 1853; 14y; pleursey; Elk Garden; s/o Jesse Davis; b. Elk Garden; reported by father. [p1;Ln10]

Davis, Elbert F.; 22 Feb 1860; 4m 10d; Croup; Lebanon; s/o Thomas & Jane Davis; b. Lebanon; reported by father. [p13;Ln9]

Davis, Emily P.; 19 Jul 1862; 4y 9 11d; "Diptherea"; Lebanon, Va.; d/o Thomas & Jane F. Davis; b. Lebanon, Va.; "Hotel Keeping"; Married; reported by father. [p16;Ln5] *(Note: the occupation of "hotel keeping" & married, obviously in reference to father).*

Davis, James F. 12 May 1862; 12y 10m 19d; Fever; Lebanon, Va.; s/o Mildred More; b. Russell County; (Occupation) "Hotel Keeping", Married; reported by Thomas Davis, her husband". [p16;Ln4] *(Note: information as stated; reference to "Hotel Keeping" was the occupation of Thomas Davis, reporting)*

Davis, William; 16 Sep 1853; 2m; Inflamation of Lungs; Lebanon; s/o Thomas & Jane Davis; b. Lebanon; reported by father. [p1;Ln17].

Deal, Celia; 11 Oct 1853; 4y; Scarlet Fever; Sandy; d/o Harvey & Louisa Deal; b. Sandy; reported by father. [p2;Ln9]

Deal, Jacob; 04 Apr 1853; 6y 8m; Cause Unknown; Sandy; s/o Harvey & Louisa Deal; b. Sandy; reported by father. [p2;Ln8]

SOME RUSSELL COUNTY RECORDS
Deaths 1853 – 1866

Dickenson, (infant); __ Jul 1861; 2d; Cause Unknown; Russell County; child of Charles H. Dickenson; b. Russell County; reported by father. [p14;Ln9]

Dickenson, Charles C.; 22 Jul 1853; 11m; Flux; Russell County; s/o John & Sarah Dickenson; b. Russell County; reported by father, John N. Dickenson. [p4;Ln45]

Dickenson, Charles C.; 03 Aug 1853; 5y; Flux; Russell County; s/o Charles C. & Catherine Dickenson; b. Russell County; reported by father. [p4;Ln17]

Dickenson, Elizabeth; 07 Jul 1853; 53y; Dyspepsia; Russell County; d/o Charles & Mary Bickley; b. Russell County; consort of Henry Dickenson; reported by husband. [p4;Ln31]

Dickenson, Emet Atwood; 12 Mar 1862; 3y; Cause Unknown; "near the Old Co. H."; s/o Jno. N. & Sarah Dickenson; b. Russell County; reported by father. [p19;Ln1]

Dickenson, H.C.; 28 Sep 1862; 2y 6m 4d; "Dytheria"; Russell County; s/o H.P. & Mary J. Dickenson; b. Russell County; reported by father. [p17;Ln20]

Dickenson, John; 17 Sep 1853; 11m 9d; Flux; Russell County; s/o Berry & Feraba Dickenson; b. Russell County; reported by father. [p3;Ln14]

Dickenson, Nancy R.; 02 Oct 1855; 1y; cause not given; Russell County; d/o Elizabeth & Samuel Dickenson; b. Russell County; reported by father. [p7.Ln7]

Dickenson, Patsy; 31 Dec 1854; 6m; Whooping Cough; Russell County; d/o John & Sary Dickenson; b. Russell County; reported by father, John N. Dickson. [p5;Ln20]

Dickenson, Thomas; __ Mar 1860; 1y 6m; Croup; Russell County; s/o Charles Dickson; reported by a Friend (unnamed). [p12;Ln38]

Dills, Peter; 03 Oct 1853; 9y 10m 25d; Flux; Copper Ridge; s/o Jas. & Sarah Dills; b.Tennessee; reported by father, James Dills. [p1;Ln16]

Dorton, Edith M.; 23 May 1854; 2y 27d; Croup; Russell County; d/o Jacob & Elizabeth Dorton; b. Russell County; reported by father. [p6;Ln11]

Dorton, Edith; 27 Jul 1853; 56y; Flux; Russell County; d/o Colbert & Hannah Fugate; b. Russell County; consort of Jacob Dorton; reported by son, Samuel B. Dorton. [p3;Ln23]

118

Dorton, John; 03 Dec 1857; 67y; Dropsy; Russell County; parents not given; a Farmer & husband; reported by son, Francis Dorton. [p9;Ln19]

Dorton, William T.; 08 May 1862; 14y; "Hemorrhoids"; Russell County; s/o Edward & Jemimah Dorton; b. Russell County; a Farmer; reported by father. [p17;Ln18]

Dotson, Charles C.J.; 15 Jun 1853; 17y 4m; Cause Unknown; Russell County; s/o James & Elizabeth Dotson; b. Russell County; reported by father. [p5;Ln11]

Dotson, George C.; 13 Jul 1853; 3y 5m; Flux; Russell County; s/o James & Elizabeth Dotson; b. Russell County; reported by father. [p5;Ln12]

Duff, Sibbie; 10 Dec 1866; 10y; Fever; Elk Garden; parents not named; b. Tazewell, Va.; reported by Rees Duff. [p19;Ln20]

Duncan, Susanah; 17 Nov 1856; 77y; cause not given; Russell County; parents not given; b. Russell County; reported by daughter, Rebecca Duncan. [p8;Ln18]

Duty, (male); 15 Apr 1857; 1m 3d; Croup; Russell County; s/o John & Sarah Duty; b. Russell County. [p9;Ln39]

Dye, Mary M.; 31 Oct 1866; 1y 8m; Croup; Elk Garden; d/o George & Elizabeth Ayers; b. Russell County; reported by George Ayers. [p19;Ln8]

Eakin, Virginiabella; 05 Oct 1858; 18d; cause not given; Russell County; d/o William & Cermantha Eakin; b. Russell County; reported by father. [p10;Ln23]

Easterly, Nathan W.; 27 Jun 1862; 22y; Killed in Battle; near Richmond; C. & Nancy Easterly; b. Russell County; "In the Army"; consort of Elizabeth E. Easterly; reported by father, Christian Easterly. [p17;Ln22]

Elliott, William W.; 10 Feb 1861; 18y 1m 20d; Camp fever; Staunton, VA; s/o Wilson Elliott; b. Elk Garden; a Farmer; Unmarried; reported by father. [p15;Ln1]

Elswick, Elizabeth B.; 09 Aug 1860; 6m 5d; Croup; Richlands; d/o John Elswick; b. Richlands; reported by father. [p13;Ln10]

Ervin, Moning; 02 May 1854; 73y; cause not given; New Garden; d/o Benjamine Chapman; *(register multilple line ditto indicates born Russell County and "reported by father"(questionable)* [p6;Ln47]

SOME RUSSELL COUNTY RECORDS
Deaths 1853 — 1866

Estep, Elizabeth; 12 Sep 1854; 25y; Fever; Russell County; d/o Absolam & Elizabeth Hammons; b. Scott County; reported by husband, Joseph Estep. [p6:Ln15]

Evans, Almeda; 02 Nov 1862; 13y; Fever; Russell County; d/o Wilson & Sarah Evans; a Housekeeper; Unmarried; reported by father. [p17;Ln23] *(sister, Nancy, listed Ln24]*

Evans, Berry; 30 Jun 1853; 93y; Old Age; Russell County; s/o Walter & Lucy Evans; b. North Carolina; a Farmer; reported by daughter (unnamed) [p4;Ln46]

Evans, Nancy; 11 Dec 1862; 17y; Fever; Russell County; d/o Wilson & Sarah Evans; b. Russell County; a Housekeeper; Unmarried; reported by father. [p17;Ln24] *(sister, Almeda, listed Ln23]*

Farmer, (female); 26 Jul 1853; 10m; Cause Unknown; Russell County; d/o John & Sarah Farmer; b. Russell County; reported by father. [p3;Ln41].

Farmer, (male); 01 Aug 1853; 4d; Cause Unknown; Russell County; s/o John & Sarah Farmer; b. Russell County; reported by father. [p3;Ln40] *(Identified by birth register as an Unnamed male (twin), born 25 Jul 1853; s/o John & Sarah Farmer)*

Farmer, Mallisa; 22 Jul 1866; 12y; Flux; Elk Garden; d/o Sol. J. Farmer & wife; b. Russell County; reported by Sol. J. Farmer. [p19;Ln19]

Farris, Mary Elizabeth; 26 Aug 1853; 1m 21d; Flux; Russell County; d/o John & Nancy C. Farris; b. Russell County; reported by mother. [p2;Ln19]

Ferguson, John Sr.; 28 Dec 1862; 87y 11m 11d; Old Age; Russell County; parents not named; a Farmer; married; reported by wife, Mary Ferguson. [p16;Ln18]

Ferguson, Mary Ann; 12 Dec 1860; 1y 10m 15d; cause not given; Elk Garden; d/o Menerva & Granville Ferguson; b. Elk Garden; reported by father. [p13;Ln14]

Ferguson, Mary; 05 Dec 1859; 24y 8m 16d; Fever; Russell County; parents not given; reported by Benjamine Ferguson *(relationship not stated)*. [p11;Ln38]

Ferguson, Rebecca; 29 Mar 1854; 24y; cause not given; d/o Andrew C. Ferguson; b. Russell County. [p7;Ln3]

SOME RUSSELL COUNTY RECORDS
Deaths 1853 — 1866

Ferguson, Sarah S.; 10 Aug 1866; 6y; Flux; Elk Garden; d/o E.M.
Ferguson; b. Russell County; reported by E.M. Ferguson.
[p19;Ln16]

Fickle, Elbert; 30 Apr 1858; 28d; Cause Unknown; Russell County; s/o
Isaac B. Fickle; b. Russell County; reported by father [p10;Ln1]

Fields, (male); 10 Sep 1860; 1d; cause/place of death not given; s/o
James J. Fields; b. Elk Garden; reported by father [p13;Ln13]

Fields, Andrew F.; 10 Aug 1861; 1y 11m(?) 10d; Croup; Elk Garden;
s/o Randolph & Rutha Fields; b. Elk Garden; reported by father.
[p15;Ln5]

Fields, Cynthia J.; 10 Oct 1859; 3y; Croup; Russell County; d/o John
Fields; reported by father. [p11;Ln9]

Fields, Elizabeth; 21 Feb 1854; 37y; Cause Unknown; Elk Garden;
parents unknown; b. Russell County; consort of William H.
Fields. [p6;Ln22]

Fields, Frances M.; 15 Apr 1860; 9m 6d; Whooping cough; Elk Garden;
d/o A.F. & Milly Fields; b. Elk Garden; reported by father.
[p13;Ln15]

Fields, James; 26 Oct 1858; 50y 6m 10d; "Breast complaint"; Russell
County; parents not given; a Farmer; Unmarried; reported by
brother, Joel Fields. [p10;Ln3]

Fields, Jeremiah; 10 Oct 1854; 9y; cause not given; New Garden; s/o
Richard Fields; b. Russell County; reported by father. [p6:Ln43]

Fields, Lilburn T.; 07 Mar 1862; 2y 6m; Dropsy; Russell County; s/o
Russell & Rachel F. Fields; b. Russell County; reported by
father. [p17;Ln25]

Fields, Richard; 07 Aug 1862; 7y; Fever; Russell County; s/o John T.
& Rosannah Fields; b. Russell County; reported by father.
[p17;Ln26]

Fields, Sarah; 30 Sep 1854; 11y; cause not given; New Garden; d/o
Richard Fields; Russell County; reported by father. [p6;Ln42]

Fields, William; __ Jan 1862; 6y; Fever; Russell County; s/o Richard
F. & Mary Fields; b. Russell County; reported by father.
[p17;Ln27]

Finney, George J.; __ Dec 1860; 19y; "Inflamation of Brain"; Russell
County; s/o Rubin Finney; b. Russell County; a Farmer. [p12;Ln2]

SOME RUSSELL COUNTY RECORDS
Deaths 1853 - 1866

Finney, Mary A.; 20 Feb 1860; 1y 1m; Flux; New Garden; d/o Lilburn & Melissa Finney; b. New Garden; reported by father. [p13;Ln12]

Fletcher, Basil; 16 Feb 1854; 43y; cause not given; New Garden; s/o John Fletcher; *(multilple line ditto indicates reported by father)*. [p6;Ln41]

Fletcher, Eliza R.; 10 Jun 1853; 3m; Flux; New Garden; d/o Jas. & Ellen Fletcher; b. New Garden; reported by father, Jas H. Fletcher. [p1;Ln34].

Fletcher, Eliza C.: 10 Jun 1853; 3m; Flux; New Garden; d/o Jas. H. & Ellen Fletcher; b. New Garden; reported by father, James H. Fletcher. [p1;Ln2]

Fletcher, Fullen; __ ____ 1853; 23y 4m 27d; Pneumonia; New Garden; s/o Jas. & Celia Fletcher; b. New Garden; farmer; unmarried; reported by brother, Lorenzo D. Fletcher. [p1;Ln1]

Fletcher, James; 20 Feb 1853; 61y 5m 25d; Pneumonia; New Garden; s/o William & Mary Fletcher; consort of Celia Fletcher; reported by son, Lorenzo D. Fletcher. [p1;Ln29]

Fletcher, Jane; 04 Apr 1853; 64y; Pneumonia; New Garden; d/o John & Mary Wallis; b. North Carolina; consort of William Fletcher; reported by son-in-law, Jno. T. Howard. [p1;Ln28]

Fletcher, Lilbern G.; 27 Sep 1861; 19y 5m 6d; Camp fever; "Alegany mountain"; s/o Major A. & Rachel Fletcher; b. New Garden; Unmarried; "Died as soldier in the War"; reported by father. [p15;Ln3]

Fletcher, Milton; __ ____ 1862; 24y; "Killed in battle"; "Kernstown in action"; s/o Ely & Agnes Fletcher; b. Russell County; a Soldier; Unmarried; reported by father. [p16;Ln16]

Fletcher, William N.; 15 Sep 1861; 23y 4m 14d; Camp fever; "Alegany mountain"; s/o Major A. & Rachel Fletcher; b. New Garden; a Farmer; Unmarried; "Died as soldier in War"; reported by father. [p15;Ln2]

Fraley, Barbary J.; 01 Feb 1862; 7y; Cold; Russell County; d/o Ephraim & Margaret Fraley; b. Russell County; reported by father. [p18;Ln39] *(sister, Sarah, listed Ln38)*

Fraley, Isabel; 09 Aug 1853; 1y 6m; Flux; Russell County; d/o George & Nancy Fraley; b. Russell County; reported by Aunt (unnamed) [p5;Ln1]

SOME RUSSELL COUNTY RECORDS
Deaths 1853 - 1866

Fraley, Margaret; 28 Jul 1862; 29y; "By a hurt"; Russell County; d/o
George & Sarah Plot; b. Russell County; a Housekeeper; consort
of Ephraim Fraley; reported by husband. [p18;Ln39]

Fraley, Mary; 22 Mar 1853; 63y; Typhoid Fever; Russell County; d/o
Jas. & Mary Turner; b. Russell County; consort of Henry Fraley;
reported by daughter (unnamed). [p4;Ln47]

Fraley, Sarah; __ May 1862; 5y; Fever; Russell County; d/o Ephraim &
Margaret Fraley; b. Russell County; reported by father.
[p18;Ln38] *(sister, Margaret, listed Ln39)*

Fraley, William; 09 Jan 1854; 9m; Measles; Russell County; s/o Boon
& Mary Fraley; b. Russell County; reported by father. [p5;Ln10]

Franklin, James; 04 Sep 1860; 70y 8m 19d; Cause Unknown; Russell
County; parents unknown; b. North Carolina; a Farmer; reported
by William L. Franklin. [p12;Ln20]

Franklin, Nancy; 06 Jan 1858; age not given; Dropsy; Russell County;
parents unknown; place of birth unknown; consort of James
Franklin; reported by son, William L. Franklin. [p10;Ln24]

Frick, Sarah; 07 Apr 1855; 9y 10m; Sore Throat; Russell County; d/o
Chris. & C. Frick; b. Russell County; reported by grandfather,
William Frick. [p7;Ln26]

Fugate, Benjamine; 22 Oct 1854; 2y 5m; Flux; Russell County; s/o
Zachariah & Nancy Fugate; reported by mother. [p5;Ln32]

Fugate, Elbert C.; 07 Sep 1853; 1m 14d; Fever; Russell County; s/o
Jos.C. & Eliz.E. Fugate; b. Russell County; reported by father,
Joseph C. Fugate [p2;Ln43] *(Ln 42 was mother, Elizabeth E.
Fugate)*

Fugate, Elizabeth E.; 09 Aug 1853; 33y 11m 13d; Childbed Fever;
Russell County; d/o John & Mary Sutton; b. Washington County,
Va; consort of Joseph C. Fugate; reported by husband. [p2;Ln42]

Fugate, Fanny; 03 Aug 1862; 57y 8m 28d; "Infalmation"; Russell
County; d/o Jos. & Mary Carter; b. Scott Co., Va.; a
Housekeeper; consort of Isaac B. Fugate; reported by husband.
[p17;Ln28]

Fugate, John B.; 02 Nov 1854; 5y 4m; Flux; Russell County; s/o
Zachariah & Nancy Fugate; reported by mother. [p5;Ln31]

Fugate, Margaret E.; 19 Aug 1866; 2y 4m; "Dyptheria"; Moccasin,
Russell County; d/o E.S. & Mary P. Fugate; b. Russell County;
reported by father. [p20;Ln18]

SOME RUSSELL COUNTY RECORDS
Deaths 1853 - 1866

Fugate, Robert H.; 16 Jun 1866; 5y 8m; "Dyptheria"; Moccasin, Russell County; d/o E.S. & Mary P. Fugate; b. Russell County; reported by father. [p20;Ln19]

Fullen, Thomas B.; 15 Oct 1861; 4y 11m 10d; Flux; Elk Garden; s/o Fowler & Ann E. Fullen; b. Elk Garden; reported by father. [p15;Ln4]

Fuller, (male); 03 Sep 1853; "3m"; Cause Unknown; Russell County; s/o Jonas & Rhoda Fuller; b. Russell County; reported by father. [p3;Ln46] *(Note: Possible error as Birth Register lists an Unnamed male Fuller, born 01 Sep 1853; s/o Jonas & Rhoda Fuller. This date indicates death at age 3 days).*

Fuller, Fleming G.; 01 Feb 1853; 24y 1m; Typhoid Fever; Russell County; s/o Isaiah & Polly Fuller; b. Russell County; consort of Martha Fuller; reported by wife. [p2;Ln35]

Fuller, Henry F.; 13 Nov 1853; 11m 24d; Measles; Russell County; s/o Noah & Cyntha Fuller; b. Russell County; reported by father, Noah H. Fuller. [p4;Ln35]

Fuller, Isaac L. Jr.; 21 Oct 1860; 18y 9m 27d; Typhoid Fever; New Garden; s/o Isaac & Susa Fuller; b. New Garden; a Farmer; Single; reported by father. [p13;Ln17]

Fuller, John; 01 May 1866; 24y; 24y; "Killed in the Army"; Richmond, Va.; s/o Jesse & Mary Fuller; b. Russell County; a Farmer; Unmarried; reported by father. [p20;Ln17]

Fuller, Julia; 08 Mar 1853; 6y; Cause Unknown; New Garden; d/o Jas. H. & Polly Fuller; b. New Garden; reported by father, James H. Fuller. [p2;Ln2]

Fuller, Polly; 22 Oct 1859; 34y 2m 17d; Fits; Russell County; d/o Adam & Polly Wisor; consort of James H. Fuller; reported by sister, Catherine Wisor. [p11;Ln43]

Gardner, Samuel P.; 21 Jul 1853; 1y 5m; Croup; Russell County; s/o William & Seny Gardner; b. Russell County; reported by father, William H. Gardner. [p3;Ln26]

Garrett, Alderson; 01 Oct 1859; 11m; Fever; Russell County; s/o William & Mary Garrett; reported by father. [p11;Ln37]

Garrett, Frances; 29 Aug 1866; 38y; Flux; Elk Garden; reported by James Bays. [p19;Ln17]

Garrett, James; 11 Oct 1854; 10y; cause not given; New Garden; s/o John J. Garrett; b. Russell County; reported by father. [p6;Ln45]

Garrett, Sarah; 01 Aug 1866; 1y; Flux; Elk Garden; d/o W.L. & Sarah Garrett; b. Russell County; reported by W.L. Garrett. [p19;Ln18]

Gent, Mary R.; 17 Jun 1861; 1y 1m 2d; Flux; New Garden; d/o Fielding & Jane Gent; b. New Garden; reported by father. [p15;Ln6]

Gentry, David: See David Jentry

Gibson, (female); 03 Oct 1854; 1m 5d; Fever; Scott County; d/o George & Casy Gibson; b. Scott Co; reported by father. [p6;Ln3]

Gibson, Helen; 10 Feb 1858; 1y 8m; Flux; Russell County; d/o Henry & Melvina Gibson; b. Russell County; reported by father. [p10;Ln6]

Gibson, Ira A.; 26 Jul 1853; 4y 2m 3d; Flux; Russell County; s/o Harvy P. & Maria Gibson; b. Russell County; reported by father. [p2;Ln31]

Gibson, Phebe; 01 Jun 1855; age and cause not given; unmarried; reported by grandson, Jefferson Baian. [p7;Ln16]

Gibson, William; 27 Aug 1866; 70y; C*(am)*mp Colic; Castlewoods; parents and birthplace unknown; a Cabinet maker; consort of Tabitha Gibson; reported by son, Mitchell E. Gibson. [p20;Ln20]

Gilbert, (female); 10 Jan 1859; 17d; Fits; Russell County; d/o William & Polly Gilbert; reported by father. [p11;Ln44]

Gilbert, (male); 15 Dec 1858; 15d; Cause Unknown; Russell County; s/o William & Mary Gilbert; b. Russell County; reported by father. [p10;Ln2]

Gilbert, Jane; 26 Jun 1855; 29y 5m; "Kings Evil"*(Scrofula\TB)*; Corner (Settlement); "wife of Jas. A. Gilbert"; b. Russell County. [p8;Ln11]

Gilmer, (Infant); died 1855, Elk Garden; b. Russell County; child of Samuel E. Gilmer; reported by father. [p8;Ln1]

Gilmer, Joseph H.; 04 Aug 1860; 5y 7m 18d; Flux; Russell County; s/o Wesley & Martha Gilmer; reported by father. [p12;Ln40]

Gilmer, Mary J.; 04 Jun 1860; 23y 2m 25d; Fever; Russell County; d/o Wesley & Martha Gilmer; a Housekeeper; reported by father. [p12;Ln39]

SOME RUSSELL COUNTY RECORDS
Deaths 1853 – 1866

Gilmer, Nancy C.; 17 Jan 1862; 28y; Consumption; near Hansonville; d/o Nathaniel & Mary Dickenson; b. Russell County; Housekeeper; consort of Daughtry Gilmer; reported by consort. [p19;Ln47]

Gilmer, Nathaniel D.; 18 Oct 1857; 6m 11d; Hives; Russell County; s/o Nancy & D. Gilmer; b. Russell County; reported by father, Daugherty Gilmer. [p9;Ln6]

Gilmer, Samuel E.; 18 Mar 1853; 12y; Flux; Waters Cedar Creek; s/o Samuel & Anna Gilmer; b. Waters of Cedar Creek; reported by father. [p2;Ln11].

Gilmore, Emily; 17 Nov 1862; 6y 5m 7d; Cause Unknown; Russell County; d/o Isaac & Mary Gilmore; b. Russell County; reported by father. [p16;Ln19]

Glenn, Fanny O.; 05 Aug 1866; 2y; "Twin"; "Dyptheria"; Moccasin; d/o William & Esther Glenn; b. Moccasin, Russell County; reported by father. [p20;Ln23] *(a twin of Jacob O. Glenn)*

Glenn, Jacob O.; 08 Aug 1866; 2y; "Twin"; "Dyptheria"; Moccasin; s/o William & Esther Glenn; b. Moccasin, Russell County; reported by father. [p20;Ln24] *(a twin of Fanny O. Glenn)*

Glenn, John L.; 02 Aug 1866; 4y; "Dyptheria"; Moccasin; s/o William & Esther Glenn; b. Moccasin, Russell County; reported by father. [p20;Ln22]

Glenn, R.F.; 27 Jul 1866; 1m; "Dyptheria"; Moccasin; s/o William & Esther Glenn; b. Moccasin, Russell County; reported by father. [p20;Ln21]

Gose, George P.; 11 Oct 1857; 3y 5m; Croup; Russell County; s/o M. & G.C. Gose; b. Russell County; reported by father, George C. Gose. [p9;Ln29]

Gose, George W.; 20 Jul 1853; 9y 2m 15d; Flux; Russell County; s/o Aaron & Nancy Gose; b. Russell County; reported by father. [p4;Ln4]

Gose, George; 07 Jun 1861; 75y; Cause Unknown; Russell County; s/o Stephen & Barbara Gose; b. Withe County, Va.; a Farmer; "married Elizabeth Gose"; reported by George C. Gose. [p14;Ln12]

Gose, Henry H.; 05 Nov 1857; 1y; "Arecepelaus"; Russell County; s/o Nancy & Aaron Gose; reported by father. [p9;Ln32]

Gose, John T.; 09 Nov 1857; 3y 4m 13d; Croup; Russell County; s/o Nancy & A. Gose; b. Russell County; reported by father, Aaron Gose. [p9;Ln31]

SOME RUSSELL COUNTY RECORDS
Deaths 1853 - 1866

Gose, Virginia(?); 25 Jul 1853; 1y 5m 5d; Flux; Russell County; d/o Aaron & Nancy Gose; b. Russell County; reported by father; [p4;Ln5] *(name appears as Nergina(?) Gose)*

Grace, Laura; 02 Apr 1854; 16y; cause not given; New Garden; d/o John Grace; b. Russell County; reported by father; [p6;Ln44]

Gray, (female); 07 Aug 1853; 1y 1m; Cause Unknown; Russell County; d/o Harvey & Nancy Gray; b. Russell County; reported by father. [p4;Ln1]

Gray, Harvey; 30 Apr 1859; 55y; Cause Unknown; Russell County; parents not given; a Farmer; consort of Nancy Gray; reported by wife. [p11;Ln11]

Gray, Jemima; __ May 1860; 5y; "Scrofula"; Russell County; d/o John E.R. Gray; reported by father. [p12;Ln25]

Gray, Martha E.; 25 Dec 1862; 6y 3m 13d; Fever; Russell County; d/o N.B. & Rebecca Gray; b. Russell County; reported by father. [p17;Ln30] *(mother, Rebecca Gray, listed Ln29).*

Gray, Rachel; 05 Jun 1857; 1m 14d; cause not given; Russell County; d/o Rachel & John Gray; b. Russell County; reported by father. [p9;Ln7]

Gray, Rebecca; 22 Jul 1862; 39y 1m 25d; Consumption; Russell County; d/o George & Elizabeth Gose; b. Russell County; a Housekeeper; consort of N.B. Gray; reported by husband [p17;Ln29] *(1860 Russell County census household #12: Napoleon B. Gray, 45; Rebecca, 39; William J., 17; Martha E., 3; Sarah Puckett, 15) (Daughter, Martha E.,listed Ln30).*

Green, John; 03 Nov 1853; 60y; Cause Unknown; Russell County; s/o Shadrick & Martha Green; b. Russell County; farmer; consort of Martha Green; reported by wife. [p4;Ln24]

Griffeth, John W.; 08 Jun 1854; 7y; Flux; New Garden; s/o Isaac Griffeth; b. Russell County; reported by father; [p6;Ln23]

Griffeth, Roben; 07 Jul 1854; 4y; ???; New Garden; s/o Isaac Griffeth; b. Russell County; reported by father; [p6;Ln25]

Griffeth, William; 11 Jun 1854; 4y; Flux; New Garden; s/o Isaac Griffeth; b. Russell County; reported by father; [p6;Ln24]

Grizzle, (male); __ Sep 1859; 9m; cause not given; Russell County; s/o John & Elizabeth Grizzle; reported by father. [p11;Ln10]

SOME RUSSELL COUNTY RECORDS
Deaths 1853 — 1866

Grizzle, James H.; 13 May 1862; 22y 4m 4d; Fever; Russell County; s/o Jessee & Nancy Grizzle; b. Russell County; a Farmer; Unmarried; reported by father. [p17:Ln32] *(sister, Malissa, listed Ln31)*

Grizzle, James; 01 Oct 1862; 29y; cause not given; Russell County; s/o William & Elizabeth Grizzle; b. Russell County; a Farmer; Unmarried; reported by father. [p17;Ln34] *(brother, John Grizzle, listed Ln33)*

Grizzle, Jesse; 17 Jul 1853; 7y 2m; Flux; Russell County; s/o William & Elizabeth Grizzle; b. Russell County; reported by father. [p4;Ln18]

Grizzle, John N.; 09 Mar 1856; 2y 3m; Fever; Russell County; s/o George & Elizabeth Grizzle; b. Russell County. [p8;Ln5]

Grizzle, John; 16 Dec 1862; 31y; Fever; Russell County; s/o William & Elizabeth Grizzle; b. Russell County; a Farmer; Unmarried; reported by father [p17;Ln33] *(brother, James Grizzle, listed Ln34]*

Grizzle, John; 04 Nov 1857; 83y 1m 24d; Dropsy; Russell County; parents not given; b. Tennessee; a Farmer & husband; reported by son, Jesse Grizzle. [p9;Ln28]

Grizzle, Malissa; 18 Aug 1862; 18y 3m 26d; Fever; Russell County; d/o Jessee & Nancy Grizzle; b. Russell County; Unmarried; reported by father [p17;Ln31] *(brother, James H., listed Ln32)*

Grizzle, Rachel; 14 Jan 1857; 1y 10m; Croup; Russell County; d/o N. & E. Grizzle. b. Russell County; reported by father, Elam Grizzle. [p9;Ln13]

Grizzle, Rebecca; 25 Dec 1857; 75y 8m 23d; Fever; Russell County; parents not given; b. Russell County; reported by husband, William Grizzle. [p9;Ln14]

Guinn, Elizabeth; 17 Jun 1853; 44y; Cause Unknown; Sandy Ridge; reported by Wiley Guinn (relationship not given). [p2;Ln5] *(Identified by 1850 Russell County census as Elizabeth Gwinn, 41, b. Wythe County, Virginia; in Hh #1606 of Wiley Gwinn, 52).*

Hackney, (male); __ Apr 1860; 20d; Cause Unknown; Russell County; s/o John W. Hackney; reported by John W. Hackney. [p12;Ln31]

Hackney, Celia; 05 Sep 1866; 2y; Croup; Clinch River; d/o Anderson & Mary Hackney; b. Clinch River, Russell County; reported by father. [p20;Ln31]

SOME RUSSELL COUNTY RECORDS
Deaths 1853 - 1866

Hackney, Jane; __ Feb 1860; age not given; Quinsey; Russell County; d/o Anderson Hackney; b. Russell County. [p12;Ln4]

Hackney, Nancy; 04 Sep 1866; 12y; "Decay of lungs"; Clinch River; d/o Anderson & Mary Hackney; b. Clinch River, Russell County; reported by father. [p20;Ln30]

Hackney, Samuel W.; 06 Aug 1861; 17y; "By lightens" (lightning ?); Russell County; s/o Joseph & Milly Hackney; reported by father. [p14;Ln23]

Hale, Elizabeth & Matthew; 02 May 1854; 10y; cause not given; New Garden; d/o & s/o Jonathan Hale; b. Russell County; reported by father. [p6;Ln31]

Hale, Malisa; 20 May 1856; 9d; cause not given; Russell County; d/o Henry & Ruthy (Hale); b. Russell County; reported by father. [p8;Ln10]

Hale, Nancy; 01 Jul 1853; 27y; Cancer; Russell County; parents not given; b. Russell County; consort of James Hale; reported by husband. [p4;Ln44]

Hale, Noah; 08 Nov 1862; 16d; Croup; Russell County; s/o William & Elizabeth Hale; b. Russell County; reported by father. [p18;Ln46]

Hall, George W.; 24 Nov 1854; 7m 3d; Cause Unknown; Russell County; s/o John & Anny Hall; b. Russell County; reported by father. [p5;Ln3]

Harden, Susanah; 08 Dec 1854; 95y 1m; Russell County; d/o William & Sarah H.; b. Russell County; reported by son, Abner Harden. [p6;Ln16]

Harmon, Elizabeth; __ Jun 1859; 42y; Dropsy; Russell County; parents unknown; b. Carter County; consort of Wilson Harmon; reported by husband [p11;Ln14]

Harmon, Robert; __ Jun 1859; 7d; Cause Unknown; Russell County; s/o Wilson & Elizabeth Harmon; b. Russell County; reported by father [p11;Ln15] *(See above listing for mother, Elizabeth Harmon)*

Harmon, William; 25 Dec 1862; 22y 6m 5d; Cause Unknown; Southern Army; s/o Henry & <u>wife</u> Harmon; b. Russell County; a Soldier; Unmarried; reported by father. [p16;Ln28]

Harrison, Axley G.; 09 Dec 1853; 3y 1m 11d; Dropsey in head; Russell County; s/o Jas. & Mary Ann Harrison; b. Russell County; reported by father, James Harrison. [p2;Ln21]

SOME RUSSELL COUNTY RECORDS
Deaths 1853 — 1866

Harrison, Elizabeth; 24 Mar 1853; 50y; Consumption; Russell County; d/o Jas. & Susan Hale; b. Russell County; consort of Samuel Harrison; reported by husband. [p2;Ln30]

Harrison, Henry; 27 Mar 1854; 15y 7m 25d; Fever; Russell County; s/o Samuel & Elizabeth Harrison; reported by father. [p5;Ln23]

Harrison, Mary; 18 Jan 1857; 26y 6m 20d; Consumption; Russell County; parents not given; reported by husband, Samuel Harrison. [p9;Ln5]

Hartsock, Emley M.; 28 May 1853; 2y 11m 12d; Bold Hives; Russell County; d/o James & Matilda Hartsock; reported by father [p3;Ln21]

Hartsock, Matilda J.; 25 Mar 1862; 15y 11m 28d; Measles; Russell County; d/o James & Matilda Hartsock; b. Russell County; a Housekeeper; Unmarried; reported by father. [p18;Ln36] *(brother, William D., listed Ln37)*

Hartsock, Matilda; 13 Mar 1859; 45y; "Chronic"; Russell County; d/o John Dorton; consort of James Hartsock; reported by husband. [p11;Ln12]

Hartsock, Sarah; 25 May 1862; 71y; Cause Unknown; Russell County; d/o James & Polly Lamas(?); b. Russell County; a Housekeeper; consort of John Hartsock; reported by husband. [p18;Ln35]

Hartsock, William D.; 09 Jun 1862; 24y; "Killed by shell"; "Portrepublic"; s/o James & Matilda Hartsock; b. Russell County; In the Army; Unmarried; reported by father. [p18;Ln37] *(sister, Matilda J., listed Ln36]*

Hawkins, Elisha; 16 Sep 1853; 11y; Flux; Russell County; s/o Elisha & Isbel Hawkins; b. Russell County; reported by brother, William B. Hawkins. [p3;Ln19]

Hawkins, Elizabeth; 26 Sep 1862; 9y; Typhoid Fever; Russell County; d/o Thomas L. & Lydia Hawkins; b. Russell County; reported by father. [p18;Ln41]

Hawkins, Ellen; 27 Nov 1857; 7m 20d; Fever; Russell County; d/o Lidia & T.L. Hawkins; b. Russell County; reported by father, Thomas L. Hawkins. [p9;Ln1]

Hawkins, Henry; 01 Dec 1862; 14y; Typhoid Fever; Russell County; s/o Thomas L. & Lydia Hawkins; reported by father. [p18;Ln43]

SOME RUSSELL COUNTY RECORDS
Deaths 1853 — 1866

Hawkins, Jane; 23 Jul 1866; 35y; "By taking Cold"; H____da_ Creek; d/o Isaiah & Mary Cumbow; b. Cedar Creek, Russell County; a Housekeeper; consort of T.T. Hawkins; reported by husband. [p20;Ln27]

Hawkins, Mary; 27 Sep 1862; 16y; Typhoid Fever; Russell County; d/o Thomas L. & Lydia Hawkins; b. Russell County; Unmarried; reported by father. [p18;Ln42]

Hawkins, Sarah; 10 May 1853; 1d; Cause Unknown; Russell County; d/o Bluford & Sidney Hawkins; b. Russell County; reported by father. [p5;Ln9]

Helbert, A.C.; 01 Sep 1862; 1m 12d; "Eresypilas"; Russell County; s/o Jacob & Mary M. Helbert; b. Russell County; reported by mother. [p18;Ln45] *(father, Jacob A. Helbert, listed Ln44).* *(Identified by birth register as A.C. Helbert, born 21 Jul 1862 in Russell County; s/o Jacob & Mary M. Helbert).*

Helbert, Jacob A.; 04 May 1862; 25y 1m 28d; Pneumonia: Russell County; s/o Sally Helbert; b. Washington County, Va; a Farmer; consort of Margaret M. Helbert; reported by wife. [p18:Ln44]

Helbert, Thomas J.; 21 Dec 1860; 6d; Croup; Russell County; s/o Jacob Helbert; b. Russell County; reported by father. [p12;Ln7]

Helton, Pleasant; 06 Sep 1853; 9m; Quinsey; Russell County; s/o John & Martha Helton; b. Russell County; reported by father. [p3;Ln38]

Hendricks, (female); 07 May 1857; 5d; cause not given; Russell County; d/o Frances & G.W. Hendricks; b. Russell County; reported by father, George W. Hendricks. [p9;Ln26]

Hendricks, Aaron; 04 Nov 1860; 15y 3m; Drowned; Elk Garden; s/o Aaron L. Hendricks; b. Elk Garden; reported by father. [p13;Ln25]

Hendricks, Andy F.; 12 Oct 1861; 49y 7m 12d; Dropsy; Elk Garden; s/o Aaron Hendricks; b. Elk Garden; a Farmer; consort of Malissa O. Hendricks; reported by wife. [p15;Ln15]

Hendricks, Elizabeth; 01 Sep 1853; 20y; cause not given; Elk Garden; d/o Col. Robert & Elizabeth Boyd; b. Lebanon; consort of A.L. Hendricks; reported by husband, Aaron L. Hendricks. [p1;Ln6]

Hendricks, Helan; 04 Apr 1861; 30y; "Apoplexy"; Russell County; d/o John & Elizabeth Bickley; b. Russell County; a Housekeeper; consort of George Hendricks; reported by husband. [p14;Ln25]

SOME RUSSELL COUNTY RECORDS
Deaths 1853 - 1866

Hendricks, Henry; 27 Mar 1862; 6m 10d; Cause Unknown; Russell County; s/o Fullen & Melissa Hendricks; b. Russell County; reported by mother. [p16:Ln30]

Hendricks, Martha J.; 25 Dec 1858; 25d; cause not given; Russell County; d/o Thomas & M.J. Hendricks; b. Russell County; reported by father. [p10;Ln26]

Henly, James H.; 24 Oct 1859; 9y 2m 18d; Fever; Russell County; s/o Stephen & Grace Henley; b. Botetourt County; reported by father. [p11;Ln16]

Henson, Elizabeth; 15 Sep 1854; 11m; Flux; Russell County; d/o James & Mary Henson; b. Russell County; reported by father. [p5;Ln21]

Herndon, James; 13 Jul 1860; 21y 3m 25d; Flux; New Garden; s/o John & Polly Herndon; b. New Garden; reported by father. [p13;Ln18]

Herndon, Sophia; 10 Nov 1861; 91y 9m 24d; Old Age; parents not named; b. New Garden; consort of Larkin Herndon; reported by daughter, Elizabeth Sample. [p15;Ln28]

Hess, (Male); 16 Oct 1853; 1d; Cause Unknown; New Garden; s/o Isaac & Susan Hess; b. New Garden; reported by father. [p1:Ln47].

Hess, Elizabeth; 05 Apr 1862; 38y 4m 2d; Consumption; New Garden; "d/o James Hess"; b. Russell County; Married; reported by "James Hess, her husband". [p16;Ln29]

Hess, Mary J.; 04 Aug 1862; 14y; Fever; Russell County; d/o William & Polly Hess; b. Russell County; reported by father. [p16;Ln21]

Hess, Mary; 25 Dec 1855; 2y 3d; "Not known"; Russell County; d/o Mathias Hess; b. Russell County; reported by father. [p7;Ln33]

Hess, Melissa; 30 Nov 1853; 13y; Inflamation Brain; Waters Clinch River; d/o Henry & Amelia Hess; b. Waters of Clinch River; reported by father. [p2;Ln12]

Hess, Nancy; 01 Aug 1859; 24y 8m; Fever; Russell County; parents not named; reported by husband, James Hess. [p11;Ln41]

Hess, Nancy; 07 Mar 1854; 12y; cause not given; Elk Garden; d/o Lucy Hess; b. Russell County; *(multilple line ditto indicates reported by father)*. [p6;Ln30]

Hickman, Mary E.; 01 Nov 1854; 3y 3m; "Burnt"; Russell County; d/o John & Sarah Hilman; b. Russell County; reported by father, John Hilman. [p6;Ln1]

SOME RUSSELL COUNTY RECORDS
Deaths 1853 – 1866

Hicks, Martha; 01 Sep 1856; 11m; cause not given; Russell County; d/o George & Rebecca (Hicks); reported by father. [p8;Ln11]

Hicks, Rebecca J.; 05 Oct 1866; 19y; Consumption; Copper Ridge; d/o James & Maria Hicks; b. Glade Hollow; a Housekeeper; Unmarried; reported by mother. [p20;Ln26]

Hill, Daniel E.; 15 Aug 1855; 6m 8d; Hives; Russell County; s/o Samuel & Hulda Hill; b. Russell County; reported by father. [p7;Ln15]

Hill, Nancy C.; 09 Nov 1855; 2y; Fever; Russell County; d/o William & M. Hill; b. Russell County; reported by father. [p7;25]

Hilman, Mary E.; *(See Mary E. Hickman)*

Hogston, Ann; 31 Jan 1861; 30y 2m 10d; Typhoid fever; Elk Garden; parents not named; consort of Franklin Hogston; reported by husband. [p15;Ln9]

Hogston, Lewis J.; 05 Oct 1861; 33y 6m 10d; Camp fever; "Allegany in Greenbrire"; s/o Lewis & Rutha Horton; b. New Garden; a Farmer; consort of Lucinda Horton; reported by wife; "died a soldier in War" [p15;Ln10] *(possible error; See: Horton, Lewis)*

Holland, Mary; 03 May 1859; 1y 2m; Croup; Russell County; d/o Alex & Mary E. Holland; reported by father. [p11;Ln42]

Holland, Samuel; 25 Nov 1860; 6m; Croup; New Garden; s/o John & Elizabeth Holland; b. New Garden; reported by father. [p13;Ln20]

Honaker, Isaac S.; 21 Sep 1859; 2y 1m 1d; Fever & Croup; Russell County; s/o H.M. & Elizabeth Honaker; reported by father. [p11;Ln13]

Honaker, Margaret E.; 23 Aug 1861; 3y 4m 25d; Croup; Russell County; John & Lucinda Honaker; b. Russell County; reported by Jno. W. Honaker. [p14;Ln26]

Horton, (male); 25 Dec 1861; 1d; cause not given; New Garden; s/o Thomas & Vina Horton; b. New Garden; reported by father. [p15;Ln8]

Horton, (male); 02 Jun 1854; 6y; cause not given; New Garden; s/o Daniel Horten; b. Russell County; reported by father. [p6;Ln35]

Horton, Charles P.; 18 Aug 1861; 23y 4m 13d; Camp fever; "Greenbrire River"; s/o Lewis & Rutha Horton; b. New Garden; a Farmer; Unmarried; reported by father; "died as soldier in the War". [p15;Ln13]

SOME RUSSELL COUNTY RECORDS
Deaths 1853 — 1866

Horton, Henry; 01 Jan 1862; 5d; Cause Unknown; Russell County; s/o Thomas P. & Sally Horton; b. Russell County; reported by father. [p16;Ln26]

Horton, James; 18 Oct 1853; 13m; Inflamation; New Garden; s/o Lewis & Lucinda Horton; b. New Garden; reported by father. [p1;Ln19]

Horton, Lewis J.; __ ___ 1862; 35y; Fever; Staunton, Va.; s/o Lewis & Ruth Horton; b. Russell County; a Soldier; Married; reported by wife, Loucinda Horton. [p16;Ln22] *(See also: Hogston, Lewis)*

Horton, William; 10 Aug 1862; 18y; Fever; New Garden; s/o Lewis & Ruth Horton; b. Russell County; a Farmer; Married; reported by father. [p16;Ln27]

Howard, George C.; 27 Sep 1860; 11m; cause not given; New Garden; s/o Hiram & Ellen Howard; b. New Garden; reported by father. [p13;Ln19]

Howard, William H.; 31 Mar 1862; 44y; "Wounded in Action"; "Kurnstown, Va."; s/o Johnson & Nancy Howard; b. Russell County; "Soldier S. Army"; Married; reported by wife, Polly Howard. [p16;Ln25]

Howell, Reubin; 06 Aug 1855; 3m 15d; Croup; Russell County; s/o George & Elizabeth Howell; b. Russell County; reported by father. [p7;Ln23]

Hubbard, (male); 04 Apr 1854; 1y; cause not given; New Garden; s/o Randolph Hubbard; b. Russell County; reported by father. [p6:Ln40]

Hubbard, (male); 10 Dec 1861; 1d; cause not given; Elk Garden; s/o Eli & Jane Hubbard; b. Elk Garden; reported by father. [p15;Ln12]

Hubbard, Jas. C.; 08 Jan 1853; 1y 8m; Cause Unknown; Russell County; s/o Jesse & Matilda Hubbord; b. Russell County; reported by mother. [p3;Ln27]

Huchison, (male); 02 Apr 1855; 1d; cause not given; Russell County; s/o Francis & Matilda Huchison; b. Russell County; reported by father. [p7;Ln20]

Hughes, James H.; 10 Sep 1866; 8y; Flux; Reed's Valley; s/o Daniel & Sarah Hughes; b. Reeds Valley; reported by father. [p20;Ln28]

Hughes, John H.; 14 Sep 1866; 17y; Flux; Reeds Valley; s/o Daniel & Sarah Hughes; b. Reeds Valley; a Farmer; Unmarried; reported by father. [p20;Ln29]

134

Hunt, Elijah; 25 Nov 1855; 3y; Croup; Russell County; s/o Josiah & Any Hunt; b. Russell County; reported by father. [p7;Ln11] *(See also: Elijah Hurt)*

Hurt, Baiadeus; 01 Sep 1862; 4y; "Diptherea"; Russell County; s/o Charles & Phebe Hurt; b. Russell County; reported by father. [p16;Ln24] *(Note: Name listed in 1860 Russell County census as Bradious Hunt, age 1, in Hh #946 of Charles & Phebe Hunt)*

Hurt, Cyrus; 10 Aug 1862; 7y; Measles; New Garden; s/o Amoses & Polly Hurt; b. Russell County; reported by father, Moses Hurt. [p16;Ln23]

Hurt, Elijah; 28 Nov 1856; 2y 8m; cause not given; Russell County; s/o Josiah & Anna Hurt; b. Russell County; reported by father. [p8;Ln15] *(See also: Elijah Hunt)*

Hurt, John H.; 12 Mar 1861; 8m 10d; Croup; New Garden; s/o Garland & Jane Hurt; b. New Garden; reported by father.

Hurt, Moses; 31 Jul 1866; 66y; Palsy; New Garden; s/o Garland & Matilda Hurt; b. Russell County; a Farmer; consort of Polly Hurt; reported by Mekin Hurt. [p19;Ln1] *(Identified by 1860 Russell County census as Moses Hurt, 56, farmer; Mary, 41; John G., 21; Mekin S., 17; Isaiah D., 16; Sally, 14; Moses, 10; Aaron, 9; Cyntha, 7; Cyrus,5; Mary P., 2; James C., 1).*

Hurt, Robert S.; 06 Jun 1854; 6y; cause not given; Russell County; s/o Mekin Hurt; b. Russell County. [p7;Ln4]

Hurt, Sally; 10 Dec 1861; 14y 4m 10d; Consumption; New Garden; d/o Moses & Polly Hurt; b. New Garden; Unmarried; reported by father. [p15;Ln11]

Hurt, Sarah W.; 03 May 1860; 14y 8m 6d; cause not given; New Garden; d/o Burgess Hurt; b. New Garden; reported by father. [p13;Ln21]

Jackson, Elizabeth; 27 Nov 1857; 80y; Cause Unknown; Russell County; married; (no other information given). [p9;ln33]

Jackson, Levina; 04 Dec 1858; 19y; Consumption; Russell County; d/o Andrew L. & Nancy Jackson; b. Russell County; Unmarried; reported by mother. [p10;Ln5]

Jackson, Marian; 1853; 79y 1m 14d; Pneumonia; New Garden; b. Hampshire Co., VA; consort of Richard Jackson; reported by husband. [p1;Ln30]

SOME RUSSELL COUNTY RECORDS
Deaths 1853 – 1866

Jackson, Mary Jane; __ Jul 1854; age and cause not given; Elk Garden; d/o James Jackson; b. Russell County; reported by father. [p6;Ln32]

Jackson, Nancy J.; 25 Dec 1860; 2y 1m 14(?)d; cause not given; New Garden; d/o A.L. & Nancy Jackson; b. New Garden; reported by father. [p13;Ln27]

Jackson, Visa; 15 May 1855; 1d; "Not known"; Russell County; d/o Michael & Visa Jackson; b. Russell County; reported by father. [p7;Ln29]

Jackson, William C.; 16 Dec 1862; 51y 8m 5d; Pneumonia; Castlewoods, Russell County; parents not named; b. Sullivan County, Tennessee; a farmer; consort of Ibby Jackson; reported by friend, Richard L.Mead. [p18;Ln7]

Jackson, William; 05 Jun 1856; 45y; Dropsy; Russell County; parents not given; b. Russell County; consort of Catherine Jackson. [p8;Ln7]

Jenks, John P. Jr.; 01 Aug 1862; 3y 8m; "Dypthera"; Lebanon; s/o John P. & Mary S. Jenks; b. Russell County; reported by father. [p18;Ln5]

Jenks, Kate; 06 Aug 1866; 1y 6m; Flux; Lebanon; d/o John & Mary Jenks; b. Lebanon, Russell County; reported by father John P. Jenks. [p20;Ln37]

Jenks, Marietta E.; 13 Aug 1862; 7y 3m 8d; "Dypthera"; Lebanon; s/o John P. & Mary S. Jenks; b. Russell County; reported by father. [p18;Ln6]

Jentry, David; 20 May 1853; 51y 5m; Fever; Russell County; parents unknown; b. Surry County, NC; a Farmer; consort of Dorothy Jentry; reported by wife. [p3;Ln35]

Jessee, (female); __ Feb 1859; 21d; Measles; Russell County; d/o Thomas & Sarah Jessee; reported by father, Thomas J. Jessee. [p11;Ln18]

Jessee, (female); 23 Dec 1861; 1m 23d; "Cold hives"; Russell County; d/o Elihu Jessee; b. Russell County; reported by mother. [p14;Ln7]

Jessee, (male); 30 Dec 1858; 21d; Croup; Russell County; s/o Charles B. & Eliza B. Jessee; b. Russell County; reported by father. [p10;Ln27] *(Birth register lists an Unnamed male Jessee born 09 Dec 1858 in Russell County; s/o Charles B. & Eliza B. Jessee).*

SOME RUSSELL COUNTY RECORDS
Deaths 1853 - 1866

Jessee, (male); 11 Dec 1857; 1d; cause not given; Russell County; s/o Mary & William F. Jessee; b. Russell County; reported by father. [p9;Ln17]

Jessee, Archer Sr.; 04 Oct 1862; 85y; General debility; Russell County; s/o John Jessee; b. North Carolina; a Farmer; consort of Mary Jessee; reported by son, John Jessee. [p18;Ln48]

Jessee, Cynthia C.; 15 Oct 1866; 5y; "Dyptherea"; Copper Creek; d/o David & Hannah Jessee; b. Copper Creek, Russell County; reported by father. [p20;Ln32]

Jessee, J.L.; 24 Sep 1866; 6y; Flux; Reeds Valley; s/o T.J. & Sarah Jessee; b. Reeds Valley; reported by father. [p20;Ln34]

Jessee, Jane; 01 Aug 1853; 51y 9m; Flux; Russell County; d/o David & Judy Price; b. Russell County; consort of Martin Jessee; reported by husband. [p4;Ln33]

Jessee, Jefferson D.; 28 Sep 1866; 4y; "a twin"; Flux; Reeds Valley; s/o T.J. & Sarah Jessee; b. Reeds Valley; reported by father. [p20;Ln35] *(twin of William B. Jessee)*

Jessee, Joseph; 28 Aug 1853; 42y; Flux; Russell County; s/o Jno. & Mary Jessee; b. Russell County; a farmer; consort of Cyntha Jessee; reported by wife. [p4;Ln9]

Jessee, Margaret; 19 Jul 1853; 1y 8m; Flux; Russell County; d/o George L. & Eliza Jessee; b. Russell County; reported by father. [p5;Ln10]

Jessee, Mary C.; 23 Dec 1860; 1m 19d; Bold Hives; Russell County; d/o Elihue K. Jessee; b. Russell County; reported by a friend (unnamed). [p12;Ln9]

Jessee, Mary; 06 Dec 1866; 46y; Apoplexy; Castlewoods; parents and birthplace unknown; a Housekeeper; consort of Abednigo Jessee; reported by husband. [p20;Ln33]

Jessee, Phillip; 26 Dec 1858; 116y; Old Age; Russell County; Married; reported by Andrew L. Jackson (relationship not given). [p10;Ln4]

Jessee, Stanford S.; 10 Jan 1862; 27y 3m 9d; "Shot in fight"; Middle Creek, KY; s/o Jefferson & Nancy Jessee; b. Russell County; a Soldier; consort of Sarah Jessee; reported by wife. [p18;Ln49]

Jessee, Velary Elizabeth; 19 Dec 1862; 11m 21d; Croup; Russell County; d/o David & Hannah Jessee; b. Russell County; reported by father. [p18;Ln4]

SOME RUSSELL COUNTY RECORDS
Deaths 1853 – 1866

Jessee, William B.; 19 Sep 1866; 4y; "a twin"; Flux; Reeds Valley; s/o T.J. & Sarah Jessee; b. Reeds Valley; reported by father. [p20;Ln36] *(twin of Jefferson D. Jessee)*

Johnson, (male); 24 Aug 1862; 10d; Cause Unknown; Russell County; s/o Jacob & Nancy Johnson; b. Russell County; reported by father. [p18;Ln1]

Johnson, Clark; 10 Dec 1854; 28d; Croup; Russell County; s/o John & Mary Johnson; b. Russell County; reported by father. [p5;Ln18]

Johnson, Emily; 11 Aug 1854; 7y 4m; Flux; Russell County; d/o Lemuel & Sarah Johnson; b. Russell County; reported by father. [p5:Ln17]

Johnson, George W.; 10 Jun 1862; 5y; Dropsy; Russell County; s/o Lemuel A. & Sarah Johnson; b. Russell County; reported by father. [p18;Ln3]

Johnson, Highlay J.; 27 Dec 1853; 1m 7d; Hives; Russell County; d/o William & Sarah Johnson; b. Russell County; reported by father. [p3;Ln18]

Johnson, Joseph; 10 Jul 1862; 68y; "Fell dead"; Russell County; s/o William & Mary Johnson; b. North Carolina; a Farmer; consort of Mary Johnson; reported by son, Joseph Johnson. [p18;Ln2]

Johnson, Mary E.; 08 May 1855; 1y; "Eresipolas" (Erysipelas); Russell County; d/o Hugh Johnson; b. Russell County; reported by father. [p8:Ln2]

Johnson, Mary; 20 Jul 1859; 1y 9m 12d; "Dierieah"; Russell County; d/o William S. Johnson; reported by father. [p11;Ln17]

Johnson, Sampson W.; 02 Nov 1853; 7y 2m 22d; Paralysis; Russell County; s/o Robert & Margaret E. Johnson; b. Russell County; reported by father. [p2;Ln18]

Johnson, Sarah; 15 Aug 1855; 1m 18d; W. Cough; Russell County; d/o Lemuel & Cornely Johnson; b. Russell County; reported by father. [p7;Ln2]

Jones, Elizabeth; 04 Dec 1854; 39y 7m 23d; Cause Unknown; Russell County; d/o Joel & Mary Ramsy; b. Russell County; consort of James V. Jones; reported by husband. [p5;Ln5]

Jones, Nancy A.; ___ Jun 1858; 1m 11d; cause not given; Russell County; d/o Green B. & Parthena Jones; b. Russell County; reported by father. [p10;Ln29]

SOME RUSSELL COUNTY RECORDS
Deaths 1853 - 1866

Jones, Polly Ann; 01 Apr 1854; 1y 6m; cause not given; Russell County; d/o Soloman Jones; b. Russell County. [p7;Ln2]

Jordan, Whitley; 14 Feb 1853; 2y 8m; Flux; Russell County; s/o Christopher & Margaret Jordan; b. Russell County; reported by father. [p2;Ln13]

Judd, Isaiah; 20 Aug 1860; 13y; Flux; New Garden; s/o I.S. & Nancy Judd; b. New Garden; reported by father. [p13;Ln26]

Kates/Katez, Elizabeth; __ Apr 1860; 17y; "Inflamation of Brain"; Russell County; d/o Robert Kates; b. Russell County; a housekeeper; reported by father. [p12;Ln8]

Kates, Martha; __ Jun 1861; 2y 8m; Inflamation of Brain; Russell County; d/o Robert B. Kates; b. Russell County; reported by father. [p14;Ln3]

Keath, Caroline; __ Oct 1862; 7y; Castlewoods, Russell County; d/o Jessee & Vina Keeth; b. Russell County; reported by father. [p18;Ln9]

Keath, Jesse; __ Jul 1861; 7y; Flux; Russell County; s/o Hugh L. & Phebe Keath; b. Russell County; reported by father. [p14;Ln19]

Keath, Mary; __ Aug 1861; 1y; Flux; Russell County; d/o Hugh L. & Phebe Keath; b. Russell County; reported by father. [p14;Ln20]

Keel, Minervy; 08 Dec 1855; 1y 8m; cause not given; Russell County; d/o Kelly & M. Keel; b. Russell County; reported by father. [p7:Ln24]

Keen, Manervy Jane; 12 Aug 1854; 8m; cause not given; Elk Garden; d/o Patten G. Keen; b. Russell County; reported by father. [p6;Ln32]

Keen, Robert P.; 20 Aug 1862; 7m; Croup; New Garden; s/o Patton G. & Polly Keen; b. Russell County; reported by father. [p16;Ln33]

Keeth, John; 02 Jan 1855; 6y 9m; Fever; Russell County; s/o Jesse & Vina Keeth; b. Russell County; reported by father. [p7;Ln13]

Keeth, Rachel; 17 Jan 1855; 3y 3m; Fever; Russell County; d/o Phebe & Hugh Keeth; b. Russell County; reported by father. [p7;Ln18]

Keeth, Sala; 01 Jan 1855; 4y; Fever; Russell County; d/o Jesse & Vina Keeth; b. Russell County; reported by father. [p7;Ln14]

SOME RUSSELL COUNTY RECORDS
Deaths 1853 - 1866

Keeth, Susan; 22 Jan 1855; 4y 11m 10d; Fever; Russell County; d/o Phebe & Hugh Keeth; b. Russell County; reported by father. [p7;Ln17]

Kelly, Hopkins; __ Jul 1858; 2m 10d; cause not given; Russell County; s/o Joseph & _____ Kelly; b. Russell County; reported by father. [p10;Ln30] *(Note: Hopkins Kelly was born 07 Feb 1858 in Russell County, a twin of Floyd P. Kelly).*

Kelly, Mary C.; 25 Jul 1860; 18m 10d; Flux; New Garden; d/o Peter & Polly Kelly; b. New Garden; reported by father. [p13;Ln28]

Kelly, William; __ ___ 1862; 22y; Fever; Southern Army; s/o William & Rebecca Kelly; b. Russell County; a Farmer; Married; reported by wife, "Rebec"(? Rebee). [p16;Ln32]

Kesnor, Isaac; 02 Aug 1853; 8y 7m 4d; Inflamation of Brain; Copper Ridge; s/o William _____; b. Washington County; reported by father, William Kesnor. [p1:Ln38]

King, Rashal; 17 Jun 1855; 82; "Fits"; Russell County; parents not given; b. Russell County; unmarried; reported by son, David Ring. [p7;Ln9]

Kiser, (male); 15 Mar 1860; 15d; Cause Unknown; Russell County; s/o Abednigo Kiser; reported by a friend (unnamed). [p12;Ln33]

Kiser, Elbert S.; __ Apr 1860; 4y 10m; Whooping Cough; Russell County; s/o Noah Kiser; b. Russell County; reported by father. [p12;Ln6]

Kiser, Elizabeth; 30 Jan 1854; 22y; Fever; Russell County; d/o Epham & Mary Kiser; b. Russell County; unmarried; reported by father. [p5;Ln2] *(Note: Listed as a male).*

Kiser, Emry; 05 Mar 1853; 9y; Pneumonia; Russell County; s/o Mayfield & Mary Kiser; b. Russell County; reported by father. [p4;Ln30]

Kiser, Ephraim; 24 Sep 1862; 35y; Fever; Castlewoods, Russell County; s/o Ephraim & Mary Kiser; b. Russell County; "In the Army"; Unmarried; reported by friend, Richard L. Mead. [p18;Ln8]

Kiser, Frances; 14 Aug 1853; 4y 6m 8d; Flux; Russell County; d/o Elihue & Jane Kiser; b. Russell County; reported by mother. [p4;Ln2]

Kiser, Malinda; 16 Mar 1853; 11y; Pneumonia; Russell County; d/o Mayfield & Mary Kiser; b. Russell County; reported by father. [p4;Ln26]

Kiser, Mary; 22 Mar 1859; 54y; Dropsy; Russell County; parents not named; b. Botetourt County; consort of Ephraim Kiser; reported by husband. [p11;Ln19]

Kiser, Mary; 24 Jul 1853; 1y 11m; Flux; Russell County; d/o James & Susan Kiser; b. Russell County; reported by father. [p4;Ln27]

Laforce, Dicy; 02 Jun 1862; 48y; "From childbirth"; Castlewoods, Russell County; d/o Joseph & Mary Kiser; b. Castlewoods, Russell County; a Housekeeper; consort of James Laforce; reported by husband. [p18;Ln13]

Lambert, Nathaniel; 12 Jun 1857; 5m 14d; cause not given; Russell County; s/o Matilda & W. Lambert; b. Russell County; reported by father, William Lambert. [p9;Ln12]

Lark, Betty F.; 10 Nov 1862; 3y 6m 2d; Fever; Lebanon; d/o Micael & Sarah Lark; b. Lebanon; reported by father. [p18;Ln16]

Lawson, James; 01 Jul 1860; 10m 6d; Flux; New Garden; s/o William & Catherine Lawson; b. New Garden; reported by father. [p13;Ln29]

Lee, George W.L.; 31 Aug 1857; 15d; cause not given; Russell County; s/o Eliza & A.M. Lee; b. Russell County; s/o A.M. Lee. [p9;Ln21]. *(Birth register lists a George W.L. Lee, born 17 Aug 1857 in Russell County; s/o Alexander & Eliza Lee.)*

Lee, James M.; 26 Dec 1862; 31y; "Stabed"; Castlewoods, Russell County; s/o James & Cloe Lee; b. Castlewoods, Russell County; a Farmer; consort of Mary E. Lee; reported by friend, Joseph Hackney. [p18;Ln15]

Lee, Mary; ___ Mar 1862; 2y; Fever; Castlewoods, Russell County; d/o David F. & Mary Lee; reported by father. [p18;Ln14]

Leece, Martha; 24 Oct 1866; 35y; Consumption; Castlewoods; d/o George & Elizabeth Gose; b. Castlewoods, Russell County; a Housekeeper; consort of William N. Leece; reported by mother. [p20;Ln25]

Leece, Samuel; 01 Jun 1862; 62y 1m 13d; Fever; Glade Hollow; s/o Jacob & Nancy Leece; b. Lexington, Va.; "a good farmer"; consort of Jane Leece, dec'd.; reported by son, William N. Leece. [p18;Ln10]

Leece, Samuel W.; 20 Apr 1862; 1y 2m 9d; Fever; Glade Hollow; s/o James A. & Ann C. Leece; b. Glade Hollow, Russell County; reported by father. [p18;Ln11]

Lesgo(?Sesco), (male); 15 Jun 1853; 1d; Cause Unknown; Scott County, Va; s/o James & Margaret Lesgo; b. Scott County; reported by father, James W. Lesgo. [p2;Ln16]

Lewis, Ira; 06 Feb 1853; 2d; Croup; Russell County; s/o Jno. & Norissa Lewis; b. Russell County; reported by father, John Lewis. [p2;Ln17] *(Note: Birth register states: Ira Lewis, b. 05 Feb 1853, Russell County; s/o John & Narsessy Lewis)*

Light, Lucinda; __ Dec 1862; 10m; Consumption; near Hansonville, Russell County; d/o Lazaras & Elizabeth A. Light; b. Russell County; reported by father. [p18;Ln21]

Light, Lydia Margaret; __ Jun 1862; 2y; Inflamation of Brain; near Hansonville, Russell County; d/o Lazaras & Elizabeth A. Light; b. Russell County; reported by father. [p18;Ln22]

Litton, Soloman; 15 Aug 1862; 80y; Old Age; Russell County; parents unknown; a Farmer; Married; reported by Vincent Browning. [p16;Ln37]

Litton, William S.; 02 Apr 1855; 3m; Cause Unknown; Elk Garden; s/o John W. Litton; b. Russell County. [p8;Ln7]

Logan, (infant); 10 Oct 1860; Stillborn; Russell County; child of Eusavius H. Logan; b. Russell County; reported by father. [p12;Ln13] *(Birth register lists a Stillborn male Logan, born 10 Oct 1860 in Russell County; s/o Eusevius & Mary Logan)*

Long, Virginia E.; 25 Aug 1862; 2y 7m; Fever; Castlewoods, Russell County; d/o Joseph & Margaret Long; b. Castlewoods, Russell County; reported by father. [p18;Ln12]

Love, Virginia; 25 Jun 1857; 15y 11m 22d; Fever; Russell County; d/o Mary H. & Oscar Love; b. Russell County; reported by father. [p9;Ln15]

Low, Dormela; 17 May 1853; 25y; pluracy; Hortons Valley; d/o John & Sarah McGraw; b. Elk Garden; consort of John B. Low; reported by husband. [p1;Ln12].

Luster/Lusten, John; 15 Nov 1854; 2y; cause not given; New Garden; s/o William Luster (or Lusten); b. Russell County; reported by father. [p6;Ln38] *(Note: Birth Register lists a John Luster, born 29 Mar 1854 in Russell County; s/o William & Sarah Luster.*

Lynch, James; 27 Aug 1858; 4m 5d; Cause Unknown; Russell County; s/o Richard H. & S.K. Lynch; reported by father. [p10;Ln7] *(Birth register lists a James Lynch, born 22 Apr 1858 in Russell County; s/o Richard & Sarah Lynch).*

SOME RUSSELL COUNTY RECORDS
Deaths 1853 — 1866

Lynch, Martha; 15 Jul 1862; 32y 3m 16d; Fever; Lebanon, Va.; d/o George & wife Cowan; b. Russell County; a "Merchant"; reported by husband, Thomas Lynch. [p16;Ln36]

Lynch, Mary C.; 18 Jun 1862; 1y 11m 19d; "Diptherea"; Lebanon, Va.; d/o Thomas & Sarah Lynch; b. Russell County; reported by father. [p16;Ln34]

Lynch, Sarah L.; 10 Jun 1862; 4y 11m 4d; "Diptherea"; Lebanon, Va.; d/o Thomas & Sarah Lynch; b. Russell County; reported by father. [p16:Ln35]

Malicote, Jas. Augustine; 09 Jul 1862; 1y 11m 10d; Inflamation of bowels; Washington County, Va.; s/o J.N. & Susan Malicote; b. Washington Co.; reported by father, Jasper N. Malicote. [p19;Ln49]

Martin, (female); 15 Nov 1857; "Dead born"; Russell County; d/o John & Elizabeth Martin. [p9;Ln35]

May, John M.; _____ 1862; 23y; Wounded in action; Southern Army; s/o Jacob & Eliza May; b. Russell County; a Soldier; Unmarried; reported by father. [p16:Ln39]

McCloud, Henry; 08 Oct 1855; 54y 8m; Fever; Corner (Settlement); s/o Daniel & Elizabeth McCloud; b. Russell County; consort of Mary McCloud. [p8;Ln16]

McClure, David; _____ 1862; 19y; Dropsy; near Staunton, Va.; s/o James & Catherine McClurey; b. Smyth Co., Va; In the Army; reported by father, James McClure. [p18;Ln20]

McClure, Elias; _____ 1862; 21y; Camp Fever; near Staunton, Va.; s/o James & Catherine McClurey; b. Smyth Co., Va; In the Army; reported by father, James McClure. [p18;Ln19]

McClure, Ezra; 17 Aug 1866; 5y; "Dyptherea"; Moccasin; s/o James & Catherine McClure; b. Moccasin, Russell County; reported by father. [p20;Ln40]

McClure, Mary Jane; 31 Aug 1866; 13y; "Dyptherea"; Moccasin; s/o James & Catherine McClure; b. Moccasin, Russell County; reported by father. [p20;Ln42]

McClure, Samuel; 19 Aug 1866; 6y; "Dyptherea"; Moccasin; s/o James & Catherine McClure; b. Moccasin, Russell County; reported by father. [p20;Ln41]

SOME RUSSELL COUNTY RECORDS
Deaths 1853 — 1866

McCoy, James; 10 Jul 1857; 72y; cause not given; Russell County; parents not given; b. Russell County; a Farmer and husband; reported by son, William McCoy. [p9;Ln3]

McCoy, Margaret; 11 Feb 1858; 5y 23d; Burn; Russell County; d/o Harvey G. & Malinda McCoy; b. Russell County; reported by father. [p10;Ln32]

McCoy, Nancy; 01 Jul 1853; 6y 9m; Flux; Russell County; d/o William W. & Eliz. McCoy; b. Russell County; reported by father. [p4;Ln40]

McCoy, Silpha; 20 Jun 1853; 7y; Flux; Russell County; d/o William W. & Eliz. McCoy; b. Russell County; reported by father. [p4;Ln39]

McFadden, Catherine; 15 Nov 1855; 32y; Cause Unknown; Corner (Settlement); parents not named; b. Russell County; consort of David McFadden. [p8;Ln12] *(Note: 2 children, Visa & Robert, reported Ln 13 & 14]*

McFadden, Margaret; 09 Nov 1866; 7y; "Bealing in the head"; Moccasin; d/o Thomas & Polly McFadden; b. Moccasin, Russell County; reported by father. [p20;Ln38]

McFadden, Robert; 15 Oct 1855; 8d; Cause Unknown; Corner (Settlement); s/o David McFadden; b. Russell County. [p8:Ln14] *(mother, Catherine, appears on Ln12; sister, Visa, Ln 13).*

McFadden, Visa E.; 08 Oct 1855; 2y 4m; Cause Unknown; Corner (Settlement); d/o David McFadden; b. Russell County. [p8;Ln13] *(death of mother, Catherine McFadden, appears Ln12; brother, Robert, Ln 14).*

McFall, David; 15 Apr 1854; 3m 37d; "Pain in the head"; Russell County; s/o James & Sarah McFall; b. Russell County; reported by father. [p6;Ln19]

McFall, Thomas; 17 Apr 1854; 15y 6m 15d; "Pain in the head"; Russell County; s/o James & Sarah McFall; b. Russell County; reported by father. [p6;Ln20]

McGee, Martha; 26 Feb 1854; 75y; cause not given; New garden; d/o Jeremiah Compton; *(register multilple line ditto indicates born in Russell County & reported by father (questionable).* [p6;Ln34] *(Possibly the person identified by 1850 Russell County census as Martha Mcgee, age 53, b. Patrick County, Va.; living in household #1640 of Jeremiah & Martha J. Compton).*

SOME RUSSELL COUNTY RECORDS
Deaths 1853 – 1866

McGlothlin, (child); 20 Dec 1858; age not given; Cause Unknown; child of Harvey & S. McGlothlin; b. Russell County; reported by father. [p10;Ln9] *(Birth register lists a Stillborn male McGlothlin, b. 12 Dec 1858 in Russell County; s/o Harvey & Nancy McGlothlin).*

McNew, Elizabeth; __ Mar 1860; 11m; Whooping cough; Russell County; d/o Alexander E. McNew; b. Russell County; reported by Alexander E. McNew. [p12;Ln21]

McReynolds, George W.; 23 Jan 1862; 22y; Wounded; Middle Creek, KY; s/o Isaac & Susan McReynolds; b. Russell County; In the Army; Unmarried; reported by father. [p18;Ln22]

McReynolds, Mary; 28 Aug 1854; 50y; Flux; Russell County; d/o Austin & Nancy Bush; b. Russell County; reported by husband, Joseph McReynolds. [p5;Ln12]

McReynolds, Polly; __ Jan 1859; 22y; Cancer; Russell County; d/o Joseph & Polly McReynolds; b. Russell County; Unmarried; reported by father. [p11;Ln20]

McReynolds, Rebecca; 11 Sep 1853; 87y 6m; Old Age; Russell County; d/o Jos. & Susannah Boring; b. Russell County; a midwife; consort of J.S. McReynolds; reported by husband, Joseph McReynolds. [p4;Ln34]

Mead, (male); __ Oct 1860; 5d; Cause Unknown; Russell County; s/o Samuel H. Mead. [p12;Ln26]

Mead, Mary J.; 22 Nov 1861; 28y 6m 11d; Typhoid Fever; Elk Garden; d/o Henson Mead; b. Elk Garden; reported by father. [p15;Ln21]

Mead, Mary; 12 Dec 1861; 14y 8m 16d; Fever; Russell County; d/o Thomas & Matilda Mead; b. Russell County; a Housekeeper; Unmarried; reported by father. [p14;Ln13]

Mead; Levina M.; 25 Sep 1860; 16y 4m 22d; "Dipthera"; Russell County; d/o Thomas Mead; Unmarried; reported by Thomas Mead. [p12;Ln27]

Meade, (female); 22 May 1859; 2d; Cause Unknown; Russell County; d/o Pressly C. & Mary A. Meade; reported by father. [p11;Ln22]

Mercer, (female); 15 Jul 1856; 5d; Hives; Russell County; d/o Daniel Mercer & Emaline; b. Russell County; unmarried; reported by Rebecca Gray. [p8;Ln3]

SOME RUSSELL COUNTY RECORDS
Deaths 1853 – 1866

Mercer, Ginsey; 14 Oct 1860; 45y; Gravel; Russell County; parents unknown; a Housekeeper; consort of Daniel Mercer; reported by a Friend(unnamed). [p12;Ln22]

Milgrim, (female); __ Aug 1860; Stillborn; Russell County; d/o John Milgrim. [p12;Ln24] *(Birth register lists a Stillborn female Milgrom, born __ Aug 1860 in Russell County; d/o Daniel & Nancy Milgram).*

Miller, John E.; 04 Jul 1866; 4y; "Dyptherea"; Moccasin; s/o Jacob & Martha J. Miller; b. Moccasin, Russell County; reported by father. [p20;Ln39]

Minnick, Margaret; __ Sep 1859; 3y; Croup; Russell County; d/o Jacob & Sarah Minnick; reported by father. [p11;Ln21]

Minton, Jane; 19 Jul 1858; 3y 9m 14d; Flux; Russell County; d/o Elizabeth Minton; b. Russell County; reported by grandfather, Richard Minton. [p10;Ln31]

Mitchell, Alexander; 30 Aug 1853; 21y 5m 3d; Flux; Russell County; s/o Elisha & Hennrey E.M. Mitchell; b. Russell County; Doctor; reported by father. [p4;Ln28] *(Identified by 1850 Russell County census as Alexander E. Mitchell, age 18, living in Hh #440 of Elisha & Henrietta Mitchel).*

Mitchell, Daniel A.; 21 Dec 1862; 3m; Croup; Russell County; s/o Charles & Maria Mitchell; b. Russell County; reported by father. [p16:Ln38]

Mitchell, Henrietta M.; 12 Sep 1853; 47y; Flux; Russell County; d/o John & Rachel Lewis; b. Greensboro, NC; reported by husband, Elisha Mitchell [p4;Ln29] *(Ln28 was son, Alexander Mitchell).*

Monk, William S.; 02 Apr 1860; 17y; Typhoid fever; Russell County; s/o James B. Monk; a Farmer; reported by father. [p12;Ln34]

Monroe, (male); 03 Aug 1853; 1d; Cause Unknown; Hawkins County, TN; s/o Mordeca & Milly Monroe; b. Hawkins County, TN; reported by father. [p2;Ln32]

Moore, Willmirth; 04 Mar 1853; 26y 11m; Consumption; Russell County; d/o John & Elizabeth Teter; b. Tennessee; consort of William Moore; reported by husband [p3;Ln25] *(Ln24 was father, John Teter; also reported by William Moore).*

Mullins, (female); 15 May 1853; 14d; Hives; Russell County; d/o Andrew & Polly Mullins; b. Russell County; reported by father, Andrew J. Mullins. [p3;Ln34] *(Birth register lists an Unnamed male Mullins, b. 01 May 1853; s/o Andrew J. & Polly Mullins).*

SOME RUSSELL COUNTY RECORDS
Deaths 1853 – 1866

Mullins, Rebecca; 14 Jul 1853; 27y; Cold; Russell County; d/o David & Susan Maggard; b. Harlan County, KY; consort of Wilson Mullins; reported by husband. [p3;Ln33]

Mullins, Wylson; 04 Jan 1855; 2m 20d; cause not given; Russell County; s/o Isham & Mary Mullins; b. Russell County; reported by father. [p7;Ln22]

Musick, (female); 11 Nov 1856; 6m; Cause Unknown; Russell County; d/o Lexious & Polly Musick; b. Russell County. [p8;Ln6]

Musick, Cummings; 10 Dec 1858; 21d; Cause Unknown; Russell County; s/o William & Isabella Musick; b. Russell County; reported by father. [p10;Ln8].

Musick, Floyd; 26 Jul 1861; 5y 1m 10d; Flux; Weavers Creek; s/o Jack & Vina Musick; b. Weavers Creek; reported by father. [p15;Ln17]

Musick, Nancy; 07 Aug 1861; 1y 9m 10d; Flux; Weavers Creek; d/o Alva & Chaney Musick; b. Weavers Creek; reported by father. [p15;Ln19]

Musick, Nancy; 17 Nov 1861; 8y 10m; Flux; Weavers Creek; d/o Elexious & Polly Musick; b. Weavers Creek; reported by father. [p15;Ln16]

Musick, Samuel; 16 Sep 1861; 9y 6m 15d; Flux; Weavers Creek; s/o Alva & Chaney Musick; b. Weavers Creek; reported by father. [p15;Ln20]

Musick, Visa; 16 Aug 1861; 11m 10d; Flux; Weavers Creek; d/o Jack & Vina Musick; b. Weavers Creek; reported by father. [p15;Ln18]

Mutter, Charles; 23 Dec 1857; 9m; Fever; Russell County; s/o Roden & Loucena Mutter; b. Russell County. [p9;Ln36]

Mutter, Eliza; 16 Mar 1855; 3m 10d; cause not given; Russell County; d/o Harvey Mutter; b. Russell County; reported by father. [p4:Ln30]

Mutter, Hugh F.; 07 Sep 1861; 20y 8m 10d; Camp fever; "Greenbrire River"; s/o Thomas & Margaret Mutter; b. Elk Garden; Unmarried; reported by father. [p15;Ln22]

Nash, James P.; 08 Apr 1859; 17y 2m; Fits; Russell County; s/o Aaron & Catherine Nash; Unmarried; reported by father, Aaron H. Nash. [p11;Ln23]

SOME RUSSELL COUNTY RECORDS
Deaths 1853 — 1866

Nash, Rolson; 15 May 1866; 8y; Cause Unknown; Castlewoods; s/o Aaron & Catherine Nash; b. Russell County; reported by father. [p20;Ln43]

Necessary, Christopher A.; 25 Sep 1855; 5y 5m; Flux; Russell County; s/o Thomas & E. Necessary; b. Russell County; reported by father. [p7;Ln12]

Neumon, Mary; 17 Jul 1853; 2y 4m; Flux; Russell County; d/o James & Mary Neumon; b. Russell County; reported by father. [p5;Ln2]

Olde, Williams; 15 Aug 1854; 4y 1m; Flux; Russell County; s/o James & Mary Odle; b. Russell County; reported by father. [p6;Ln12] *(listed as Williams Jodle, s/o James & Mary Odle).*

Osborn, Nancy B.; 25 Aug 1854; 1y 6m 25d; Croup; Russell County; d/o William & Anny Osborn; b. Scott County; reported by father. [p5;Ln4]

Osborn, Solomon; 05 Jun 1857; 65y 9m; cause not given; Russell County; parents not given; a Farmer; reported by wife, Cloe Osborn. [p9;Ln23]

Osborn, Stephen; __ May 1860; 10m 9d; Whooping cough; Russell County; s/o David Osborn; b. Russell County; reported by father. [p12;Ln14]

Osborne, (male); 27 Sep 1861; 5d; "Cold hives"; Russell County; s/o David Osborne; b. Russell County; reported by father. [p14;Ln6]

Osborne, John C.; 27 Jul 1853; 5y 6m; Flux; Russell County; s/o Samuel & Unity Osborn; b. Russell County; reported by mother. [p5;Ln 8]

Owen, Elbert H.D.; 22 Jul 1866; 16y 2m 20d; "Dyptherea"; Moccasin; s/o Jacob & Hannah Owen; b. Moccasin, Russell County; a Farmer; Unmarried; reported by brother, Joseph Owen. [p20;Ln44]

Owens, Elisha M.; 26 Dec 1853; 1m 8d; Croup; Russell County; s/o Rufus & Nancy Owens; b. Russell County; reported by father. [p2;Ln14] *(Birth register states: Elisha M. Owens, born 18 Nov 1853, Russell County; s/o Rufus M. & Nancy A. Owens).*

Owens, Eliza E.; __ Jun 1858; 5y; Flux; Russell County; d/o Jacob & H.F. Owens; b. Russell County; reported by father. [p10;Ln33]

Owens, James H.; 18 Jan 1862; 18y; Fever; Moccasin, Russell County; s/o John W. & Elizabeth Owens; b. Russell County; single; reported by mother [p18;Ln25] *(father, John W. Owens, Ln23].*

SOME RUSSELL COUNTY RECORDS
Deaths 1853 — 1866

Owens, John W.; 19 Nov 1862; 47y; Fever; Moccasin, Russell County; s/o John & Nancy Owens; b. Russell County; a Farmer; consort of Elizabeth Owens; reported by consort. [p18;Ln23] *(Identified by 1860 Russell County census household #1142 as John W. Owens, 46; farmer; born Tennessee; Elizabeth, 46; Samuel B., 19; Nancy A., 17; James, 15; Susan, 14; Sarah E., 9; Thomas W., 7; Hannah M., 4; Susannah McFarlane, 66. (Death register p18 lists: son, Joseph C., Ln24; son, James H., Ln25; daughter, Susan J., Ln 26)*

Owens, Jos. C.; 23 Nov 1862; 22y; Fever; Moccasin, Russell County; s/o John W. & Elizabeth Owens; b. Russell County; a Farmer; consort of Darthula Owens; reported by mother. [p18;Ln24] *(Identified by 1860 Russell County census household #1143 as Joseph C. Owens, 21, farmer; born VA; Darthula H., 18; born VA. Census indicates they "married within the census year". They were living next door to his parents, John W. & Elizabeth Owens)*

Owens, Susan J.; 19 Jan 1862; 14y; Fever; Mocassin, Russell County; d/o John W. & Elizabeth Owens; b. Russell County; Single; reported by mother [p18;Ln26] *(father, John W. Owens, Ln24)*

Painter, John M.; 13 Jan 1853; 4m 4d; Cause Unknown; Russell County; s/o Jas. & Sarah A. Painter; b. Russell County; reported by father, James Painter. [p3;Ln1]

Parks, Aaron C.; 05 Oct 1862; 11m 24d; Croup; Elk Garden; s/o Hezekiah & <u>wife</u> Parks; b. Russell County; "reported by father, Hezekiah Parks" [p16;Ln45] *(Hezekiah Parks, died 06 Sep 1862; (See listing) which indicates a possible error, as stated).*

Parks, Hezekiah; 06 Sep 1862; 53y 6m 2d; Consumption: Russell County; parents unknown; a Farmer; Married; reported by "Wm. Parks, his wife"*(sic)* [p16;Ln 44] *(1860 Russell County census Hh #282: Hezekiah Parks, 50; Rodah, 50; Amandah, 28; Elizabeth, 27; William, 23; Aaron, 22; Lucinda, 18; Lutitia, 17; Ludema, 12; Matilda, 4; Vanburen Parks, 4; William Parks, 1).*

Parks, Louisa; 20 Aug 1862; 21y 11m 22d; Consumption; Russell County; d/o William & <u>wife</u> Parks; b. Russell County; reported by Wm. Parks. [p16:Ln43]

Patrick, Ambrose; __ Dec 1862; 17y; Fever; Reeds Valley; s/o Isham & Lydia Patrick; b. Washington County, Va.; a Farmer; Single; reported by father. [p18;Ln29]

Patrick, Mary; 06 Feb 1857; 2y 6m 20d; cause not given; Russell County; d/o Lydda & John Patrick; b. Russell County; reported by father. [p9;Ln9]

SOME RUSSELL COUNTY RECORDS
Deaths 1853 – 1866

Payne, John G.; 28 Aug 1862; 21y; "Action in Battle"; "Manassas, Va."; s/o "Mary (widow) Payne"; a Soldier; Unmarried; reported by mother. [p16:Ln40]

Perry, Eliza; 23 Jun 1854; 32y 11m; Fever; Russell County; d/o James & Sary Perry; b. North Carolina; reported by father. [p5;Ln6]

Perry, Polly; 19 Jan 1853; 8y; Cause Unknown; Russell County; d/o Nathan & Mary Perry; b. Russell County; reported by father. [p3;Ln29]

Perry, Senah; 25 May 1853; 43y; Cause Unknown; Russell County; parents unknown; b. North Carolina; consort of James Perry; reported by husband. [p3;Ln32]

Phelps, Samuel; 30 Aug 1854; 11m 25d; Flux; Russell County; s/o Samuel & Rialy Felps; reported by father, Samuel Phelps. [p5;Ln24] *(listed as Samuel Felps)*.

Phipps, (male); 14 Jan 1854; 17m 2d; Hives; Russell County; s/o Alexander & Elizabeth Phipps; b. Russell County; reported by father. [p6;Ln17]

Pinion, (male); 06 Aug 1853; 4d; Cause Unknown; New Garden; s/o William & Amelia Pinion; b. New Garden; reported by father. [p1;Ln45] *(Birth register lists; Unnamed male Pinon, born 02 Apr 1853, Russell County; s/o William & Milly Pinion)*.

Pippin, Margaret J.; 04 Jul 1858; 12y 4m 22d; Flux; Russell County; d/o Zachariah & Nancy Pippin; b. Russell County; reported by father. [p10;Ln34]

Pool, (female); 22 Jan 1857; 20d; cause not given; Russell County; d/o J. & H. Pool; b. Russell County; reported by father Hardy Pool. [p9;Ln8]

Pool, Jemima; 15 Oct 1858; age not given; "Diebetes"; Russell County; d/o Piety Pool; consort of of Hardy Pool; reported by husband. [p10;Ln35]

Porter, Eliza J.; 10 Oct 1862; 28y 3m 18d; Measles; Copper Creek, Russell County; d/o Moses & Jemima Dorton; b. Russell County; consort of John R. Porter; reported by "Friend", Moses Dorton. [p18;Ln27]

Porter, Elizabeth; 16 Oct 1854; 6y 9m; Fever; Russell County; d/o George & Rosy Porter; b. Russell County; reported by father, George A. Porter. [p5;Ln13]

SOME RUSSELL COUNTY RECORDS
Deaths 1853 – 1866

Porter, George; __ Sep 1862; 3y; Debility; Copper Creek, Russell County; s/o John R. & Eliza J. Porter; b. Russell County; reported by "Friend:, Moses Dorton. [p18;Ln28]

Porter, Henry; 04 Nov 1856; 14y; cause not given; Russell County; s/o Francis & Elizabeth Porter; b. Russell County; reported by father. [p8;Ln9]

Porter, Mary L.; 17 Feb 1861; 7y; "Dipthera"; Russell County; d/o Thomas M. Porter; b. Russell County; reported by father. [p14;ln5]

Porter, Mary C.; 03 Apr 1859; 23y; "Chronic"; Russell County; d/o Charles & Mary C. Kilgore; b. Scott County; consort of William D. Porter; reported by husband. [p11;Ln24]

Porter, Mary; 05 Dec 1866; 32y 8m 8d; Consumption; Copper Creek; d/o Moses & Jemima Dorton; b. Russell County; a Housekeeper; consort of L.G.W. Carty; reported by husband. [p20;Ln11]

Porter, Oscar; 27 Apr 1857; 1m 15d; cause not given; Russell County; s/o Mary C. & William Porter; b. Russell County; reported by father. [p9;Ln20] *(Birth register lists Oscar Porter, born 03 Mar 1857 in Russell County; s/o William D. & Mary C. Porter).*

Powers, Lucy; 15 Jan 1853; 4y 3m; Bold Hives; Russell County; d/o Reubin & Catherine Powers; b. Russell County; reported by father. [p4;Ln20]

Powers, Martha J.; 10 Sep 1859; 23y; Breast complaint; Russell County; parents not named; consort of John M. Powers; reported by friend, William N. Leece(?). [p11;Ln45]

Powers, Sarah C.; __ ___ 1858; age not given; Dropsy; Russell County; d/o James & Sarah E. Powers; reported by father. [p10;Ln36]

Powers, Sarah E.; __ ___ 1858; age not given; "Consummption"; Russell County; parents not given; consort of Jas. Powers; reported by husband. [p10;Ln38]

Price, Aaron; 28 Dec 1862; 7m; Croup; Russell County; s/o James & Sally Price; b. Russell County; reported by father, John M. Price. [p16:Ln42]

Price, Andy; 10 Jun 1859; 15y 4m; Flux; Russell County; s/o Mark & Ellen Price; reported by father. [p11;Ln46].

SOME RUSSELL COUNTY RECORDS
Deaths 1853 - 1866

Price, Daniel; 17 May 1854; 90y 10m 5d; Dropsy; Russell County; parents not listed; b. South Carolina; a Farmer & Husband; reported by son, Oliver Price. [p5;Ln8]

Price, Hannah; 19 Aug 1862; 36y 5m; Fever; Elk Garden; parents unknown; b. Russell County; reported by brother, John M. Price. [p16;Ln41]

Price, John; 02 Dec 1866; "66m"(sic); Flux; Cedar Creek; s/o Thomas & Mary Price; b. Elk Garden; consort of Rebecca Price; reported by wife, Rebecca Price [p20;Ln45] *(age of 66m misstated for 66 years. 1860 Russell County census household #116 lists: John Price, 58; Rebecca, 42; Thomas J., 15; William W.L., 13; Sarah E.J., 9; John R.S., 5; Henry B.F., 3).*

Price, Phoebe H.; 02 Jul 1853; 32y 7m 2d; Consumption; Russell County; d/o Jas. & Rachel Lee; consort of Oliver H. Price; reported by husband. [p2;Ln24]

Prophet, David; 09 Oct 1866; 15y; "Shot by accident"; New Garden; s/o Edward Prophet & wife; b. Russell County; reported by Edward Prophet. [p19:Ln14]

Pruner, George; __ Oct 1862; 2y 6m; "Dupthera"; Lebanon; s/o George & Catherine Pruner; b. Lebanon, Va.; reported by father. [p19;Ln48]

Pruner, James; 01 Apr 1855; 15y; cause unknown; Lebanon; s/o George A. Pruner; b. Russell County; reported by father. [p8;Ln3]

Pucket, (female); 02 Apr 1854; 4d; cause not given; Russell County; d/o David Puckett; b. Russell County. [p7;Ln1]

Pucket, Major; 26 Feb 1854; 17y; cause not given; s/o Daniel Puckett; b. Russell County; reported by father. [p6;Ln36] *(name written as Majar Pucket. Identified by 1850 Russell County census as Major Puckett, age 14; living in Hh #1602 of Daniel & Mahala Puckett).*

Pucket, Sally; 10 Oct 1862; 6m 2d; "Diptherea"; Russell County; d/o Jeremiah & Margaret Puckit; b. Russell County; reported by father. [p16;Ln46]

Puckett, Charles; 25 Jul 1866; 1m 6d; "Dyptherea"; Copper Ridge; s/o D. & S. Puckett; b. Copper Ridge, Russell County; reported by neighbor, Elijah Hicks [p20;Ln46] *(an Elias Hicks lived in 1860 census household #340 with #342 being household of Daniel & Sydney J. Puckett).*

Puckett, Martha; 14 Sep 1861; 8y 1m 12d; Flux; Copper Ridge; d/o Jeremiah & Margaret Puckett; b. Copper Ridge; reported by father. [p15;Ln23]

Purcell, Mary J.; __ Jan 1860; 12m; Croup; Russell County; d/o James Purcell; reported by father. [p12;Ln23]

Ramey, Isaac; 07 Aug 1855; 18y; cause not given; Russell County; s/o John & Emley Ramey; b. Russell County; reported by father. [p7:Ln28]

Ramsey, Charles L.; 01 Oct 1866; 10y; Flux; Lick Creek, Russell County; s/o Joel & Margaret Ramsey; b. Lick Creek; reported by father. [p21;Ln56]

Ramsey, Silvester; 07 Oct 1866; 9y; Flux; Lick Creek, Russell County; s/o Joel & Margaret Ramsey; b. Lick Creek; reported by father. [p21;Ln57]

Rasnake, George; 22 Oct 1866; 1y 6m; Cause Unknown; Castlewoods; s/o James & Rebecca Rasnake; b. Castle's woods, Russell County; reported by father. [p21;Ln53]

Rasnake, Margaret; 10 Aug 1862; 30y 6m 1d; Consumption; Russell County; d/o Jacob & Judia Rasnake; b. Russell County; Married; reported by husband, Fayette Rasnake. [p16;Ln50] *(Ln49 was son, William Rasnake).*

Rasnake, William; 11 Jun 1862; 3y 1m 2d; "Diptherea"; Russell County; s/o Fayette & Margaret Rasnake; b. Russell County; reported by father. [p16;Ln49] *(mother's death reported Ln50).*

Redwine, Crockett; 15 Jun 1855; 16y; cause unknown; New Garden; s/o Soloman Redwine; b. Russell County. [p8;Ln5]

Redwine, Priscilla; 10 Feb 1862; 45y; Fever; Russell County; d/o "Aldersons"; b. Washington (Co.) Va.; Married; reported by husband, Roling R. Redwine. [p16;Ln52]

Reynolds, Bernard; 31 May 1862; 21y; General debility; Stanton, Va.; s/o Bernard & Lucy Reynolds; b. Russell County; In the Army; Single; reported by mother. [p18;Ln30]

Reynolds, Elizabeth; 28 Dec 1855; 21y 5m 21d; cause not given; parents not given; b. Russell County; consort of Phillip J. Reynolds; reported by Aunt, Rachel Reynolds. [p7;Ln10]

Reynolds, Ira; 08 Jul 1858; 4m 22d; Croup; Russell County; s/o B. & C. Reynolds; b. Russell County; reported by father, Bernard Reynolds. [p10;Ln12]

SOME RUSSELL COUNTY RECORDS
Deaths 1853 — 1866

Reynolds, Johnson; 14 Jul 1861; 22y 6m 26d; Consumption; s/o Ira Reynolds; b. Elk Garden; Unmarried; reported by father, [p15;Ln24]

Reynolds, Joseph B.; 27 Nov 1853; 23y 5m 4d; Consumption; New Garden; s/o Abram & Nancy Reynolds; b. Wythe County, VA; a farmer; unmarried; reported by father. [p1;Ln43]

Reynolds, Milley; 31 Mar 1859; 44y; "Chronic": Russell County; d/o James & Sarah Chaffin; b. Russell County; consort of William Reynolds; reported by son, Noah Reynolds. [p11;Ln25]

Reynolds, Sarah; __ ___ 1860; 81y; "Phithisic & cold"; Russell County; d/o ___ Pippin; a Housekeeper; consort of Henry Reynolds, Dec'd.; reported by Stephen Gose. [p12;Ln15]

Richardson, Anna M.; 24 Dec 1861; 2y 6d; Croup; Swords Creek; d/o Christopher & Maria Richardson; b. Swords Creek; reported by father. [p15;Ln25]

Richardson, George F.; 19 Mar 1862; 4y 2m 5d; "Diptherea"; Russell County; s/o Thomas J. & Jane Richardson; b. Russell County; reported by father. [p16;Ln48] *(Ln47 was brother, James B. Richardson)*

Richardson, Henry; 21 Nov 1860; 4y 8d; Flux; New Garden; s/o Samuel & Mary Richardson; b. New Garden; reported by father. [p13;Ln37]

Richardson, James B.; 13 Feb 1862; 7y 6m 1d; "Diptherea"; Russell County; s/o Thomas J. & Jane Richardson; b. Russell County; reported by father. [p16;Ln47] *(Ln48 was brother, George F. Richardson)*

Richardson, Margaret J.; 30 Jul 1856; 6m; cause not given; Russell County; d/o William & Margaret Richardson; b. Russell County; reported by father. [p8;Ln13]

Richardson, Mary A.; 01 Sep 1853; 4y; Flux; New Garden; d/o Christopher & Amanda Richardson; b. New Garden; reported by father. [p1;Ln42]

Rickman, Henry; 01 Dec 1862; 3m 10d; "Diptherea"; Russell County; s/o Thomas & <u>wife</u> Rickman; b. Russell County; reported by father. [p16;Ln51] *(register error indicates married and reported by <u>her</u> husband, Thomas R. Rickman).*

Riley, (female); 09 Mar 1857; 1m; Croup; Russell County; d/o Thomas & Mary Riley; b. Russell County. [p9;Ln38]

SOME RUSSELL COUNTY RECORDS
Deaths 1853 — 1866

Riley, Celia; 15 Jun 1853; 33y 2m 2d; Consumption; New Garden; d/o Jno. & Eliza Johnson; b. New Garden; consort of Thomas J. Riley; reported by husband. [p1:Ln40]

Riley, Susan; 10 Oct 1853; 80y; Pneumonia; New Garden; (no other information). [p1;Ln41].

Ritchie, Mary; 18 Sep 1854; 12y 11m; Fever; Russell County; d/o John & Casy Ritchie; reported by father. [p6;Ln2]

Roberts, (male); 17 Nov 1854; 3m; Croup; Russell County; s/o Garlin & Ester Roberts; reported by father. [p5;Ln34]

Robertson, Charles; 16 Sep 1854; 8y 13d; Flux; Russell County; s/o Berry & Cyntha Roberson; reported by father. [p5;Ln26]

Robertson, Rebecca; 05 Sep 1854; Flux; Russell County; d/o Berry & Cyntha Robertson; reported by father. [p5;Ln28]

Robertson, Sarah; 25 Sep 1854; 6y; Flux; Russell County; d/o Berry & Cyntha Roberson; reported by father. [p5;Ln27]

Robins, George; *(See George Robinson; d. 17 Apr 1856)*.

Robins, Henderson; 08 Jul 1860; 25y 1m 25d; Flux; New Garden; s/o Elizabeth Robins; b. New Garden; a Farmer; consort of Sara J. Robins; reported by "his wife". [p13;Ln35]

Robins, Lorenzo D.; 17 Dec 1854; 20y; cause not given; New Garden; s/o Celia Robins; *(multilple line ditto indicates reported by father)*. [p6;Ln39]

Robins, Robert E.; 10 Jul 1860; 1y 9m; Flux; New Garden; s/o Sarah J. Robins; b. New Garden; reported by "Morther". [p13;Ln34]

Robins, Silas; 15 Sep 1854; New Garden; 7y; Cause Unknown; s/o William Robins; b. Russell County; reported by father. [p6;Ln26]

Robins, William B.; 09 Jun(?) 1860; 14y 6m 21d; Flux; New Garden; s/o Elizabeth Robins; b. New Garden; reported by mother. [p13;Ln39]

Robinson, Cynthia F.; 28 Oct 1860; 20y; Consumption; New Garden; d/o Celia Robinson; b. New Garden; Single; reported by "her mother". [p13;Ln36]

Robinson, Emory; 20 Apr 1855; 2y; cause unknown; Elk Garden; s/o John W. Robinson; b. Russell County. [p8;Ln4]

SOME RUSSELL COUNTY RECORDS
Deaths 1853 – 1866

Robinson, George W.; 12 Dec 1853; 5y 9m 22d; Flux; New Garden; s/o Jas. & Celia Robinson; b. New Garden; reported by Uncle, Elijah Ferrell. [p1;Ln46].

Robinson, George; 17 Apr 1856; 6y; Fever; Russell County; s/o William & Celia Robinson; b. Russell County; reported by Jackson Mutter [p8:Ln1] *(listed as George Robins, s/o William & Celia Robin<u>son</u>)*

Robinson, Hannah; 04 Jun 1853; 4m; "Colery Morbus"; Russell County; d/o Mathew & Nancy Robinson; b. Russell County; reported by father. [p4;Ln19]

Roman, Elizabeth; 07 Sep 1861; 11y 9m 21d; Flux; New Garden; d/o James Roman; b. New Garden; reported by father. [p15;Ln26]

Roman, Lorenzo D.; 15 Sep 1858; 3y; Flux; Russell County; s/o Richard & Tempa Roman; b. Russell County; reported by father. [p10;Ln11]

Roman, William F.; 29 Jul 1860; 2y 20d; Flux; New Garden; s/o Richard & Tempy Roman; b. New Garden; reported by father. [p13;Ln38]

Routh, Catherine; 03 Jun 1862; 43y; Fever; Lebanon, Russell County; d/o Peter & Amy Kitts; b. Granger County, Tennessee; a Housekeeper; consort of Asa Routh; reported by husband. [p19;Ln2]

Routh, Eliza Kate; 03 Sep 1862; 1y 10d; Measles; Lebanon, Russell County; d/o Asa & Catherine Routh; b. Lebanon, Russell County; reported by husband*(sic; father)*. [p19;Ln3]

Russell, Hiram C.F.; 12 Feb 1853; 4y 1m 1d; Pneumonia; Russell County; s/o William & Ann Russell; b. Washington County; reported by father. [p2;Ln34]

Salyers, Mahala; 27 Jul 1854; 5y; Flux; Russell County; d/o Jesse & Nancy Salyers; b. Russell County; reported by father. [p5;Ln19]

Salyers, Samuel; 10 Aug 1854; 13y 2m 13d; Fever; Russell County; s/o James & Elizabeth Salyers; b. Russell County; reported by father. [p6;Ln10]

Sample, (male); 24 Jul 1865; 1m; cause not given; s/o William Sample; b. Russell County. [p19;Ln5] *(Identified by Birth register as Unnamed Male Sample, born 24 Jul 1865, Russell County; s/o William & Rody Samples)*

SOME RUSSELL COUNTY RECORDS
Deaths 1853 — 1866

Samples, James; 23 Aug 1853; 53y 9m; Flux; New Garden; s/o William & Nancy Samples; b. New Garden; a farmer; consort of Elizabeth Samples; reported by wife. [p1;Ln20]

Samples, Mary E.; 16 Feb 1862; 4y 1m; Croup; Russell County; d/o William & Roda Samples; b. Russell County; reported by father. [p17;Ln62]

Samples, Nancy; 12 Nov 1859; 80y; Fever; Russell County; parents not given; consort of James Samples; reported by friend, Moses Ball. [p12;Ln1]

Sanders, Jane; 15 Nov 1853; 70y; Cause Unknown; Russell County; parents unknown; birthplace unknown; consort of John Sanders; reported by husband. [p3;Ln6]

Sanders, William; 26 Dec 1853; 30y; Measles; Russell County; s/o John & Jane Sanders; b. Russell County; a Farmer; reported by father, John Sanders. [p3;Ln6]

Senter, Martha; 21 Aug 1854; 2y 19d; Fever; Russell County; d/o Stephen & Sarah Senter; b. Russell County; reported by father. [p6;Ln18]

Senter, Mary E.; 25 Oct 1853; 5y 8m 12d; Scarlet Fever; Russell County; d/o Stephen H. & Sarah Senter; reported by father. [p3;Ln5]

Senter, Wiley W.; 27 Sep 1853; 3y 7m 16d; Scarlet Fever; Russell County; s/o Stephen H. & Sarah Senter; b. Russell County; reported by father. [p3;Ln4]

Sergent, Hugh; 26 Dec 1858; age not given; Fever; Russell County; s/o Isaac & Mary Sargent; b. Russell County; Unmarried; reported by father. [p10;Ln10]

Sexton, (female); 16 Feb 1861; 7y; Cause Unknown; Russell County; d/o Harvey Sexton; b. Russell County; reported by father. [p14;Ln4]

Sexton, (male); __ Feb 1860; Stillborn; Russell County; s/o Harvey Sexton; b. Russell County; reported by father. [p12;Ln11] *(Birth register lists a Stillborn male Sexton, b. __Feb 1860 in Russell County; s/o Harvey & Catherine Sexton).*

Sexton, Ellsbury; 05(?) Apr 1866; 20y; "Cold & exposure"; "In hospital in Richmond"; s/o William & Elander Sexton; b. "Ken."; a Farmer; Unmarried; reported by father, William A. Sexton. [p21;Ln50]

SOME RUSSELL COUNTY RECORDS
Deaths 1853 — 1866

Sexton, Martha; 04 Oct 1866; 18y; "Decay of lungs"; Castle's Woods, Russell County; d/o William & Elander Sexton; b. "Ken."; a Spinster; Unmarried; reported by father, William A. Sexton. [p21;Ln49]

Sexton, Millard F.; 25 Oct 1856; 3d; cause not given; Russell County; s/o Henry & Catherine Sexton; b. Russell County; reported by father. [p8;Ln17]

Shell, (male); 05 Jul 1853; 1d; Cause Unknown; Russell County; s/o Aaron & Rhody Shell; b. Russell County; reported by father. [p2;Ln37]

Shell, James H.; 09 Aug 1862; 23y 10m 5d; "Killed"; Bull Run; s/o Aaron & Roda Ann Shell; b. Russell County; Soldier; Single; reported by father. [p19;Ln34]

Shell, Sarah; 17 Apr; 1854; 70y; Fever; Russell County; d/o Aaron(?) & Catherine Shell; b. Russell County; "a wife"; reported by son, Aaron Shell. [p6;Ln5]

Shoemaker, George W.; 03 Sep 1855; 19y; Consumption; Russell County; s/o James Shoemaker; b. Russell County; reported by father. [p7;Ln31]

Shoemaker, Mary J.; 17 Aug 1861; 1y 1d; Flux; New Garden; d/o Benjamine Shoemaker; b. New Garden; reported by father. [p15;Ln29]

Shoemaker, Sarah E.; 07 Jul 1862; 17y; Fever; near Hansonville, Russell County; d/o Reynolds & Rachel Shoemaker; b. Russell County; a Housekeeper; Single; reported by father. [p18;Ln32]

Short, William; 20 May 1854; 16y 2m; Flux; Russell County; s/o William & Lear Short; reported by Uncle, Daniel Short. [p5;Ln33]

Shumaker, Lenana; 12 Oct 1866; 10y(?); Gravel; Russell County; reported by Francis Shumaker. [p19;Ln7]

Simerly, (male); 22 Jul 1859; 1m 15d; Cause Unknown; Russell County; s/o James & Tabitha Simerly; reported by father. [p11;Ln30]

Simerly, Mary E.; 04 Jan 1859; 3y 11m; Croup; Russell County; d/o James & Tabitha Simerly; reported by father. [p11;Ln29]

Skeen, Jane; 25 Mar 1862; 11y 8d; "Casuality"; Castlewoods, Russell County; d/o Ephraim & Alzira Skeen; b. Russell County; reported by mother. [p18;Ln31]

SOME RUSSELL COUNTY RECORDS
Deaths 1853 - 1866

Smith, Fanney; 24 Mar 1859; 66y; Fever; Russell County; reported by daughter, Nancy Dye. [p12;Ln2]

Smith, George; 02 Sep 1862; 72y 6m; "Wars"; Russell County; s/o Ake Smith; b. Russell County; Married; reported by son, John W. Smith. [p16;Ln54]

Smith, Henry A.; 29 Jun 1860; 10m; Flux; New Garden; s/o Matison & Martha Steele; b. New Garden; reported by father. [p13;Ln47]

Smith, John H.; 21 Nov 1853; 12y; Measles; Russell County; s/o John & Nancy Smith; b. Russell County; reported by friend, William Bickley. [p4;Ln14]

Smith, John T.; 28 Feb 1862; 56y; Cause Unknown; Russell County; s/o Harry & Mary M. Smith; b. Russell County; a "Phycician"; Married; reported by wife, Mary D. Smith. [p16;Ln56]

Smith, Jos. L.; 16 Feb 1859; 18y 2m; "Thrown from horse"; Russell County; s/o John & Rebecca Smith; Unmarried; reported by father. [p11;Ln26]

Smith, Joseph H.; __ Feb 1860; 19y 3m 8d; "by a fall"; Russell County; s/o John Smith; b. Russell County; a Farmer; reported by father. [p12;Ln5]

Smith, Mary M.; 13 Dec 1862; 82y; Old Age; Russell County; parents unknown; reported by Charles A. Smith. [p17;Ln60]

Smith, Matilda; __ Dec 1858; 5m; cause not given; Russell County; d/o William & Matilda Smith; reported by father. [p10;Ln37]

Smith, Nancy J.; 04 Mar 1860; 20y; Child bed: New Garden; d/o John M. Combs; b. New Garden; consort of William H. Smith; reported by husband. [13;Ln43]

Smith, Pendleton; __ Sep 1861; 12y; Flux; Russell County; s/o William & Matilda Smith; b. Russell County; reported by father. [p14;Ln18]

Snapp, Catherine; 04 Nov 1860; 31y; Consumption; Russell County; d/o Rev. David Jessee; a Housekeeper; consort of Elkanah R.D. Snapp; reported by William D. Snapp. [p12;Ln35]

Snapp, Lucy; 22 May 1853; 46y; Parlysis(?); 46y; Russell County; d/o Daniel & Judith Price; b. Russell County; consort of John Snapp; reported by brother, Oliver H. Price. [p2;Ln25]

SOME RUSSELL COUNTY RECORDS
Deaths 1853 – 1866

Snapp, Samuel L.; 28 Feb 1859; 2y 1m; Cause Unknown; Russell County; s/o E.D. & Catherine Snapp; reported by father, Elkanah D. Snapp. [p11;Ln27]

Snead, Louisa; 08 Jun 1857; 1m 6d; Croup; Russell County; d/o Jane Snead; b. Russell County. [p9;Ln37]

Southerland, Polly; 01 Mar 1853; 4y; Pneumonia; Sandy; d/o Henry & Margaret Southerland; b. Sandy; reported by father. [p2;Ln6]

Spurgeon, Catherine; 23 Feb 1853; 59y; Inflamation; Russell County; d/o Christopher & Eliza Lark; b. Pennsylvania; consort of Samuel Spurgeon; reported by son-in-law, Ader Fields. [p2;Ln41]

Stamper, Frankline; 15 Sep 1866; 6y; Flux; Castlewoods; s/o James & Mary Stamper; b. Castle's Woods; reported by father. [p21;Ln48]

Stanley, Henly; 23 Oct 1853; 2y 7m; Scarlet Fever; Russell County; s/o William & Anna Stanley; reported by father. [p3;Ln9]

Stanley, John; 13 Oct 1853; 1y 1m; Cause Unknown; Russell County; s/o William & Anna Stanley; b. Russell County; reported by father. [p3;Ln8]

Stapleton, (female); __ Jul 1859; 4d; Cause Unknown; Russell County; d/o William & Esther (Stapleton); reported by father. [p11;Ln28]

Stapleton, (female); __ Jan 1861; 1d; Cause Unknown; Russell County; d/o George Stapleton; b. Russell County; reported by a friend (unnamed). [p14;Ln8]

Statzer, John M.; 05 May 1866; 19y; "shot by soldiers"; Moccasin; s/o Andrew & Nancy Statzer; b. "Car's Creek", Russell County; a Farmer; Unmarried; reported by father. [p20;Ln47]

Steele, (infant); 05 Mar 1861; 1d; Cause Unknown; Russell County; child of Thomas P. Steele; b. Russell County; reported by father. [p14;Ln11]

Steele, Malissa E.; 08 Dec 1860; 1y 8m; Flux; New Garden; d/o Sparrel & Elizabeth Steele; b. New Garden; reported by father. [p13;Ln46]

Stephens, Elizabeth; 01 Feb 1860; 2y; Flux; New Garden; d/o Owen Stephens; b. New Garden; reported by father. [p14;Ln3]

Stiltner, Richard; 10 Jun 1855; 8y 10d; "Not known"; Russell County; s/o James Stiltner; b. Russell County; reported by father. [p7;Ln32]

Stinson, Aaron; 28 Feb 1862; 26y 10m 1d; Fever; "Army (of) Va."; s/o "Rachel Stinson (widow)"; b. Russell County; Unmarried; reported by Rachel Stinson "her wife"(sic). [p16;Ln55]

Stinson, Edward D.; 10 Aug 1861; 2y 2m 5d; Flux; Copper Ridge; s/o John & Nancy Stinson; b. Copper Ridge; reported by father. [p15;Ln27]

Stinson, Henry P.; 07 Oct 1860; 17y 1m 10d; Disease of Heart; Elk Garden; s/o James & Adah Stinson; b. Elk Garden; reported by father. [p13;Ln41]

Stinson, Henry; 30 May 1860; 10y 8m 6d; Drowned; New Garden; s/o Rachel Stinson; b. New Garden; reported by "his mother". [p13;Ln40]

Straugh/Strangh, Mary; 12 May 1855; 1y 5m; Cause Unknown; New Garden; b. Russell County; d/o Michiel Straugh (or Strangh). [p8;Ln10]

Strow, Mary; 10 Apr 1860; 3y; Flux; New Garden; d/o Michael Strow; b. New Garden; reported by father. [p13;Ln44]

Stump, (female twin); 11 Apr 1860; 1d; Flux; New Garden; d/o Joseph & Peggy Stump; b. New Garden; reported by father. [p14;Ln1]

Stump, (female twin); 10 Sep 1860; 5m; cause not given; New Garden; d/o Joseph & Peggy Stump; b. New Garden; reported by father. [p14;L2]

Stump, Shade; 01 Oct 1853; 20 days; Croup; New Garden; s/o Joseph & Margaret Stump; b. New Garden; reported by father. [p1;Ln5] *(Double entry also listed with same information [p1;Ln37]*

Suit, (female); __ Nov 1861; 21d; Cause Unknown; d/o Daniel & Rebecca Suit; b. Russell County; reported by father. [p14;Ln22]

Suit, (infant); 03 Oct 1857; 1m; cause not given; Russell County; child of Nancy & Johnson Suit; b. Russell County; reported by father [p9;Ln10] *(Birth register lists an Unnamed female Suit, born 05 Sep 1857 in Russell County d/o Johnson & Nancy Suit)*

Suit, John; 30 Aug 1854; 2y 5m; Flux; Russell County; s/o Pleasant & Mary Suit; reported by father. [p5;Ln30]

Suit, Ranson; 02 Nov 1855; 6y; Cause Unknown; Elk Garden; s/o Pleasant Suit; b. Russell County. [p8;Ln8]

SOME RUSSELL COUNTY RECORDS
Deaths 1853 - 1866

Sutherlan, Mary J.; __ Jul 1861; 9y; Flux; Russell County; d/o Alexander & Mary Sutherlan; b. Russell County; reported by father. [p14;Ln17]

Sutherland, Phoebe; __ Apr 1860; 3y; Fever; Russell County; d/o Jesse Sutherland; b. Russell County; reported by a friend (unnamed). [p12;Ln3]

Sutton, John B.; 07 Feb 1856; 3y 1m 6d; cause not given; Russell County; no other information given. [p8;Ln16]

Sykes, Emeline F.; 15 Jul 1860; 8y 1m; Flux; New Garden; d/o Celia Sykes; b. New Garden; reported by mother. [p13;Ln42]

Sykes, James; 10 Feb 1855; 72y 4m; Dropsy; New Garden; s/o John Sykes; b. "Old Virginia"; a Farmer; consort of Mary Sykes. [p8;Ln9]

Tate, Elisha; 19 Jun 1858; 57y 2m 5d; Consumption; Russell County; parents unknown; place of birth unknown; a Farmer; consort of Eliza Tate; reported by Eliza Tate. [p10;Ln39]

Taylor, (female); 05 Dec 1853; 3m; Croup; Elk Garden; d/o Michael & Mary Taylor; b. Elk Garden; reported by father. [p1;Ln11].

Taylor, James A.; 25 Oct 1862; 19y; Cause Unknown; Southern Army; s/o Isaac & Catherine Taylor; b. Russell County; a Soldier; Unmarried; reported by father. [p17:Ln63]

Taylor, James C.; 12 Oct 1866; 11y; Flux; Elk Garden; s/o Emby & Nancy Taylor; b. Russell County; reported by Emby Taylor. [p19;Ln6] *(See also: Nancy Taylor)*

Taylor, Margaret; 11 Nov 1853; 21y 5m; Flux; Russell County; d/o Charity Williams; b. Russell County; reported by grandfather, James Williams. [p3;Ln10]

Taylor, Nancy; 05 Nov 1866; 37y; Flux; Elk Garden; d/o James & Clersy Kindrick; b. Russell County; reported by Emby Taylor (relationship not stated). [p19;Ln2] *(The 1860 Russell County census household #619 lists: Emby Taylor, 36; Nancy P., 36; Elihu V., 14; Parris, 12; Robert W., 11; Samuel W., 9; Julia Ann E., 8; Rachel J., 5; James C., 4; Clarisa V., 2; unnamed male, 4/12).*

Taylor, Paris; 20 Nov 1866; 17y; Flux; Elk Garden; s/o Emby & Nancy Taylor; b. Russell County; reported by Emby Taylor. [p19;Ln3] *(See: Nancy Taylor)*

Taylor, Robert; 05 Oct 1866; 15y; Flux; Elk Garden; s/o Emby & Nancy
Taylor; b. Russell County; reported by Emby Taylor. [p19;Ln4]
(See: Nancy Taylor)

Taylor, Samuel; 09 May 1854; 3m 1d; Croup; Russell County; s/o
Charles & Nancy Taylor; b. Russell County; reported by father.
[p6;Ln8] *(See Nancy Taylor).*

Taylor, Wade; 16 Oct 1866; 13y; Flux; Elk Garden; s/o Emby & Nancy
Taylor; b. Russell County; reported by Emby Taylor. [p19;Ln5]
*(Identified by 1860 Russell County census as Samuel W. Taylor,
age 9). (See: Nancy Taylor)*

Taylor, William; 20 Jun 1860; 75y 1d; Typhoid Fever; Clinch
Mountain; parents not named; b. Clinch Mountain; consort of
Polly Taylor; reported by wife. [p14;Ln7]

Teters, John; 11 Apr 1853; 85y; Cold; Russell County; s/o John
Teter; b. Pensylvania; Occupation, "Founder"; reported by son-
in-law,William Moore [p3;Ln24] *(See also: Willmirth Moore)*

Thomas, Rosannah; 27 Dec 1853; 3y 2m; Cause Unknown; Sandy; d/o Eli
C. & Ellen Thomas; b. Sandy; reported by father. [p2;Ln7]

Thompson, (female); __ ___ 1853; 3y 10m 4d; measles; New Garden; d/o
Patton & Mary Thompson; b. New Garden; reported by father.
[p1;Ln3] *(1850 Russell County census lists a Matilda C.
Thompson, age 10/12, in Hh# 205 of Patton & Mary Thompson.
Matilda Thompson does not appear in the 1860 household.
Possibly died 29 Mar 1853 and listed [p1;Ln35] in error as s/o
Patton & Mary Thompson.)*

Thompson, (infant); 01 Jul 1861; 1d; cause not given; New Garden;
child of Patten & Mary Thompson; b. New Garden; reported by
father. [p15;Ln34]

Thompson, (Male); 29 Mar 1853; 3y 10m 4d; Measles; New Garden; s/o
Patton & Mary Thompson; b. New Garden; reported by father.
[p1;Ln35] *(a possible error and a double listing for unnamed
daughter (Matilda C.) of Patton & Mary Thompson from [p1;Ln35].
Age indicates a twin but a male is not present in the 1850
household #205 of Patton & Mary Thompson).*

Thompson, Alfred; 09 Sep 1861; 30y 2m 25d; Flux; Elk Garden; s/o
Thomas Thompson; consort of Jane Thompson; reported by father.
[p15;Ln31]

Thompson, Hawkins; 10 Aug 1861; 21y 29d; Camp fever; "Monterey,
Va."; s/o Emory & Phoebe Thompson; b. New Garden; Unmarried;
reported by his father; "Died as a soldier in War". [p15;Ln30]

SOME RUSSELL COUNTY RECORDS
Deaths 1853 — 1866

Thompson, Joannah; 13 Mar 1862; 40y; Consumption; Russell County; d/o Abram & Jemimah Owens; b. Russell County; Married; reported by husband, Jacob Thompson. [p17;Ln63]

Thompson, John; 08 Aug 1853; 6m 11d; Flux; Russell County; s/o George & Elizabeth Thompson; b. Russell County; reported by father, George W. Thompson. [p3;Ln16]

Thompson, Mary; 15 Aug 1861; 37y 5m 10d; Consumption; New Garden; d/o Isaac & Lusa Fuller; consort of Patten Thompson; reported by husband. [p15;Ln32] *(Ln33 was daughter, Nancy J. Thompson; Ln 34 an infant, age 1 day).*

Thompson, Nancy J.; 10 Jul 1861; 3y 6m 12d; Flux; New Garden; d/o Patten & Mary Thompson; b. New Garden; reported by father. [p15:Ln33] *(Ln32 was mother, Mary Thompson}*

Tignor, Rebecca J.; 16 Jul 1860; 8y 5m 7d; Flux; Corner (Settlement); d/o Patrick & Nancy Tignor; b. Corner (Settlement); reported byfather. [p14;Ln5]

Todd, Lucy; 05 Jun 1860; 76y; Flux; Corner (Settlement); parents unnamed; b. Corner (Settlement); a Widow; reported by son, Joseph Todd. [p14;Ln4]

Turner, Mary; 13 Dec 1862; 72y; Fever; Castlewoods, Russell County; parents unknown; b. Russell County; consort of James Turner; reported by friend, R.L. Mead. [p19;Ln37]

Turner, Nancy; 25 Dec 1862; 7y; Fever; Castlewoods, Russell County; d/o Hugh & Elizabeth Turner; b. Russell County; reported by friend, R.L. Mead. [p19;Ln38]

Turner, Nancy; 13 Aug 1853; 7y 4m; Flux; Russell County; d/o Charles & Eliz. Turner; b. Russell County; reported by father. [p4;Ln25]

Vance, (male); 05 Feb 1854; "Deadborn"; Russell County; s/o David & Elizabeth Vance; reported by mother. [p6;Ln21]

Vanover, Martha J.; 29 Dec 1853; 1y 1m 2d; Scarlet Fever; Russell County; d/o Jno. & Keziah Vanover; b. Russell County; reported by father, John Vanover. [p4;Ln23]

Vermillion, (male); 04 Aug 1862; 14d; Croup; Russell County; s/o Elihu & Eliza Vermillion; b. Russell County; reported by father. [p17;Ln65]

SOME RUSSELL COUNTY RECORDS
Deaths 1853 — 1866

Vermillion, Jessee; 09 Feb 1862; 75y; Dropsy; Copper Creek, Russell County; s/o Wilson & Nancy Vermillion; b. North Carolina; a Farmer; consort of Nancy Vermillion; reported by daughter, Rebecca Jessee. [p19;Ln35]

Vermillion, Mary; 18 May 1866; 38y; "Child bed"; Elk Garden; d/o John Browning & wife; b. Russell County; Married; reported by J.J. Bays. [p19:Ln12]

Vermillion, Nancy; 05 May 1862; 71y; Fever; Copper Creek, Russell County; d/o Fleming & Rebecca Burk; b. Russell County; a Housekeeper; consort of Jessee Vermillion; reported by daughter, Rebecca Jessee. [p19;Ln36]

Vermillion, Rachel; 23 Feb 1865; *(age stated as)* 00; cause not given; Elk Garden; d/o Lihugh & Rebecca Vermillion; b. Russell County. [p19;Ln1] *(Birth register lists a Rachel Vermillion, born 15 Sep 1865, New Garden, Russell County; d/o Lihugh & Mary Vermillion. Notation in birth register states, "died").*

Vermillion, Rachel; 11 Aug 1866; 1y; Flux; Elk Garden; d/o Elihu Vermillion & wife; b. Russell County; reported by J.J. Bays. [p19;Ln13]

Vicars, James; 16 Dec 1855; 67y; Dropsy; Russell County; parents not given; b. Russell County; reported by son, Samuel Vicars. [p7;Ln3]

Vicars, Mary S.; 03 Dec 1855; 5y 10m 21d; Fever; Russell County; d/o Robert & Phebe Vicars; b. Russell County; reported by father. [p7;Ln4]

Vicars, Mary; 10 Aug 1854; 3y 8m 4d; Flux; Russell County; d/o William & Susan Vicars; b. Russell County; reported by father. [p5;Ln16]

Vicars, Paul; 18 Aug 1855; 28y; Fever; Russell County; s/o Lidda & Robert Vicars; b. Russell County; consort of Susanah Vicars; reported by wife. [p7;Ln1]

Vincell, Catherine; 11 Nov 1866; 30y; Flux; Elk Garden; d/o John & Nancy Vincell; b. Russell County; Single; reported by John Vincell. [p19;Ln10]

Vincell, Sallie; 27 Oct 1866; 35y; Flux; Elk Garden; d/o John & Nancy Vincell; b. Russell County; Single; reported by John Vincell. [p19;Ln9]

SOME RUSSELL COUNTY RECORDS
Deaths 1853 - 1866

(Vincil), William Barten; 10 Apr 1854; 1y; cause not given; New Garden; s/o William Vincil; reported by father. [p6;Ln27] *(listed as William Barten, s/o William Vincil).*

Vincil, William; 28 Oct 1854; cause not given; New Garden; s/o Laurenzo D. Vincil; b. Russell County; reported by father. [p6:Ln33]

Wallis, Christopher; 17 Aug 1853; 6y 6m 22d; Flux; New Garden; s/o James & Jane Wallis; b. New Garden; reported by father. [p1;Ln44]

Wallis, Sarah; 07 Jan 1858; 85y; Old Age; Russell County; parents not given; reported by husband, Andrew L. Jackson. [p10;Ln13]

Ward, Anna; 03 Jan 1860; 1m 2d; cause not given; New Garden; d/o William T. & Polly Ward; b. New Garden; reported by father. [p14;Ln10]

Ward, Enoch; 27 Jul 1853; 6y 11m; Flux; New Garden; s/o William & Mary Ward; b. New Garden; reported by father. [p2;Ln4]

Ward, Soloman; 27 Jul 1853; 9y 9m; Flux; New Garden; s/o William & Mary Ward; b. New Garden; reported by father. [p2;Ln3]

Ward, Thomas; 23 Dec 1859; 2y; Fever; Russell County; s/o William & Mary Ward; reported by father. [p12;Ln3]

Weddle, Albert; 20 Mar 1857; 3y; cause not given; Russell County; s/o Mary & J.C. Weddle; b. Russell County; reported by father. [p9;Ln4]

Wheeler, James H.; 17 Oct 1862; 1y 6m; "Dypthera"; Castlewoods, Russell County; s/o James C. & Malissa Wheeler; b. Russell County; reported by father. [p19;Ln46]

Wheeler, James D.; 24 Dec 1862; 2y; "Dypthera"; Castlewoods, Russell County; s/o Pleasant H. & Anny Wheeler; b. Russell County; reported by mother. [p19;Ln39]

Wheeler, Joseph L.; 12 Oct 1862; 12y; "Dypthera"; Castlewoods, Russell County; s/o James C. & Malissa Wheeler; b. Russell County; reported by father. [p19;Ln43]

Wheeler, Mary Jane; 03 Oct 1862; 9y; "Dypthera"; Castlewoods, Russell County; d/o James C. & Malissa Wheeler; b. Russell County; reported by father. [p19;Ln41]

Wheeler, Mary; 06(?) Dec 1862; 64y 4m 1d; "Palsy"; Castlewoods, Russell County; parents not named; b. Russell County; consort of James Wheeler; reported by husband. [p19;Ln40]

Wheeler, Sarah J.; 11 Oct 1862; 7y; "Dypthera"; Castlewoods, Russell County; d/o James C. & Malissa Wheeler; b. Russell County; reported by father. [p19;Ln42]

White, Darthula; 12 Jul 1860; 3m 9d; Flux; Elk Garden; d/o Robert A. & Darthula White; b. Elk Garden; reported by father. [p14;Ln8]

White, Rachel; 25 May 1862; 2y; Croup; Russell County; d/o John B. & Rachel White; b. Russell County; reported by father. [p17;Ln68]

Whited, Harvey; ___ ___ 1862; 23y; "Exastus"; Russell County; s/o R.M. & <u>wife</u> Whited; b. Russell County; a Farmer; Married; reported by father. [p17;Ln69]

Whited, John T.; 06 Jun 1860; 3y 2m; Flux; New Garden; s/o Robert M. & Ann Whited; b. New Garden; reported by father. [p14;Ln11]

Whited, Moses S.; 09 Jul 1860; 3y 5m 9d; Flux; Elk Garden; s/o Jos. W. & Elizabeth Whited; b. Elk Garden; reported by father. [p14;Ln9]

Whitt, John Senr.; 28 Dec 1853; 76y; Cause Unknown; Indian Creek; b. North Carolina; Occupation, Miller; consort of Mary Whitt; reported by son, James Whitt. [p1;Ln14].

Willey, Cowan; ___ Sep 1862; 1m; Croup; Castlewoods, Russell County; s/o Andrew & Elizabeth Willey; b. Russell County; reported by father. [p19:Ln44]

Williams, (male); 19 Apr 1853; 1d; Measles; Russell County; s/o John & Elizabeth Williams; b. Russell County; reported by father. [p2;Ln27] *(Ln26 shows mother's death from measles 10 days later).*

Williams, (female); 18 Mar 1853; "3y"; Cause Unknown; Russell County; d/o Andrew & Nancy Williams; b. Russell County; reported by Andrew Williams. [p2;Ln47] *(Birth Register lists an unnamed female Williams, (born dead), 18 Mar 1853; d/o Andrew & Nancy Williams.*

Williams, (male); 15 Aug 1853; 1y 6m; cause not given; Cedar Creek; s/o George & Charity Williams; b. Cedar Creek; reported by father, George W. Williams. [p1;Ln7].

Williams, (male); 27 Aug 1855; 3y; Cause Unknown; near Lebanon; s/o George W. Williams; b. Russell County. [p8;Ln15]

SOME RUSSELL COUNTY RECORDS
Deaths 1853 – 1866

Williams, Charles H.; 30 May 1866; 2y; Croup; Copper Creek, Russell County; s/o Joseph & Dallis Williams; b. Copper Creek; reported by father, Joseph H. Williams. [p21;Ln54]

Williams, Elizabeth; 29 Apr 1853; 26y 2m 18d; Measles; Russell County; d/o Jeremiah & Anna Fields; b. Russell County; consort of John Williams; reported by husband, John D. Williams. [p2;Ln26]

Williams, Emonet F.; 02 Jan 1866; 4y; Disease of heart; New Garden; s/o Samuel D. & Elizabeth Williams; b. Russell County; reported by Samuel Williams. [p19;Ln15]

Williams, George; _____ 1862; 22y; "of wounds in action; in Southern Army; s/o William Williams; b. Russell County; a Soldier; Unmarried; reported by father. [p17;Ln67]

Williams, Margaret A.; _____ 1860; 30y; Compsumption; Russell County; d/o Stephen Gose; consort of James Williams; reported by Stephen Gose. [p12;Ln16]

Williams, Shadrick; 27 Dec 1862; 26y; Fever; Augusta County, Va.; s/o George & Elizabeth Williams; b. Russell County; a Soldier; Unmarried; reported by father. [p19;Ln45]

Wilson, Catherine; 17 May 1853; 13y; "Cholie" (?); Russell County; d/o Samuel & Sarah Wilson; b. Russell County; reported by father. [p4;Ln22]

Wise, (Stillborn male); 30 Apr 1862; Russell County; s/o John & Margaret Wise; b. Russell County; reported by father. [p17;Ln66]

Wiser, Silvester A.; 06 Jun 1860; 1y 2m 3d; Croup; New Gaeden; s/o John & Mary Wysor; b. New Garden; reported by father. [p14;Ln12]

Wisor, Albert C.; 06 Jun 1859; 6m; Croup; Russell County; s/o John & Mary Wisor; reported by sister, Catherine Jackson. [p12;Ln4]

Wisor, Beverley; 31 Jan 1856; 6m; Cause Unknown; d/o William & Catherine Wisor; b. Russell County; reported by Sarah Snader. [p8:Ln4] *(Birth register lists; Beverley Wisor, born 31 Jan 1856, Russell County; d/o William & ____ Wisor).*

Wisor, Cordilla; 10 Apr 1861; 1y 7m 10d; Croup; New Garden; s/o John & Mary Wisor; b. New Garden; reported by mother. [p15;Ln35]

Witt, James O.; 02 Jun 1861; 9m 15d; Elk Garden; Croup; s/o John & Rosana Witt; b. Elk Garden; reported by father. [p15;Ln36]

168

SOME RUSSELL COUNTY RECORDS
Deaths 1853 — 1866

Wolf, Thomas; 06 Mar 1854; 3m 18d; Hives; Russell County; s/o John & Elizabeth Wolf; b. Russell County; reported by father. [p6;Ln7]

Wright, (male); 16 Nov 1853; age not given; Cause Unknown; Russell County; s/o Paris & Mary Wright; b. Russell County; reported by mother. [p4;Ln42]

Wright, Fanny; 01 Jul 1853; 3y; Flux; Russell County; d/o Robert & Sarah Wright; b. Russell County; reported by father. [p4:Ln43]

Wright, Margaret; 01 Jul 1853; 1y; Flux; Russell County; d/o John & Sucha Wright; b. Russell County; reported by mother. [p4;Ln41]

Wright, Viney E.; 01 Aug 1853; 1y 2m; Flux; Russell County; d/o William & Caroline Wright; b. Russell County; reported by grandfather, John Wright. [p3;Ln42]

SOME RUSSELL COUNTY RECORDS
Deaths 1853-1866
Slave & Free Black

Alexander; (Former slave ?); 11 Sep 1866; 12y; Flux; Mocassin, Russell County; s/o Lanna; b. Russell County; reported by "Former mistress", Mary E. Browning. [p20;Ln8]

Banner, Betsey; Slave; __ Sep 1862; 1y 3m; Cause Unknown; Russell County; d/o Queen; reported by Owner, Stephen Banner. [p17;Ln21]

Bickley, Ceason; Slave; 03 Nov 1853; 65y; Flux; Russell County; parents unknown; b. North Carolina; reported by Owner, John Bickley. [p4;Ln8]

Bickley, Fletcher; Slave; __ Jul 1853; 11y; Flux; Russell County; s/o Isaac & Jinna; b. Russell County; reported by Owner, Marion T. Bickley. [p4;Ln37]

Bundy, Thomas; (Free Colored); 09 Jul 1853; 11m; Cause Unknown; Russell County; s/o Samuel & Sarah Bundy; b. Russell County; reported by father. [p3;Ln11]

Burdine, Henry; Slave; 06 Sep 1853; 1y 10d; Russell County; "Colery Infantium"; parents unknown; reported by master, N.E. Burdine. [p2;Ln23]

Burdine, Nancy C.; (Free, Colored); 15 Sep 1866; 4y; "Dyptherea"; Russell County; d/o Robert & Nancy C. Burdine; b. Russell County; reported by father. [p20;Ln6]

Burdine, Robert; (Free, Colored); 02 Sep 1866; 2y 3m; "Dyptherea"; Russell County; d/o Robert & Nancy C. Burdine; b. Russell County; reported by father. [p20;Ln5]

Burdine, Sarah Ann; (Free, Colored); 10 Sep 1866; 6y; "Dyptherea"; Russell County; d/o Robert & Nancy C. Burdine; b. Russell County; reported by father. [p20;Ln4].

Counts, Jane; Slave; 05 Dec 1862; 13y; Fever; Russell County; d/o Jane ____; b. Russell County; Unmarried; reported by Owner, James Counts. [p18;Ln47]

Dickenson, David; (Free Colored); 21 Apr 1866; 25y; Castlewoods; parents unknown; a Servant; reported by "Former master", T.T. Dickenson. [p20;Ln15]

Dickenson, Jane; Slave; 25 Nov 1862; 35y; Fever; Russell County; d/o Edmund & Susan; Housekeeper; consort of Sam Boyd; reported by Owner, Henry Dickenson. [p17;Ln19]

Dickenson, John D.; (Free Colored); __ Sep 1866; 1m; Croup; Castlewoods; parents unknown; reported by "Former master", T.T. Dickenson. [p20;Ln16]

SOME RUSSELL COUNTY RECORDS
Deaths 1853-1866
Slave & Free Black

Dickenson, Mary J.; (Free Colored); 10 May 1866; 3y; Croup; Lick Creek, Russell County; d/o Charles & Priscilla Dickenson; b. Lick Creek; reported by father. [p21;Ln55]

Dorton, Robert; Slave; 15 Aug 1853; 7y 3m 14d; Flux; Russell County parents unknown; b. Russell County; reported by Owner, Moses Dorton. [p3;Ln22]

Ferguson, William; Slave; 31 Dec 1853; 3d; Cause Unknown; Cedar Creek; reported by Owner, Anthony M. Ferguson. [p1;Ln39]

Ferrell, Moses; Slave; 22 Apr 1860; 22y; Typhoid Fever; New Garden; parents not named; b. New Garden; reported by Owner, Elijah Ferrell. [p13;Ln11]

Fletcher, (female); Slave; 16 Apr 1860; 10m 13d; Whooping cough; New Garden; parents not given; b. New Garden; reported by Owner, Major A. Fletcher. [p13;Ln16]

Fugate, Samuel; Slave; 30 Nov 1853; 20y 20d; Typhoid Fever; Russell County; parents unknown; b. Russell County; reported by Owner, Isaac Fugate. [p2;Ln44]

Hanson, Lucy; Slave; 29 Jun 1853; 20y; Typhoid Fever; Russell County; parents unknown; Owner, Sidney Hanson; reported by James M. Hanson. [p2;Ln20]

Hendrick, Peter; Slave; 15 Apr 1857; age not given; Smothered: s/o Dolly Hendricks. [p9;Ln41]

Herndon, Chany; Slave; 25 Feb 1860; 60y; Dropsy; New Garden; reported by Owner, Sophia Herndon. [p13;Ln22]

Hooze, Jane; Slave; 21 Aug 1854; 6y 4d; Cause Unknown; Russell County; d/o Jane Hooze; reported by Owner, Oliver Hooze. [p5;Ln22]

Howard, Charles; Slave; 10 Mar 1860; 42y 2m; Measles; New Garden; reported by Owner, Johnson Howard. [p13;Ln 23].

Irvin, Philip; slave; 100y; Hayters Gap; b. North Carolina; reported by Owner, Benjamine Chapman. [p1:Ln8]

Lampkins, Abram; Slave; 13 Jun 1860; 45y; cause not given; Elk Garden; b. Elk Garden; reported by Owner, John W. Lampkins. [p13;Ln31]

Lampkins, Nancy; Slave; 31 Jul 1860; 17y; Consumption; Elk Garden; b. Elk Garden; reported by Owner, John W. Lampkins. [p13;Ln32]

172

SOME RUSSELL COUNTY RECORDS
Deaths 1853-1866
Slave & Free Black

Lampkins, Sarah; Slave; 12 Nov 1860; 53y; Dropsy; Elk Garden; b. Elk Garden; reported by Owner, John W. Lampkins. [p13;Ln33]

Leece, Alice; Slave; 15 Jul 1862; 3d; Cause Unknown; Reeds Valley; d/o Prisser; b. Reeds Valley; reported by Owner, William N. Leece. [p18;Ln17]

Leece, Mariet; Slave; 01 Sep 1854; 8m; Hives; Russell County; d/o Mary Leece; b. Russell County; reported by Owner, Samuel Leece. [p6;Ln6]

Litton, James; Slave; 16 Sep 1860; 70y; Dropsy; Elk Garden; b. Elk Garden; reported by Owner, James F. Litton. [p13;Ln30]

Melissa; (Former Slave ?); 09 Nov 1866; 7m; Flux; Mocassin, Russell County; s/o Lanna; b. Russell County; reported by "Former mistress", Mary E. Browning. [p20;Ln9]

Nash, Neel; Slave; 28 Dec 1853; 36y; "Hung hinself"; parents unknown; b. Russell County; reported by Owner, Aaron Nash. [p3;Ln43]

Osborn, Eizy; Slave; 01 Nov 1854; 9m; Croup; Russell County; d/o Celia Osborn; b. Russell County; reported by Owner, Soloman Osborn. [p5;Ln14]

Right, Samuel; slave; 21 Dec 1853; 24y 4m 12d; cause unknown; Elk Garden; b. Washington County, VA; reported by Owner, John W. Litton. [p1;Ln9]

Samples, Philis; slave; 14 Aug 1853; 60y; Dropsey; New Garden; reported by Owner, Nancy Samples. [p1;Ln18]

(Slave), (female); 10 Sep 1862; 10d; reported by Owner, Andy Ferguson. [p16;Ln17]

(Slave), (infant); __ Apr 1861; 3d; Russell County; child of Eliza; b. Russell County; reported by Owner, Stephen Banner. [p14;Ln10]

(Slave), (infant); __ ___ 1862: b. Russell County; reported by Owner, Elizabeth Johnson. [p16;Ln31]

(Slave), (male triplets ?); 01 Dec 1861; 1d; Elk Garden; cause not given; b. Elk Garden; reported by Owner, Andy F. Hendricks. [p15;Ln14] *(Register indicates 3 male slaves, age 1 day)*

(Slave), (male); 20 Jun 1854; 13y 9m; Fever; Russell County; s/o Milly D.; b. Russell County; reported by Owner, James Dickenson. [p5;Ln7]

(Slave), (male); 11 Mar 1857; 1d; "Over lain"; reported by Owner, James Hendricks. [p9;Ln34] *(See: Peter Hendricks (Slave); a possible double entry)*

(Slave), (male); 01 Dec 1857; 1y; Cause Unknown; s/o Deley Hendricks. [p9;Ln42]

(Slave), (male); __ Apr 1860; 10m; Russell County; reported by Owner, Joseph Hackney. [p12;Ln19]

(Slave), (Unnamed female); 18 Feb 1853; 8y; Inflamation of Brain: New Garden; Owner, John W. Smith. [p1;Ln33]

(Slave), (Unnamed); 18 Jun 1853; 10m; Croup; New Garden; b. New Garden; reported by Owner, Zadock N. Gardner. [p1;Ln21]

(Slave), **Aggy**; 01 Feb 1859; 33y 8m; Measles; Russell County; reported by Owner, Isaac Gilmer. [p11;Ln39]

(Slave), **Caroline**; 11 Dec 1859; 5m; Cause Unknown; d/o Dilsa; reported by Owner, Martha Hendricks. *(Note: A.L. Hendricks also listed as Owner)* [p11;Ln40]

(Slave), **Amy**; __ ___ 1862; 2m; cause not given; Russell County; b. Russell County; reported by Owner, Charles A. Smith. [p17;Ln61]

(Slave), **Caroline**; 01 Jun 1858; 11m; cause not given; Russell County; d/o Temperance; b. Russell County; reported by Owner, Jefferson Jessee. [p10;Ln28]

(Slave), **David**; 05 Aug 1853; 4y; Flux; Russell County; parents unknown; b. Russell County; reported by Owner, Dale Carter. [p2;Ln39]

(Slave), **Edmund**; 12 Jul 1855; 80y; Old Age; Russell County; reported by Owner, Caleb Hawkins. [p7;Ln6]

(Slave), **Emeline**; 15 Aug 1861; 1y 3m 5d; Flux; New Garden; b. New Garden; reported by Owner, Wilson E. Campbell. [p14;Ln31]

(Slave), **Florence**; Elk Garden; age not given; "Diptherea"; b. Russell County; reported by Owner, Mary D. Smith. [p17;Ln59]

(Slave), **George**; 12 Feb 1857; 1y; cause not given; s/o Celia; b. Russell County; reported by Owner, A. M. Lee. [p9;Ln22]

(Slave), **Isaac**; 20 Oct 1858; 33y; "Consummistion"; Russell County; parents unknown; place of birth unknown; reported by Owner, Abel Alderson. [p10;Ln15]

SOME RUSSELL COUNTY RECORDS
Deaths 1853-1866
Slave & Free Black

(Slave), Jackson; __ Aug 1860; 6m; Croup; Russell County; reported by Owner, Cloey Osborn. [p12;Ln12]

(Slave), Jane; __ Jun 1860; 4y; Croup; Russell County; reported by Owner, Aaron H. Nash. [p12;Ln36]

(Slave), Jane; 08 Sep 1856; 4y; cause not given; Russell County; reported by Owner, John Dickenson. [p8;Ln19]

(Slave), Jennie; 27 Apr 1861; 17m; Cause Unknown; Lebanon; b. Russell County; reported by Owner, William Beverly. William B. Aston. [p14;Ln2]

(Slave), Jeny; 06 Aug 1861; 12y; "By lightens" (lightning ?); parents unknown; b. Tennessee; reported by Owner, Joseph Hackney. [p14;Ln24]

(Slave), John S.; 01 Aug 1853; 7y; Fever; Russell County; s/o Viny Gilson (Gibson ?); reported by Owner, Thomas Gibson. [p5;Ln29]

(Slave), Julia; __ Dec 1857; 40y; cause not given; reported by Owner, Isaac Munsey. [p9;Ln27]

(Slave), Louisa F.; 25 Aug 1854; 3y; Flux; Russell County; d/o Julia Frick; reported by Owner, Oliver H, Frick. [p5;Ln25]

(Slave), Manda; __ Jul 1860; 1y 4m; "Phthisic"; Russell County; reported by Owner, Aaron H. Nash. [p12;Ln37]

(Slave), Margaret; __ Aug 1862; 7m; Tumor; Castlewoods, Russell County; d/o Mary; b. Russell County; reported by Owner, Pleasant Horn. [p19;Ln33]

(Slave), Margaret; 02 Apr 1856; 4m; cause not given; Russell County; d/o Florence; reported by Owner, A.H. Nash. [p8;Ln20]

(Slave), Martin H.; 29 May 1854; 1y 2d; Flux; Russell County; s/o Mary Horn; b. Russell County; reported by Owner, Pleasant Horn. [p5;Ln11]

(Slave), Mary; 01 Oct 1855; 27y; cause not given; Russell County; reported by Owner, Caleb Hawkins. [p7;Ln5]

(Slave), Mary; 30 Sep 1862; 18y 1m 10d; Fever; Russell County; b. Russell County; reported by Owner, A.G. Smith. [p16;Ln53]

(Slave), Mary; 13 Nov 1859; 50y; Dropsy; Russell County; parents unknown; b. Henry County; reported by Owner, Banner Berry. [p11;Ln1]

SOME RUSSELL COUNTY RECORDS
Deaths 1853-1866
Slave & Free Black

(Slave), Moses; 20 Jul 1858; 73y; "Chronic dirrare"; Russell County; reported by Owner, Thomas D.P. Dickenson. [p10;Ln22]

(Slave), Nelson; 18 Dec 1858; 70y 8m; Quinsey; Russell County; reported by Owner, A.C. Ferguson. [p10;Ln14]

(Slave), Rebecca; 07 Apr 1855; 70y; Old Age; Russell County; parents unknown; reported by Owner, John Dickenson. [p7;Ln8]

(Slave), Romulous; __ ___ 1862; age not given; Elk Garden; b. Russell County; reported by Owner, Mary D. Smith (widow of John T. of Ln56). [p16;Ln57]

(Slave), Sarah; 06 Mar 1857; 7y; "Burnt"; Russell County; parents not given; reported by Owner, Anderson(?) Hendricks. [p9;Ln30]

(Slave), Stanley; __ ___ 1862; age not given; "Diptherea"; Elk Garden; b. Russell County; reported by Owner, Mary D. Smith. [p17;Ln58]

(Slave), William; 04 Nov 1858; 2y 10m 5d; Hives; Russell County; s/o Mary; b. Russell County; reported by Owner, Pleasant Horn. [p10;Ln25]

Smith, (female); Slave; 20 Apr 1860; 15d; cause not given; Lebanon; b. Lebanon; reported by Owner, A.G. Smith. [p13;Ln45]

Smith, Andrew; Slave; 10 May 1853; 19y; Typhoid Fever; Clifton; reported by Owner, Charles A. Smith. [p1;Ln23]

Smith, Cheshire; Slave; 29 May 1853; 10y; Typhoid Fever; Clifton; reported by Owner, Charles A. Smith. [p1:ln27]

Smith, Emeline; Slave; 29 May 1853; 17y; Typhoid Fever; Clifton; reported by Owner, Charles A. Smith. [p1;Ln26]

Smith, Iseril; Slave; 17 Apr 1853; 50y; Typhoid Fever; Clifton; reported by Owner, Charles A. Smith. [p1;Ln22]

Smith, James; Slave; 26 May 1853; 5y; Typhoid Fever; Clifton; reported by Owner, Charles A. Smith. [p1;Ln25].

Smith, Lydia; Slave; 26 May 1853; 67y; Typhoid Fever; Clifton; reported by Owner, Charles A. Smith. [p1;Ln24].

Tigner, (female); Slave; 30 Jul 1860; 2m; Whooping Cough; Corner (Settlement); reported by Owner *(not named but possibly Patrick Tignor from Ln5]*. [p14;Ln6]

Blessing
Crockett & Mary 107

Blizzard
Sidner 107
Sidner & Ruth 107
Sidney & Lucy 107

Boggs
Eli & Mary 107
Rebecca 107
William & Rebecca 107

Bond
Charles F. & Mary J. 108

Boothe
John 108

Boring
Jos. & Sarah 145

Boswell
William T. & Hannah 108

Bowman
John & Elizabeth 108
Peter 108
Peter & Nancy 108

Boyd
Charles & Martha 109
Charles D. & Martha 109
Charles P. & Martha 108
Col. Robert & Elizabeth 131
Jas. & Prissila 108
John H. 108
Jonathan & Mary 108
Robert A. 109

Bradley
Clary 109
Ephraim 109

Bradshaw
John 109
John & Jane 109
William & Jane 109

Breeding
William & Elizabeth 109

Browning
Jno. C. & Elizabeth 109
John 165
Mary E. 171
Vincent 142
William McK & Susan 109

Buchanan
Jno. V. 110

Bumgarner
William & Elizabeth 110

Bundy
Daniel & Rebecca 110
Sampson & Sarah 110

Burk
Fleming & Rebecca 165
Isaiah & Martha 110
John & Nancy 110
William & Mary 110
Winton & Dorcas 110

Bush
Austin & Nancy 110, 145

Campbell
Henry 111
Henry & Milly 110
Jas. & Mahala J. 110

Candler
Singleton & Adeline H. 111

Carrell
James P. & Lila 111
Thomas 116
Thomas & Jane 111

Carter
Jos. & Mary 123

Cartey
John & Nancy 111

Carty
G.L.G.W. & Mary 111
John B. & Delila 111
L.G.W. 151
Thomas J. & Caroline 111

Castle
Elijah 111
Ralph & Sarah 111
Ralph S. 111
Zachariah 111

Chaffin
James & Sarah 154

Chafin
Oliver & Rebecca 112

Chapman
B.F. & Charity 112
Benjamine 119
William 112

Chatron
William & Lucinda 112

Childers
David & Martha 112

Clark
Daniel & Leah 112
J.P. & Elizabeth 112
Patrick & Eliza 112
Robert 112

Claypole
James 112

Claypool
James N. & Chairty 112
James N. & Chirty 112

Claypoole
John 113

Clifton
Martin J. 113

Cloud
John 113

Cockran
Marvel 113
Marvell 113

Coleman
Jas. & Martha 113

Colley
John & Ann 113
Joshua & Didama 113
Richard 113

Collins
William H. & Mary 113

Colly
John & Anny 113

Combs
Alexander & D. 113
Cullin Jr. & Desty 114
Feeling & Sarah 114
John M. 159
Thompson 114
William & Ana 114

Compton
Jeremiah 144
Jerry & Martha 114

Cooper
William & R. 114
William P. & Tabitha 114

Corvin
John & Melvina 114

Couch
Jeremiah & Margaret 114, 115
Jeremiah & Peggy 114
John & Eliza 114
John & Fanny 114, 115

Counts
Canaan & Ann 115
David & Nancy 115

John & Margaret 113
John J. 115
John J. & Eliza A. 115
John Sr. 115
John W. & Elizabeth 115
Joshua 115
Joshua & Martha 115
William & Patsey 115

Cowan
George 115, 143

Cox
John & Mary 116

Crook
David & Nancy 116

Cross
Modecai & Jane 116

Culbertson
Tyre & Martha 116

Culverson
E.J. & Matty 116

Cumbo
William & Eliza A. 116

Cumbow
Charles & Darthula 116
Darthula 116
Isaiah & Mary 116, 131

Cunningham
Thomas & Louisa 117

Dale
Hayman & Eliza D. 117
Hiram & Fanny 117

Darnold
Mary 117

Davis
Andrew & Elizabeth 110
Jesse 117
Thomas 117

Thomas & Jane 117
Thomas & Jane F. 117

Deal
Harvey & Louisa 117

Dickenson
Berry & Feraba 118
Charles C. & Catherine 118
Charles H. 118
H.P. & Mary J. 118
Henry 118
Henry & Eliza 107
John N. & Sarah 118
Nathaniel & Mary 126
Samuel & Elizabeth 118

Dickson
Charles 118

Dills
James & Sarah 118

Dorton
Edward & Jemimah 119
Francis 119
Jacob & Elizabeth 118
John 130
Moses 151
Moses & Jemima 150, 151
Samuel B. 118

Dotson
James & Elizabeth 119

Duff
Rees 119

Duncan
Rebecca 119

Duty
John & Sarah 119

Dye
Nancy 159

Eakin
William & Cermantha 119

Easterly
Christian & Nancy 119
Elizabeth E. 119

Elliott
Wilson 119

Estep
Joseph 120

Evans
Walter & Lucy 120
Wilson & Sarah 120

Farmer
John & Sarah 120
Sol. J. 120

Farris
John & Nancy C. 120

Ferguson
Andrew C. 120
Benjamine 120
E.M. 121
Granville & Menerva 120
Mary 120

Ferrell
Elijah 156

Fickle
Isaac B. 121

Fields
A.F. & Milly 121
James J. 121
Jeremiah 107
Jeremiah & Anna 168
Joel 121
John 121
John T. & Rosannah 121
Randolph & Rutha 121
Richard 121
Richard F. & Mary 121
Russell & Rachel F. 121
William H. 121

Finney

Lilburn & Melissa 122
Rubin 115, 121

Fletcher
Celia 122
Ely & Agnes 122
James H. & Ellen 122
Jas. & Celia 122
John 122
Lorenzo D. 122
Major A. & Rachel 122
William 122
William & Mary 122

Fraley
Boon & Mary 123
Ephraim 123
Ephraim & Margaret 122, 123
George & Nancy 122
Henry 123

Franklin
James 123
William L. 123

Frick
Chris. & C. 123
William 123

Fugate
Colbert & Hannah 118
E.S. & Mary P. 123, 124
Isaac B. 123
Joseph C. 123
Joseph C. & Elizabeth E. 123
Zachariah & Nancy 123

Fullen
Fowler & Ann E. 124

Fuller
Isaac & Louisa 164
Isaac & Lusa 124
Isaiah & Polly 124
James H. 124
James H. & Polly 124
Jesse & Mary 124
Jonas & Rhoda 124
Martha 124

Noah H. & Cyntha 124

Gardner
William H. & Seny 124

Garrett
John J. 125
W.L. & Sarah 125
William & Mary 124

Gent
Fielding & Jane 125
James 114

Gibson
George & Casy 125
Harvey P. & Maria 125
Henry & Melvina 125
Mitchell E. 125
Tabitha 125

Gilbert
Jas. A. 125
William & Mary 125
William & Polly 125

Gilmer
Daughtery & Nancy 126
Daughtry 126
Samuel & Anna 126
Samuel E. 125
Wesley & Martha 125

Gilmore
Isaac & Mary 126

Glenn
William & Esther 126

Gose
Aaron & Nancy 126, 127
Elizabeth 126
George & Elizabeth 127, 141
George C. & M. 126
Stephen 105, 154, 168
Stephen & Barbara 126

Grace
John 127

Gray
Harvey & Nancy 127
John & Rachel 127
John E.R. 127
N.B. 127
N.B. & Rebecca 127
Nancy 127
Rebecca 145

Green
Shadrick & Martha 127

Griffeth
Isaac 127

Grizzle
Elam & N. 128
George & Elizabeth 128
Jesse 128
Jesse & Nancy 128
John & Elizabeth 127
William 128
William & Elizabeth 128

Guinn
Wiley 128

Hackney
Anderson 129
Anderson & Mary 128, 129
John W. 128
Joseph 141
Joseph & Milly 129

Hale
Henry & Ruthy 129
James 129
Jas. & Susan 130
Jonathan 129
William & Elizabeth 129

Hall
John & Anny 129

Hammons
Absolom & Elizabeth 120

Harden
Abner 129

William & Sarah H. 129

Harmon
Henry 129
Wilson 129
Wilson & Elizabeth 129

Harrison
James & Mary Ann 129
Samuel 130
Samuel & Elizabeth 130

Hartsock
Daniel & Darky 112
James 130
James & Matilda 130
John 130

Hawkins
Bluford & Sidney 131
Elisha & Isabel 130
T.T 131
Thomas L. & Lydia 130, 131
William B. 130

Helbert
Jacob 131
Jacob & Mary M. 131
Margaret M. 131
Sally 131

Helton
John & Martha 131

Hendricks
Aaron 131
Aaron L. 131
Fullen & Melissa 132
George 131
George W. & Frances 131
Malissa O. 131
Thomas & M.J. 132

Henley
Stephen & Grace 132

Henson
James & Mary 132

Herndon
John & Polly 132
Larkin 132

Hess
Henry & Amelia 132
Isaac & Susan 132
James 132
Lucy 132
Mathias 132
William & Polly 132

Hicks
George & Rebecca 133
James & Maria 133

Hill
Samuel & Hulda 133
William & M. 133

Hilman
John & Sarah 132

Hogston
Franklin 133

Holland
Alex & Mary E. 133
John & Elizabeth 133

Honaker
H.M. & Elizabeth 133
John & Lucinda 133

Horn
Ichabod 106

Horten
Daniel 133

Horton
Lewis & Lucinda 134
Lewis & Ruth 134
Lewis & Rutha 133
Lucinda 133, 134
Thomas & Vina 133
Thomas P. & Sally 134

Howard

Hiram & Ellen 134
John T. 122
Johnson & Nancy 134
Polly 134

Howell
George & Elizabeth 134

Hubbard
Eli & Jane 134
Randolph 134

Hubbord
Jesse & Matilda 134

Huchison
Francis & Matilda 134

Hughes
Daniel & Sarah 134

Hunt
Josiah & Any 135

Hurt
Amoses & Polly 135
Burgess 135
Charles & Phebe 135
Garland & Jane 135
Garland & Matilda 135
Josiah & Anna 135
Mekin 135
Moses & Polly 135
Polly 135

Jackson
A.L. & Nancy 136
Andrew L. 137, 166
Andrew L. & Nancy 135
Catherine 136
Ibby 136
James 136
Michael & Visa 136
Richard 135

Jenks
John P. & Mary S. 136

Jentry

Dorothy 136

Jessee
Abednigo 137
Charles B. & Eliza B. 136
Cyntha 137
David & Hannah 137
Elihu 136
Elihu K. 137
George L. & Eliza 137
Jefferson & Nancy 137
John 137
John & Mary 137
Martin 137
Mary 137
Rebecca 165
Rev. David 159
Sarah 137
T.J. & Sarah 137, 138
Thomas & Sarah 136
William F. & Mary 137

Johnson
Hugh 138
Jacob & Nancy 138
John & Eliza 155
John & Mary 138
Lemuel & Cornely 138
Lemuel & Sarah 138
Mary 138
Robert & Margaret E. 138
Samuel A. & Sarah 138
William & Mary 138
William & Sarah 138
William S. 138

Jones
Green B. & Parthena 138
James V. 138
Soloman 139

Jordan
Christopher & Margaret 139

Judd
I.S. & Nancy 139

Kates
Robert 139

Keath
Hugh L. & Phebe 139

Keel
Kelly & M. 139

Keen
Patten G. 139
Patten G. & Polly 139

Keeth
Hugh & Phebe 139
Jesse & Vina 139

Kelly
Joseph 140
Peter & Polly 140
William & Rebecca 140

Kesnor
William 140

Kilgore
Charles & Mary C. 151

Kindrick
James & Clersy 162

Kiser
Abednigo 140
Elihue & Jane 140
Epham & Mary 140
Ephraim 141
Ephraim & Mary 140
James & Susan 141
Joseph & Mary 141
Mayfield & Mary 140
Noah 140

Kitts
Peter & Amy 156

Laforce
James 141

Lamas
James & Polly 130

Lambert
William & Matilda 141

Lark
Christopher & Eliza 160
Micael & Sarah 141

Lawson
William & Catherine 141

Lee
Alexander M. & Eliza 141
David F. & Mary 141
James & Cloe 141
Jas. & Rachel 152
Mary E. 141

Leece
Jacob & Nancy 141
James A. & Ann C. 141
Jane 141
William N. 141

Lesgo/Sesco
James W. & Margaret 142

Lewis
John & Narsessy 142
John & Rachel 146

Light
Lazaras & Elizabeth A. 142

Litton
John W. 142

Logan
Eusavius H. 142

Long
Joseph & Margaret 142

Love
Oscar & Mary H. 142

Luster
William 142

Lynch
Richard H. & S.K. 142
Thomas 143
Thomas & Sarah 143

Maggard
David & Susan 147

Malicote
Jasper N. & Susan 143

Martin
John & Elizabeth 143

May
Jacob & Eliza 143

McCloud
Daniel & Elizabeth 143
Mary 143

McClure
James & Catherine 143

McCoy
Harvey G. & Malinda 144
William 144
William W. & Elizabeth 144

McFadden
David 144
Thomas & Polly 144

McFall
James & Sarah 144

McGlothlin
Harvey & S. 145

McGraw
John & Sarah 142

McNew
Alexander E. 145

McReynolds
Isaac & Susan 145
J.S. 145
Joseph 145

Joseph & Polly 145

Mead
Henson 145
R.L. 164
Richard L. 136, 140
Samuel H. 145
Thomas 145
Thomas & Matilda 145

Meade
Pressly C. & Mary A. 145

Mercer
Daniel 146
Daniel & Emaline 145

Milgrim
John 146

Miller
Jacob & Martha J. 146

Minnick
Jacob & Sarah 146

Minton
Elizabeth 146
Richard 146

Mitchell
Charles & Maria 146
Elisha 146
Elisha & Hennrey E.M. 146

Monk
James B. 146

Monroe
Mordeca & Milly 146

Moore
William 146, 163

More
Mildred 117

Mullins
Andrew J. & Polly 146

Isham & Mary 147
Wilson 147

Musick
Alva & Chaney 147
Elexious & Polly 147
Jack & Vina 147
Lexious & Polly 147
William & Isabella 147

Mutter
Harvey 147
Jackson 113, 156
Roden & Loucena 147
Thomas & Margaret 147

Nash
Aaron H. & Catherine 147

Necessary
Thomas & E. 148

Neumon
James & Mary 148

Odle
James & Mary 148

Osborn
Cloe 148
David 148
Samuel & Unity 148
William & Anny 148

Osborne
David 148

Owen
Jacob & Hannah 148
Joseph 148

Owens
Abram & Jemima 164
Darthula 149
Elizabeth 149
Jacob & H.F. 148
John & Nancy 149
John W. & Elizabeth 148, 149
Rufus & Nancy 148

Painter
James 107
John & Sarah A. 149

Parks
Hezekiel 149
William 149

Patrick
Isham & Lydia 149
John & Lydda 149

Payne
Mary 150

Pennick
Joshua & Anna 111

Perry
James 150
James & Sary 150
Nathan & Mary 150

Phelps
Samuel & Rialy 150

Phipps
Alexander & Elizabeth 150

Pinion
William & Amelia 150

Pippin
(F/O Sarah Reynolds) 154
Zachariah & Nancy 150

Plot
George & Sarah 123

Pool
Hardy 150
Hardy & J. 150
Piety 150

Porter
Francis & Elizabeth 151
George A. & Rosy 150
John R. 150
John R. & Eliza J. 151

Thomas M. 151
William & Mary C. 151
William D. 151

Powers
James 151
James & Sarah E. 151
John M. 151
Reubin & Catherine 151

Price
"James" & Sally 151
Daniel & Judith 159
David & Judy 137
John M. 151, 152
Mark & Ellen 151
Oliver 152
Oliver H. 159
Rebecca 152
Thomas & Mary 152

Prophet
Edward 152

Pruner
George & Catherine 152
George A. 152

Puckett
Daniel 152
Daniel & Sydney 152
David 152
Jeremiah & Margaret 153

Puckit
Jeremiah & Margaret 152

Purcell
James 153

Ramey
John & Emley 153

Ramsey
Joel & Margaret 153

Ramsy
Joel & Mary 138

Rasnake
Fayette 153
Fayette & Margaret 153
Jacob & Judia 153
James & Rebecca 153

Redwine
Roling R. 153
Soloman 153

Reynolds
Abram & Nancy 154
Bernard & C. 153
Bernard & Lucy 153
Henry 154
Ira 154
Noah 154
Phillip J. 153
Rachel 153
William 154

Richardson
Christopher & Amanda 154
Christopher & Maria 154
Samuel & Mary 154
Thomas J. & Jane 154
William & Margaret 154

Rickman
Thomas 154

Riley
Thomas & Mary 154
Thomas J. 155

Ritchie
John & Casy 155

Roberts
Garlin & Esther 155

Robertson
Berry & Cyntha 155

Robins
Celia 155
Elizabeth 155
Sarah J. 155
William 155

188

SOME RUSSELL COUNTY RECORDS
Index to Deaths: Parents & Persons Reporting

Robinson
Celia 155
Jas. & Celia 156
John W. 155
Mathew & Nancy 156
William & Celia 156

Roman
James 156
Richard & Tempa 156

Routh
Asa 156
Asa & Catherine 156

Russell
William & Ann 156

Salyers
James & Elizabeth 156
Jesse & Nancy 156

Sample
Elizabeth 132
William 156

Samples
Elizabeth 157
James 157
William & Nancy 157
William & Rhoda 157

Sanders 157
John 157
John & Jane 157

Sargent
Isaac & Mary 157

Senter
Stephen & Sarah 157

Sexton
Harvey 157
Henry & Catherine 158
William & Elander 157, 158

Shell
Aaron 158

Aaron & Catherine 158
Aaron & Rhoda Ann 158

Shoemaker
Bjamine 158
James 158
Reynolds & Rachel 158

Short
Daniel 158
William & Lear 158

Shumaker
Francis 158

Simerly
James & Tabitha 158

Skeen
Ephraim & Alzira 158

Slave
Alexander 171
Banner, Betsey 171
Bickley, Creason 171
Bickley, Fletcher 171

Smith
Ake 159
Charles A. 159
Harry & Mary M. 159
John 159
John & Nancy 159
John & Rebecca 159
John W. 159
Mary D. 159
William & Matilda 159
William H. 159

Snader
Sarah 168

Snapp
Elkanah D. & Catherine 160
Elkanah R.D. 159
John 159
William D. 159

189

Snead
Jane 160

Southerland
Henry & Margaret 160

Spurgeon
Samuel 160

Stamper
James & Mary 160

Stanley
William & Anna 160

Stapleton
George 160
William & Esther 160

Statzer
Andrew & Nancy 160

Steele
Matison & Martha 159
Sparrel & Elizabeth 160
Thomas P. 160

Stephens
Owen 160

Stiltner
James 160

Stinson
James & Adah 161
John & Nancy 161
Rachel 161

Straugh
Michiel 161

Strow
Michael 161

Stump
Joseph & Margaret 161
Joseph & Peggy 161

Suit

Daniel & Rebecca 161
Johnson & Nancy 161
Pleasant 161
Pleasant & Mary 161
Ralph & Nancy 111

Sutherlan
Alexander & Mary 162

Sutherland
Jesse 162

Sutton
John & Mary 123

Sykes
Celia 162
John 162
Mary 162

Tate
Eliza 162

Taylor
Charles & Nancy 163
Emby 162
Emby & Nancy 162, 163
Isaac & Catherine 162
Michael & Mary 162
Polly 163

Teter
John 163
John & Elizabeth 146

Thomas
Eli C. & Ellen 163

Thompson
Emory & Phoebe 163
George & Elizabeth 164
Jacob 164
Jane 163
Patton 164
Patton & Mary 163, 164
Thomas 163

Tignor
Patrick & Nancy 164

Todd
Joseph 164

Tolbert
Nancy 110

Turner
Charles & Elizabeth 164
Hugh & Elizabeth 164
James 164
Jas. & Mary 123

Vance
David & Elizabeth 164

Vanover
John & Keziah 164

Vermillion
Elihu 165
Elihu & Eliza 164
Jesse 165
Lihugh & Rebecca 165
Nancy 165
Wilson & Nancy 165

Vicars
Robert & Lidda 165
Robert & Phebe 165
Samuel 165
Susannah 165
William & Susan 165

Vincell
John & Nancy 165

Vincil
Lorenzo D. 166
William 166

Wallis
James & Jane 166
John & Mary 122

Ward
William & Mary 166
William T. & Polly 166

Weddle
J.C. & Mary 166

Wheeler
James 167
James C. & Malissa 166, 167
Pleasant H. & Anny 166

White
John B. & Rachel 167
Robert A. & Darthula 167

Whited
Jos. W. & Elizabeth 167
R.M. 167
Robert M. & Ann 167

Whitt
James 167
Mary 167

Willey
Andrew & Elizabeth 167

Williams
Andrew & Nancy 167
Charity 162
George & Elizabeth 168
George W. 167
George W. & Charity 167
James 162, 168
John & Elizabeth 167
John D. 168
Samuel D. & Elizabeth 168
William 168

Wilson
Samuel & Sarah 168

Wise
John & Margaret 168

Wisor
Adam & Polly 124
Catherine 124
John & Mary 168
William & Catherine 168

Witt
John & Rosana 168

Wolf
John & Elizabeth 169

Wright
John 169
John & Sucha 169
Paris & Mary 169
Robert & Sarah 169
William & Caroline 169